Changement

"When I make a word do a lot of work like that," said Humpty Dumpty, "I always pay it extra."

"...You see, it's like a portmanteau...there are two meanings packed up into one word."

Lewis Carroll,
Through the Looking Glass, 1871

"Changement," as used in the title of this book, is a reasonably well paid and awfully convenient word for suggesting not only the constant, forever ongoing nature of the process of change itself, but the challenges associated with the *management* of change.

Peter H. Burgher,
Changement, 1979

Changement

Understanding and Managing Business Change

Edited by
Peter H. Burgher
Arthur Young & Company

Lexington Books
D.C. Heath and Company
Lexington, Massachusetts
Toronto

LIBRARY
The University of Texas
At San Antonio

Library of Congress Cataloging in Publication Data
Main entry under title:
Changement
  1. Organizational change.   I. Burgher, Peter H.
HD58.8.C46   658.4'06   78-19576
ISBN 0-669-02569-0

Published simultaneously in Canada

Printed in the United States of America

International Standard Book Number: 0-669-02569-0

Library of Congress Catalog Card Number: 78-19576

Contents

Observe constantly that all things take place by change, and accustom thyself to consider that the nature of the universe loves nothing so much as to change the things which are, and to make new things like them.

Marcus Aurelius, *Meditations,* c. A.D. 174

One change always leaves the way prepared for the introduction of another.

Machiavelli, *Il Principe,* 1513

What man has made, man can change.

Fred M. Vinson, speech, 1945

We are not seeking change for the sheer fun of it. We must change to meet the challenge of altered circumstances. Change will occur whether we like it or not. It will be either change in a good and healthy direction or change in a bad and regrettable direction. There is no tranquillity for us.

We can choose not to accept the challenge of change, of course; but then we shall fall very rapidly into the ranks of the museum nations, and tourists from more vigorous lands will come from afar to marvel at our quaint ways.

John W. Gardner, *No Easy Victories,* 1968

In a world of accelerant change, next year is nearer to us than next month was in a more leisurely era. This radically altered fact of life must be internalized by decision-makers in industry, government and elsewhere. Their time horizons must be extended.

Alvin Toffler, *Future Shock,* 1970

In managing change in the organization, the strategy is to know how to spot the need for it, how to judge when it isn't necessary, and how to know what result you want the change to accomplish.

Man generates changes in technology, methods, and organization, but probably the most complex change...is transformation in people themselves. "People change" occurs on at least two levels—in mores and in psychological mutation in individuals, due to age, changes in their environment, and other factors.

John S. Morgan, *Managing Change,* 1972

The innovative organization, the organization that resists stagnation rather than change, is a major challenge to management, private and public. That such organizations are possible, we can assert with confidence; there are enough of them around. But how to make such organizations general, how to make them productive for society, economy, and individual alike, is still largely an unsolved task.

Peter F. Drucker, *Management,* 1974

Preface

For nearly twenty years as an independent certified public accountant, I have been fascinated with the subject of change. First as an auditor, then as a consultant, and subsequently as the managing partner of a substantial practice, I have been in a position to observe many organizations in the process of change. I have also had the opportunity to observe many people in that same process. For some it was clearly an exhilarating experience; for others it was difficult, tiresome, and frustrating. Gradually, as it became more and more my responsibility to help others in our organization to meet the challenges of change, I have developed some thoughts and theories about how to approach change constructively.

At the same time I have observed an increasing fascination on the part of businessmen, students, and teachers with the process of change. Perhaps the single most significant event that focused the attention of our society on the subject of change in recent years was the publication in 1970 of Alvin Toffler's remarkable book, *Future Shock*. Toffler's central thesis is that there has been an exponential increase in the rate of change in our world. Although the heavenly philosophers of the sixteenth and seventeenth centuries were also deeply interested in change, their emphasis was on change in the social order of things. It remained for Toffler to draw our attention to the implications of the change that is taking place in our physical and scientific (or evidential) conditions.

If you separate the existence of knowledge from its application, Toffler's book points out dramatically that both our fund of knowledge and our rate of using the resources of our environment have changed radically. The philosopher Malthus also addressed himself to the implications of change in his dire predictions that our population would soon overrun its environment. More recently, the Club of Rome Report extrapolated what were essentially Malthusian predictions, using what have since proved to be defective computer programs, that we will soon exceed our ability to support ourselves. Although many anthropologists suggest that our society and our environment are actually in relatively stable equilibrium, there are, nonetheless, dramatic social and ecological changes taking place about us.

As a student of change, I have concentrated my interest primarily on change in our society and, in an even more limited way, on change as it affects our business institutions. Starting about 1970, writers on the subject of change have increased their output almost as impressively as the exponential rate of change they describe. In reviewing what has been written on the subject, I discovered that much of what I would have wanted to say about change had already been said by others. I noted, however, tha' very few writers had tried to bring together the many different viewpoints and experiences that have been expressed about such things as the identification of the attributes of change, the management of change as an ongoing activity, the human dynamics of social change, or how to harness change as a positive force. In fact, despite the existence of so many well-written articles and papers about change, I found no one presentation that completely satisfied me. Over a period of several years, my study of the subject of change became more intensive, and from that study evolved this book.

Collected here are what I believe to be some of the most interesting and provocative writings on change—and especially the management of change in business institutions—that have been published in recent years. These selections are representative, and by no means exhaustive. I have attempted to unify these contributions with introductory comments suggesting how they relate to one another, or emphasizing important points.

I am indebted to Pamela Hartman and Elaine Russman for their able and diligent assistance in performing the research necessary for this project. Together we reviewed more than a thousand articles and books in business periodicals, psychological journals, scientific annals, social science abstracts, and other sources. Their insight into the process of change and the high quality of their thinking have added measurably to this project. In addition, I express my thanks to Henry C. Marksbury, who reviewed the manuscript and made many valuable suggestions, and to Lois McIntyre, Andrea Stryker-Rodda, and May Allstrom, all of whom contributed in many ways to the preparation of the manuscript, the checking out of facts, the reading of proofs, and the securing of necessary permissions. Special thanks are due to Albert Newgarden, without whose encouragement, advice, and assistance this book would have been less cogent and much less fun to produce. Finally, I must express my thanks to my partners and to my wife, Elinor, for their patience during the preparation of this work.

Prologue: The Purposes of This Book

The significant question facing management today is not how to prevent change—that would be self-destructive and may be impossible—but rather how to understand change, how to accommodate change, and how to bring constructive influences to bear on the process of change. That statement, paraphrased from a *New York Times* news item of several years ago, sums up as well as anything I could originate my own views on the challenge of managing change in modern business organizations.

The American businessman has no equal in technological problem solving. Since the industrial revolution, business people all over the world have been striving to develop, learn, and use better management techniques. Today these same techniques are being applied, sometimes dramatically, to deal with governmental, social, and community tasks and problems. In education, for example, both universities and intermediate schools have only recently begun to benefit from the use of modern budgeting, financial control, and output evaluation techniques. And all of us, these days, are more aware of the impact of change in such areas as environmental control and health care. In the past few years the United States Congress has appropriated large sums of money for improvement of our law enforcement, judicial, and penal systems, and significant changes have resulted from the expenditure of these monies. In other countries of the world, such efforts to effect significant change in the larger institutions of society have yet to be started.

Notwithstanding the fact that our economic and social progress increasingly meets the needs and demands of our society, there is a real danger that what have come to be called our "expectations" are increasing at an even faster pace and placing all our institutions—not just business, but labor, education, and government as well—in jeopardy. If we examine the ways in which business institutions can adapt to changes within their own organizations and in society generally, perhaps we can find some better ways of coping with the larger, environmental changes that are all around us.

Our employees, and many of our managers as well, are disturbed by the size and strength of our business and other social institutions. Some feel that our institutions are too deeply embedded in the past, or that they have become too large or too rigid to serve the needs for which they were originally conceived. Fringe elements resort occasionally to force and terror to accomplish change in our institutions, while the vast mass of our society, our employees and fellow workers, are feeling (and expressing) increasing dissatisfaction with our business and governmental institutions. This dissatisfaction manifests itself in many ways. Some say we should deregulate our business institutions, while others feel equally certain that all our institutions need more, not less, control (for example, by government).

There are, however, some brighter aspects of today's situation which we should also acknowledge. First, American enterprise continues to rely heavily on profits as the basic motivation and measurement of effectiveness in our economic system. Although it can be argued that our profit system is no longer as effective as it once was, it has not lost its importance as a prime and moving force.

The relationship of business, government, and other social institutions to their members and employees is changing. Employees no longer react to such institutions or those who manage them according to the expected patterns of the past. New emphasis has been placed upon the responsibility of an organization to its members and employees—an emphasis far transcending the paternalism of prior days.

There is significant change in the marketplace as well. Consumer demands are shifting more and more rapidly, and products, services, and distribution systems have to be adapted accordingly. There is still, however, the discipline of the marketplace. We accept as a given that no company can long produce goods or services that the public does not want or is not willing to pay for. Technological obsolescence, or excess or insufficient capacity, still leads to low price–effectiveness and thus permits displacement within the market. As economists would put it, price elasticity decreases as the rate of technological obsolescence increases—yet we all know that the latter often forces increased competition in terms of the former.

The fact that American business has been relatively successful in managing change in the marketplace should be an important source of strength as we confront the many other kinds of change discussed in this volume. Despite the increasing uncertainty noted above, business has developed systems that deal well with the kinds of economic change the marketplace brings. These types of change are easiest to manage because they are tangible. New products, new packaging, and new distribution techniques have evolved rapidly, and are increasingly relied upon as other changes affect the marketplace.

The modern American corporation probably has more extensive and more elaborate internal control systems than any institution in history, yet most of the public is unaware of the existence and importance of these controls. Accounting controls have evolved to a high level of sophistication and reliability over the past fifty to seventy–five years. The responsibilities of independent auditors and corporate directors are acknowledged to be greater than ever before. Modern risk management techniques spread both the cost of losses and the potential for protection against losses on a worldwide scale. The increasing emphasis of our legal system on the prevention as well as the redress of wrongs has affected business management and the corporation significantly.

The relationship of business to society has changed. Our business institutions and business people are no longer automatically accepted as the good guys. Business and other sectors of our society are developing different priorities and goals, which are often in conflict. Still, the ethical demands of our society, its mores and taboos, continue to be effective—at least as effective as our laws—in imposing the community's consensus upon our business and governmental institutions. The power of public opinion is still very great.

American business has been successful in dealing with attitudinal change. Students of Frederick W. Taylor's era, seventy-five years ago, did not recognize that attitudinal change was as important as other, more tangible kinds of change in managing to meet the evolving needs of our society. Today we are more aware of the limited success that business has had in managing change in the relationships between employees and the business itself. Thus, exceptionally high employee turnover rates continue to characterize certain industries and certain enterprises. There is even less success in managing change in the relationships between business and society.

Many business people have tried to ignore what is happening in our society in the belief that it is only a temporary condition and that the pendulum will swing back sooner or later. People are fond of assuming that the American way will prevail. The business community has failed to identify what changes it should support or seek to create and has dealt primarily in generalities. Too often our business leaders have cast themselves in reactive roles and have been unable to take positive action to improve their environment and their relationships, even within their own organizations.

What are the problems that have caused this stunning lack of success in managing certain types of change in our business institutions? First, business' perception of change is probably incorrect. Change is still too often viewed as a transition between conditions or periods of stability. Business' approach to change frequently takes the form of predicting the state of things to come at some future time, rather than viewing change as a constant, ongoing, and evolutionary process. Too often business people fail to recognize the full dimensions of "the problem," limiting themselves instead to the pragmatic perception of a particular set of changes. Even more than other sectors of our society, business has failed to recognize that change is the only constant that can be relied upon.

Managers within our business institutions are apprehensive about change. Change is often viewed as a response to pressure from outside, and in fact is usually brought into business organizations by outsiders, or by people who are identified and thought of as outsiders, who do not let change develop from within. Fear of change causes many managers to ignore or fight change instead of attempting to deal with it constructively. Day-to-day work pressures often prevent managers from taking positive steps toward achieving desirable long-term change in their organizations.

Against this background, let us consider the purposes of this book. The twenty-nine chapters address themselves to various aspects of the process of change in business organizations, under five main parts—identifying change, understanding change, creating change, managing change, and social change.

For each part, a brief introduction states the unifying thesis. Within each part, interpretive comments are provided for each chapter to emphasize key points of that selection and to help relate each chapter to the whole.

It is hoped that this volume amounts to something more than the sum of its parts. At the same time, although there is a unifying viewpoint expressed in both the editor's selection of and commentary upon the various chapters, it must be acknowledged that the breadth and diversity of views represented by the individual contributions to this volume represent, in the editor's judgment, its real virtue and strength. Finally, since the business microcosm mirrors our society as a whole, many of the principles discussed in these pages can undoubtedly be applied to other social institutions as well.

Part I
Identifying Change

Change often hurts, but the consequences of failure to change can hurt far worse.

An essential element in the management of change is the ability to recognize change as it starts to take place. Many people, and nearly all societies, fail to recognize change until the hurt begins. This is probably because our ecological needs include a high degree of stability. Stability translates for most people into continuity and, accordingly, the absence of change. If we analogize the business organization to the human organism, we can readily see that change is constantly taking place even under the guise of stability. Cells are damaged and renewed, aging and replacement occur, and the organism gradually adapts itself to its changing condition. The business organization often does the same, but usually not without difficulty. Changes often take place within the business organization as a result of people's failure to follow prescribed procedures. Outside changes, although not identified as such, cause reactions within the organization, and conscious efforts are needed to adopt new approaches to the business' problems.

Many successful business managers have adopted the technique of identifying and harnessing the changes that are constantly going on within the organizations they seek to change in other ways. By converting people's needs for adaptation to constructive ends, the organization can be made to adapt to new conditions, too. Basic to this approach is the ability to identify changes within and outside the organization that can be used for this purpose.

The chapters in this section illustrate several different viewpoints on the identification of change. The material reflects insights into change from a number of disciplines, including marketing, financial accounting, motivation, technology, and management theory. This broad–ranging selection is intended to provide a perspective on change from each of these disciplines.

1

A Marketing Man Takes Marketers to Task: An Interview with Philip Kotler

Although marketing is but one of many disciplines involved in managing a modern business enterprise, the marketing function often serves as a laboratory for analyzing and exploring the implications of change. The following material, excerpted from a Business Week *interview with Philip Kotler, professor of marketing at Northwestern University, identifies a number of areas of change affecting the marketing function. In describing some of the elements of a new marketing environment, Dr. Kotler identifies aspects of change that are helpful in understanding the phenomenon of change as a whole. He emphasizes the need for continuing self-examination as a part of the process of identifying and managing change.*

One of Philip Kotler's pet peeves—he has many—is the complacency of most marketing men. "Look at economics, sociology, psychology, and almost every other major discipline, and you will find a ferment of challenging and often conflicting ideas," says the forty-four-year-old marketing professor at Northwestern University. "Then look at marketing. It has the distinction of being singularly uncontroversial within its ranks, while being endlessly controversial outside its ranks"—thanks to such outside critics as economist John Kenneth Galbraith, lawyer–consumerist Ralph Nader, and journalist Vance Packard. "At a time like this when so many of our old marketing assumptions about competition, markets, and growth are no longer valid," Kotler adds, "there should be someone on the inside lighting fires and challenging basic thinking. There are no native–son radicals."

Except, that is, for Kotler himself. One of marketing's most persistent and perceptive critics, Kotler is a frequent public speaker and a prolific, award–winning writer who has cranked out a stream of professional articles and three major books, including *Marketing Management: Analysis, Planning, and Control,* the most widely used marketing text in graduate business schools.

Amid signs that the country's worst recession in forty years has finally hit bottom, Kotler visited with a *Business Week* editor and discussed what

---

he calls the "whole new marketing environment" that confronts and increasingly confounds American business. Judging by the rapid growth of consumerism, expanding government regulation over consumer products, and rising public disenchantment with business in general, it would even seem that the so-called marketing concept is in trouble and is not doing its job—that is, creating satisfied customers.

Kotler insists that the concept itself is fine. The problem, he says, is with the huge proportion of companies that still fail to practice the concept. They tend to be too inflexible and too closed to new ideas and approaches, Kotler claims. "I see only a struggle to maintain the stance and posture that were successful in the past," Kotler says. "And I don't care how hard marketing men try—and they are great rationalizers—we just are not going to return to those boom time periods of growth we enjoyed in the 1950s and 1960s. But very few companies recognize or respond to this."

What is the proper response?

For one thing, companies have to abandon the notion of marketing being simply the stimulation of demand or a response to demand. Marketing has got to evolve toward "demand management" or the management of growth. For instance, we are seeing more and more companies like General Electric, Shell Chemical, Crown Zellerbach, and Scovill prune lower-margin products out of their lines and concentrate far more attention on higher-margin products. That is a start—but only a small one. The bigger urgency is for better long-range planning to avert this later need for pruning out a product line.

Planning means different things to different companies. What, to your mind, is "better planning"?

Many marketers are still content to have annual sales forecasts masquerade as marketing planning, when their real need is solid strategic planning. This is a road map for getting you from point A to point B and achieving some predetermined result. I always come back to a favorite definition of modern marketing—which is the process of making selling unnecessary. That is what marketing planning should be about, but seldom is.

What is the biggest error that companies make in their marketing planning?

A failure to stay loose. Today more than ever before, you have to plan for change, not stability. Pillsbury, for instance, puts out a good line of premium-priced bakery products, mixes, and so on. Recently, some Pillsbury brand managers started saying, "Today's shopper is worried about inflation and wants prices held down. So we've got to shift to lower-priced lines." At first, top management fought this idea. The feeling was that Pillsbury had to have premium branding all the way, and that any consumer resistance could be overcome with extra advertising and sales promotion. That reflects a failure to adjust to the new demands of the economy. Now within the last few months, Pillsbury is starting to reconsider—but there is still that hesitation.

At a time when the public is complaining so much about inflation and high prices, what are the pricing implications of today's trend toward a refinement or reduction of product lines?

When you analyze causes, marketing practices tend to be increasingly inflationary. On the one hand, of course, they produce volume, and that should generate mass economies that bring costs and prices down. The problem comes when you get heavy market segmentation, as we have had in the last fifteen or twenty years. Marketing men just went too far with this. And customers have ended up paying a big premium for all those styles, colors, sizes, and options. That is inflationary. It increases costs, increases prices, and does not always increase profits.

From an economic standpoint, however, the trouble with a lot of today's product–line pruning is that many companies are dropping lower-margin, commodity-type products and stocking with higher–priced specialty lines, since they produce more profit. While that may help company profit margins, the broader effect can be inflationary, because you are minimizing production economies.

As a major force reacting on marketers, where is consumerism headed?

Being dynamic, of course, consumerism is pulling in many new directions all the time. Yet in the large picture, there does appear to be a new and very important "societal phase" emerging. Back in the late 1960s and early 1970s when consumerism first burst on the scene, it focused mainly on product durability and integrity. While these are still leading considerations, consumerism is now going beyond that and getting into the effect of products and services on our quality of life. If you smoke, then I want you to go to another part of the theater, bus, plane, or train. Or if you drive a big car, that means you are polluting my air, and I may not like that. Who knows? In some future millennium this may lead to smokeless cigarettes or noisefree jackhammers.

Is marketing research keeping pace with that kind of change?

Unhappily no, because of the person who directs much of today's marketing research. Often it's an older sales manager who is being put out to pasture. Or the person may have been picked purely for his administrative skills. Too often, the people who make these appointments feel that you do not have to understand marketing research—you must just be able to manage it. So you get average people in charge, getting average results.

There are, of course, many able and well-managed research departments—
for instance, those at Pillsbury, Du Pont, Quaker Oats, and Procter &
Gamble. But there are too many others that are simply mediocre.

*In marketing research and other intangible areas of marketing—advertis-
ing, sales promotion, and so on—there is the even larger problem of cost-
benefit measurement of analyzing what you get out of all that money you
pour into a given function. Is there any headway here?*

Sad to say, we are still in the Dark Ages when it comes to productivity
analysis in marketing. And this is where the future of marketing lies if we
are going to offer the public the lower-priced products and greater value
that it is demanding. The difficulty is that corporate financial controls are
exercised by financial people, and they are seldom sympathetic to marketing. They think in terms of payout, amortization, and so on.

Is there a solution?

What we are starting to see in a few companies like Nestlé, General Foods,
Du Pont, Johnson & Johnson, TWA, and American Cyanamid is either a
special outside marketing auditor or someone in the corporate controller's
office. These experts are trained in both marketing and finance and can
interrelate the tangible and intangible benefits of marketing.

The same way that a company audits its books every so often, the
outside auditor does a periodic audit of marketing practices to determine
whether a product line and its pricing are right for the current marketing environment, whether the product and customer mix are what they should be,
and whether the company is on target with its broader marketing objectives
and goals in terms of its overall marketing budget. The inside controller is
more concerned with itemizing and analyzing actual expenses and how the
profit and loss sheet adds up in terms of company spending for advertising,
sales promotion, and so on. In short, the inside controller might pick up
where the outside auditor leaves off. We need more of this in marketing.

2 Prepare for the Financial Accounting Revolution

Frank T. Weston

One aspect of management that has been particularly subject to the impact of change in recent years is financial reporting and accounting, and pressures for change in this area are still being brought to bear from many different directions. Although the effects of such change may be most readily apparent in the increasing complexity of corporate financial reports, these changes have had a profound impact on the way in which American business conducts its affairs.

Frank T. Weston, CPA, is a retired partner of Arthur Young & Company and served for a number of years on the Accounting Principles Board of the American Institute of Certified Public Accountants. This chapter summarizes some of Mr. Weston's thoughts about impending changes in the financial accounting area. In reading it, you are encouraged to consider the nature of the changes described, rather than the specific accounting issues themselves, some or all of which may already appear old hat—so fast is the rate of change in this area. Mr. Weston's admonition to adopt a positive view toward change, and to respond in an orderly manner, anticipating the impact of revolutionary ideas, is sound advice at any time.

Corporate managers in the United States are about to encounter an exciting challenge: a significant revolution in financial accounting and reporting in a relatively short period of time. They would be well advised to respond to this revolution in a positive and orderly manner.

The revolution is a product of the complex interaction of such organizations as the Financial Accounting Standards Board, the American Institute of Certified Public Accountants, the Securities & Exchange Commission, the Cost Accounting Standards Board, the New York Stock Exchange and other major securities exchanges, the Financial Executives Institute, and, last but not least, the federal and state judicial systems.

The revolution can be traced in large part to the advent of consumerism in financial reporting. The pace is accelerated by the installation of activists as SEC commissioners and staff members and by the continual prodding from the press and members of the academic community. Other environ-

This chapter is based on an article that originally appeared in *Harvard Business Review,* September–October 1974. Copyright © 1974 by the President and Fellows of Harvard College; reprinted by permission. All rights reserved.

mental factors—the current and cumulative impact of inflation, the growing importance of accounting and reporting policies on the international scene, and the steady stream of litigation concerning financial accounting and reporting—have contributed to the momentum. Add to all these factors the efforts of the accounting profession to restructure the process by which financial accounting standards are established, through the creation of the Financial Accounting Standards Board (FASB), and the stage is set for major changes in the next few years.

The nature and extent of the forthcoming revolution, particularly those changes expected in the near future, are outlined below. At the risk of being tagged a false prophet a year or two from now, I also indicate the timetable that a corporate manager may anticipate. Some slippage in that timetable may occur, especially in those areas involving major changes from present practice. However, the trend is clear.

Price–level–adjusted Statements

One of the first changes undoubtedly will occur in the area of price-level-adjusted financial statements. The continued high rate of inflation has convinced many people in the corporate, professional, and public sectors that statements based on historical...dollar conventions are no longer realistic indicators of financial position or operating results. Responsive to these views, the FASB held hearings...to obtain the opinions of interested parties as to whether price–level–adjusted statements should be required to supplement historical–dollar data.

I believe that the FASB will establish a standard requiring the provision of such supplemental data.... Satisfactory experience with the Accounting Principles Board's 1969 test study and the continued high rate of inflation militate against delay in requiring such important information to be furnished to stockholders.

Financial Forecasts

Another subject receiving considerable attention is forecasts of operating results. The SEC changed its position early in 1973, eliminating its prohibition on inclusion of forecast data in any document filed with it. The commission is expected to issue guidelines late in 1974 for voluntary preparation and publication of forecasts.

To make clear to readers of forecasts the extent of responsibility for them which CPAs are assuming, the American Institute of CPAs is attempting to develop a statement of standards regarding its involvement with the forecasts. For the present, however, the CPAs probably will concern themselves only with the reasonableness of the underlying assumptions, the adequacy of the compilation, and the consistency of accounting principles applied. They will, of course, take no responsibility for the "achievability" of the forecast—that is, whether the actual operating results will coincide with the prediction.

A report of the AICPA's study group on the objectives of financial statements, issued in October 1973, recommends that financial forecasts be provided when they will enhance the reliability of predictions made by users of financial statements. The FASB is reviewing this report, but it is unlikely to focus separately on the forecast issue in the near future.

I expect that a number of corporations will begin to issue forecasts of 1975 earnings early next year in connection with their 1974 annual reports. These forecasts will be updated quarterly in 1975 if necessary, but in any case whenever a significant change in circumstances warrants a material change in the forecast.

As the practice of making public forecasts becomes more widespread, I would not be surprised to see—barring a major economic dislocation— most corporations listed on the major stock exchanges issuing forecasts by mid-1976. By that time, managements of companies not publishing forecasts should feel the pressure to join the movement.

Leases

The FASB is tackling the controversial subject of accounting for leases....The project covers accounting by both lessees and lessors, as well as the treatment of leveraged leases.

However, the FASB will probably experience great difficulty in arriving at a conclusion on this subject. I anticipate that its conclusion will require capitalization of many leases, based on the theory that the inclusion of property-right resources and obligations in the balance sheet is consistent with the purposes of that statement and with the objectives of financial accounting....

Elimination of Alternatives

Other developments expected soon are attempts to achieve greater consistency of treatment in financial accounting and reporting through elimination of alternatives.

R&D Costs

The FASB held hearings in March 1974 on the treatment of R&D expenditures and subsequently issued an exposure draft of a proposed standard that

requires the current expensing of most of such costs when incurred. I anticipate that the final standard will be issued late in the fall of 1974, to be effective for periods beginning after December 31, 1974. The exposure draft
stated that any changes required by the standard must be made on a retroactive basis. Accordingly, if the standard is not substantially altered, corporations will disclose in their 1974 financial statements—and for any fiscal
years ending before December 31, 1975—the current and retroactive effects
of the standard. Naturally, the impact of this change will be most significant for corporations that have been deferring R&D costs.

Future Losses

In May 1974 the FASB held a hearing on the question of establishing reserves for future losses. I expect the board to issue two exposure drafts on
this subject before March 1, 1975. The first will concern the treatment of
catastrophe losses in the property and casualty insurance industry.
Although the FASB has not indicated which way it will move on this subject, I think the board will acknowledge the long–term risk–taking aspects
of the industry and permit (or possibly require) property and casualty
companies to provide reserves for catastrophes whenever a reasonable basis
for determination of probability exists.

The other exposure draft will deal with reserves established by companies other than insurers for uninsured losses—such as plant fires or explo-
sions—and losses from expropriation of foreign assets. The FASB is likely
to conclude that, unless the probabilities of occurrence are relatively high
and the uncertainties regarding the amount and timing of the potential
losses are fairly low, loss reserves of this type should not be provided. I
believe that standards on these matters will become operative for fiscal
periods beginning after June 30, 1975.

Currency Translation

The significant and unexpected fluctuations in foreign exchange rates in
recent years have made the accounting treatment of foreign currency translation very important to multinational corporations. Because of the effects
of inflation and deflation abroad, the subject is closely related to
price–level–adjusted financial statements.

The FASB held hearings on the subject last June. I expect the board to
issue for exposure a proposed standard on translation this fall, if it has not
already done so by the time this article appears. Because of the complexity
of the subject and the variety of current practice, the ultimate standard—

if issued early next year—will probably not affect fiscal years beginning before January 1, 1976....

At this point it is difficult to predict which approach the board will adopt: the dual-rate translation method or the current rate method. Considering its approach to accounting for R&D costs, however, I think the board will favor the dual-rate (monetary-nonmonetary) approach and the immediate reflection of the resulting adjustments in the income statement.

Fuller Disclosure

Another area in which changes will be quite extensive is disclosure of additional information.

Lines of Business

In August 1974 the FASB conducted hearings on the disclosure of operations of business segments. In my view, given today's widespread diversification in business enterprises, the board will find it very difficult to conclude that such disclosure should not be required in financial statements. The emphasis on providing useful investment data is overpowering.

The ideal, a completely segmented presentation of income statements, balance sheets, and statements of changes in financial position, would be most useful to investors. However, practical difficulties of implementation abound. The major problem is in defining lines of business, or segments. The treatments of intersegment transfers and common costs are also troublesome.

The board, in my opinion, will decide that line-of-business operating results should be submitted on a supplemental basis, using rather broad criteria for line-of-business definitions....After a year or two of experience, more detailed criteria may be specified, together with the inclusion of certain balance sheet and funds flow data.

Current Values

Two important and far-reaching development in the offing are the disclosure of current-value information concerning assets and liabilities in the balance sheet and the reflection of changes in current values in a separate part of the income statement. The AICPA study group took the position that an objective of financial statements is to provide information useful for predicting, comparing, and evaluating earning power and cash-flow generating ability. It urged that the current values of assets and liabilities be reported whenever they are significantly different from historical costs.

It is unlikely that the FASB will take a position on this broad subject in the near future. On the board's agenda is a project titled "Conceptual Framework for Accounting and Reporting." As an initial step, the board held a hearing in September 1974 on the report of the objectives study group....

In my opinion, the trend toward inclusion of current-value information is irreversible. During the next few years, information on certain assets will be included on a piecemeal basis, reflecting, for example, the current value of assets soon to be liquidated or sold. Later, information about the current value of investment assets—that is, income-producing assets—will be added. The next step will be inclusion of the replacement costs of operating assets.

Other Information

Obviously, developments of this nature take time. Coincident with them, even more data useful to investors will no doubt be added gradually to financial statements. Various analytical ratios could be shown—current ratio, debt/equity ratio, and inventory turnover ratio, for example. Rates of return, by lines of business and in total, could be indicated on both historical-cost and current-value bases.

Role for the Manager

It should be clear from this recitation of impending changes that consumerism has finally arrived in the financial accounting and reporting arena. The needs of users are receiving greater attention, and the wishes of preparers—and, to a certain extent, those of attestors (CPAs)—are being subordinated. How can the corporate manager prepare himself to meet the demands of this revolution? Here are some suggestions:

1. Designate an individual in the organization as a clearing house to keep up-to-date on developments.

2. Undertake some imaginative testing of the various proposals as soon as their direction is reasonably assured. (Many large companies are experimenting with price-level-adjusted statements and current-value data, and some may publish this information in the near future.)

3. Coordinate the departments to be affected by these changes, such as the tax, public relations, stockholder relations, and legal departments.

4. Keep the management group, particularly the board of directors, informed of developments, so that it can react in a proper and timely fashion.

5. Participate in the public hearings and submit position papers.

6. Keep an open mind as to the consequences of these proposals on the efficient allocation of capital resources in the economy, recognizing the needs and desires of users.

To the extent that managers of business enterprises participate effectively in this revolution, its results will be that much more beneficial. By anticipating the impact of the revolutionary ideas and by adopting a positive rather than a defensive posture, the manager can play a decisive role in shaping their development. Viewed in this light, revolutions can be not only exciting but also productive.

3

Breed Change, Don't Just React to It

Henry B. Schacht

The ability to anticipate changes in one's environment is important to competitive success. Humans and other organisms can respond only to changes that have already occurred, but business organizations can identify likely future changes and prepare for their eventual impact. Since each enterprise operates in an environment that differs in many respects from most others, there is no one approach that will suffice for every organization. There are, however, some generalizations that can be relied upon in any effort to identify and respond to the changes that are likely to affect our businesses.

One view is that the business organization should be instrumental in creating changes in its own environment, rather than merely reacting to change. This, of course, requires an identification of those changes that will be useful and socially acceptable. In a speech before the Sales Executives Club of New York, Henry B. Schacht, president of the Cummins Engine Company, expressed some provocative ideas about the "care and feeding" of change. Although some of the matters he dealt with in that speech, republished here, are no longer of open concern to American business organizations, the concepts surrounding them are still important. Although much of what he says appears to relate specifically to marketing, he goes well beyond the narrow concerns of marketing in suggesting that to ensure survival, business should create changes that are responsive to its own needs.

Change is a subject that is getting considerable attention. It is a complex and little-understood process that is being addressed increasingly by those who thoughtfully contemplate what is going on in today's society.

Few businessmen are experts on the subject; I certainly am not. However, I would guess that the process of change is the single most important subject for a businessman to comprehend today. More importantly, the acceleration of the rate of change and the inevitable conflicts it produces must be understood clearly.

Some people, and some organizations, look forward to and thrive on change; others fear and resent change. My belief is that the latter will atrophy and die in the world of today. Let us take a look at what I think is a constructive approach to change.

This chapter is based on a speech presented before the Sales Executives Club of New York in March 1972. Published by special permission of the author.

Any social organization, and particularly any business organization, should seize upon change as an opportunity. It should look forward to change. It should thrive on change. But, most of all, it should create change rather than react to changes created by others. Given this as a statement of frame of mind, let me offer some general thoughts about what I think is going on in today's society and move to what all this might mean to the outlook for tomorrow's corporation.

We believe there are fundamental changes at work today, and that they provide unique opportunities. These changes stem from the acceleration of knowledge and advances in communications and travel that permit a more rapid and widespread dissemination of knowledge. These trends increase demands for an improved standard of living from less-developed nations as they become aware of the growing and unsupportable disparity in wealth in various parts of the world. This demand will provide opportunity in the form of new markets, and challenge in the form of aggressive awakened nations and work forces offering new competition.

At the same time, educational levels are rising throughout the world. We will experience a growing demand for more self-determination. This will result in a rise in nationalism. Nations will demand a stronger voice in their own resource deployment.

We forecast several important characteristics of the future business climate:

1. Resources of all kinds, including money and skilled people, will become increasingly expensive, scarce, and mobile as the worldwide competition for them heightens.

2. The proportion of scarce resources made available to the "private" sector will shrink as worldwide demands for social capital goods increase dramatically.

3. Ideas will become obsolete more rapidly, and products will have ever shorter lives in the marketplace as the pace of technology quickens.

4. National competencies are changing. The more developed countries are beginning to concentrate their investment and job content in high technology, systems, and knowledge industries. The developing nations are assuming more and more of the laboring, capital-intensive kinds of industry characterized by low product differentiation. Such changes will be moderated by legitimate national concerns about employment and resource utilization.

Implications for Business

Worldwide Operations

Major businesses must be truly worldwide in every respect. Resources must be focused to take advantage of new emerging markets wherever they occur.

Developed nations will always be key markets because of their size and because of their need for U.S.-type products. The developing countries represent the areas where the most rapid growth will occur in the next few decades. The first companies into these new markets will enjoy unique and long-lasting advantages.

U.S. corporations must develop the most cost-effective manufacturing systems available to serve any market, regardless of geographic location. U.S. corporations cannot afford to duplicate each facility in every country. Plants must be developed as an integral part of a total manufacturing network. This system will provide the most stable employment base possible as well as the lowest possible cost to the end user—thus moderating the impact on any single plant of fluctuations in national markets, and thus providing fuller and more effective use of valuable manpower and equipment. There will be limits to this policy dictated by the uncertainties of trade and distance, but the potential is great.

Flexibility

U.S. management attitudes and assets must be geared to the pace of the coming decade. Technology must be in the forefront, and we must constantly be in a position to incorporate new ideas into products designed to meet specific market needs. We must fully understand the complex and changing needs of the worldwide marketplace, anticipating rather than reacting.

Assets must be flexible enough to introduce new products quickly. The era of deep vertical integration, which implies technology static enough to generate long-term payouts, is ending. It was successful in the past; its time has passed. Balance sheets must be capable of handling large and sudden financial demands occurring at unexpected intervals.

Conservation of Capital

U.S. corporations must concentrate their available capital in those areas where it can generate the greatest return. This means investment in the high technology areas of research, distribution, and proprietary manufacturing. We also must be aware of the trade-offs between fixed and working capital, the necessity to both buy and make our requirements, the critical importance of cost reduction activities, and our goal of stable employment. We must be courageous enough to discard that which is obsolete and relentless enough to seek constructive change, remembering that our basic mission is to serve the needs of our customers throughout the world.

In General

All this implies a smaller world where commerce takes place independent of national boundaries. Successful corporations will need to look for markets wherever they occur and will need to marshal resources in the most effective combination possible, without regard to geographic boundaries. Only through freer trade between nations can we hope to meet the rising aspiration levels of all people.

There is some fear that this degree of free trade will mean a major threat to the U.S. economy, and we see among us a renewed desire for protective tariff barriers. However, attempts to restrict trade artificially have always been unhappy. For us such efforts will result in greater damage to those behind the trade barriers and bring about the eventual decline in the very standard of living we are trying to protect.

The United States has the skilled workforce and the economic strength to compete effectively in world markets, provided we never forget that the areas where we will have advantages are likely to change. Management of these changes is difficult, but it is also of top national priority. In today's world the need for continuous and responsive change is irrefutable.

The mechanics of free trade, such as currency valuations, barter arrangements, and tariff agreements, all need to be constantly reviewed and updated. Recent events are encouraging, though in no sense a final solution. As to the future, we need to be sensitive not only to our own programs but to those of our trading partners as well.

Our economic system is based on the concept that scarce assets should flow to areas of greatest demand, and within those areas to the most efficient and productive portions. This means that individual firms must change their product mixes to meet changing market demands, and must change their emphases in response to competitive pressures, costs, and developing competencies. Nations must do the same.

A business enterprise operates with an inherent franchise from society granted on the basis that it provides desired goods and services. Failure to provide these goods and services at competitive costs means forfeiture of the franchise to someone else. No corporation has the "right" to be in business. The inherent franchise must be earned continually. In the coming years, we must extend the scope of the franchise concept from national to international.

If others are able to produce goods more efficiently, we should accept the benefits for our consumers and turn our own efforts to areas where either we can compete more effectively or increase productivity and reduce costs to meet competition. For the United States, this means concentrating more and more on high technology and complete systems of doing work. Not only is this where our ultimate skills lie, but it is in keeping with the expanding educational levels of our population. This will require a higher degree of national sophistication in controlling change than we have yet shown to make the transition tolerable. It will also require a greater awareness of trends in international finance and trade. We are only beginning in both of these areas.

The growing needs of the world are now real, and the trends we have described are irreversible. This is the world in which we all will live; I find it exciting, challenging, and full of opportunity.

Marketing in the Future

What does all this mean for the marketing posture of a company? We have implied several things; let us expand:

1. The outlook has to be worldwide; nothing less will do in today's society, regardless of the type of product involved. I am very distrustful of the "international division." It usually turns out to be an international division of a domestic enterprise, by definition.

We must market independently of production sources. Marketing systems must not be tied to any particular production location. They are independent considerations so long as we begin with a correct perception of the needs of the marketplace and a fundamental grasp of how fast the needs are changing.

I am also opposed to marketing organizations being located in plants. This leads to sales forces calling on plants rather than on customers. Logistics and sourcing are important, but they must not be the concern or prerogatives of the customer if we are to deliver lowest possible cost. Ideas, needs, new products all operate independently of national boundaries. We must do the same.

2. The definition of product is changing dramatically. The sale of hardware is diminishing as hard goods become more and more nondifferentiated. I speak from an industrial bias, but I believe there are implications for soft-goods producers also. Speaking from the industrial side, I believe that the distribution system per se is becoming the product. The trend is more prominent in mature economies, but it is also happening in developing countries. Let me take the example with which I am most familiar—Cummins Engine Company.

We traditionally have been marketers of hardware—diesel engines. The changes that we have talked about have led us to try to carefully redefine this implied strategy.

In the last analysis, all that our ultimate customer really cares about is moving something from point A to point B at the lowest possible cost. He does not really care what the hardware looks like or who makes what. Ultimately he is interested only in the lowest total cost.

Total cost is important. As we move into an era of more and more sophisticated cost analysis and data availability, I believe the emphasis will change rapidly toward costs that are not now easily identified with the initial purchase. If we are really selling only cost of performance, several interesting things develop. Let us stay with my engine company by way of illustration.

1. We must know very precisely what needs to be done. This has resulted in our simulating on computers each mile of the interstate highway system in the United States. We can now tell you precisely how much work is done and on any given trip what is the correct hardware combination.

2. We must have accurate cost records to verify and assign costs to each performance variable. This necessitated the purchase of a record-keeping company that specializes in installing cost record systems in our customer's work places.

Downtime for any equipment is becoming a critical cost. This has necessitated gearing our 2,000 U.S. outlets with quick diagnosis capabilities, quick repair practices, increased hours of operation and so on.

Cost of repair is soaring as labor costs skyrocket; skilled repairmen become more scarce, and facility costs disappear into the heavens. This has necessitated a dramatic switch in the role of the service unit. We are attempting to turn the high-cost mechanic into a diagnostician who will find the trouble and replace the entire offending part with a rebuilt assembly. The defective assembly will be sent to a central rebuild station for repair, using assembly-line techniques and factory labor, rather than being rebuilt by expensive mechanics in an expensive on-scene facility. This puts the customer in and out much more quickly, makes better use of labor, and reduces the number of new facilities required. We have recently increased our U.S. rebuild operations from one to four and have two planned for overseas locations.

So our systems approach results in a careful definition of work done, careful simulation of product solutions, careful specification of hardware, good record keeping to verify costs, quick and readily available service operations at low cost, and quick turnaround times. The tie-in to R&D and manufacturing is obvious. The ultimate goal is also obvious: motive power at guaranteed cost.

In marketing a system, the hardware remains important, but the particular configuration of hardware is less critical. We are moving to sell a total package that meets the ultimate needs of the customer; that really is our product, and it really is distribution.

Aggressive companies have made customer service their real product for years. From a customer's point of view, IBM sells service rather than hardware; housewives buy Sears products because they know they can get them serviced; Motorola's TV concept is much the same.

Industrial companies must follow suit. The more nondifferentiated the product, the more important the service. Yet selling a service is really not enough. You must understand what the customer really wants. You must deliver this to him at the lowest cost possible, *not* the lowest cost available under the current system. There is a world of difference. Let me illustrate.

Cummins elected to try to change the system rather than work the current system harder. The jury is still out, but we could have trained more mechanics and built more buildings instead. Why didn't we? Back to that early dialogue.

1. The rising cost of resources means that metropolitan buildings and land are priced out of the marketplace, no matter how many we might have bought.

2. The rising cost of education means there are going to be less and less people willing to be mechanics, not more—regardless of how we want it to be.

Therefore our answer:

3. Change the system to work with the trends. This is what I mean by facing change rather than reacting.

The differentiation of the total product will be more and more in the "soft" side of the business: the technology and the distribution. Proprietary manufacturing will always be important and will tax all of our resources—both people and dollars. The hardware will change dramatically under the pressure of technology and instant communications.

Under these circumstances the challenge to the marketing capabilities of the corporation will be severalfold.

1. Insist on marketing what the customer truly needs, irrespective of what he is currently saying. Present him with more cost–effective solutions to his real needs (old words), *but* recognize that what he really needs is changing very, very fast and probably faster than your capability to respond with hardware. Therefore find ways to make your obsolete hardware look better until the next round is available. Total cost gives you more room.

2. Beware: hardware in search of a market is a philosophy to which nobody subscribes but which everybody follows. It has to go. The cost of a mistake is severe; the cost of persisting with a mistake is disaster.

3. Ensure that the system has the flexibility to market a rapidly changing mix. The new hardware is obsolete before the customer gets it; the system of marketing is not.

4. Be flexible enough to market what the customer needs, regardless of who makes it. If somebody else makes a product your customer needs, market it through your system and take the marketing margin. If you look carefully, it is a darn good return on investment. Laugh at your critics and

doubters all the way to the bank. Save your scarce corporate development and manufacturing money for areas where you can leapfrog and differentiate.

5. Recognize that in all too many cases a product that you sell for $100 out of your back door with full markup costs the customer $200. Do something about it.

6. Look worldwide. Emerging nations will undergo dramatic growth in the next decade as they search for a higher and higher standard of living. Emerging nations offer the chance for a preemptive position.

7. Finally, tackle change as opportunity, and most of all follow your natural instincts. Have fun. If it is not fun in this changing world, it really is not worth doing.

4

Evaluating Signals of Technological Change

James R. Bright

Technological change is a phenomenon with which we are all becoming increasingly comfortable. In Toffler's Future Shock *and other catalogs of change we have explored the new technology at length, and sometimes in depth as well. But merely to understand the changes that have already come about is not enough to equip us to respond effectively to the changes that still lie ahead.*

One interesting approach is the process of purposefully anticipating future technological innovation, estimating the political, social, and other factors influencing its progress, and preparing for the business opportunities created thereby.

James R. Bright is a professor of technology management and an associate dean of the Graduate School of Business at the University of Texas at Austin; he is also president of Industrial Management Center, Inc., a consulting firm specializing in the implications of technological change. In this chapter Professor Bright identifies a number of techniques that can be used to make technological change visible and useful. Although many of the examples he uses are drawn from a military context, you should have little difficulty making analogies to your own experience.

The folly of ignoring technological advances is readily apparent. For their well-being, all institutions in our society, particularly industry and government, must anticipate radical technological changes that sweep aside existing practices and open new opportunities, or create new problems. The company that neglects this task runs a serious risk. To the thoughtful and imaginative manager the need is obvious. The question is: how can he meet it?

A common assumption is: our research and development department is automatically doing this job by serving as the technological lookout agency for the company. Discussions with several hundred research and engineering managers during the past eight years have convinced me, however, that this role is played neither widely nor well in many R&D departments. The reasons are:

1. Most R&D departments are expected to concentrate on product development and refinement and new applications. They tend to keep their eyes on the technological workbench immediately before them—on the

technology of today, on the one-year to five-year time horizon and on the company's immediate concerns. Management's expectations, corporate custom, and conditioning by traditional practices do not often encourage them to study the technological environment outside their immediate areas of activity.

2. While many alert R&D managers (and some marketing managers) are extremely concerned about the need for long-range, broadband technological surveying and are eager to assume the responsibility for undertaking it, they lack support from higher levels. They try their best to keep up to date by reading the professional literature, attending association meetings, and making personal contacts. Unhappily, their managements have not recognized the necessity for such work, and they usually lack the funds and the manpower to conduct systematic surveys outside their companies' product areas. When, by energy or chance, a company's R&D manager does identify matters of great but not imminent concern, who will listen? How can he bring his information or suspicions to top management's attention so that the company's collective wisdom can be applied to further assessment? Of course, if he walks in with a new product in hand, he has little trouble getting a hearing. But persuading top management to explore a totally new technology, to undertake systematic investigation of an alien concept that might cause a current product to be superseded, is something else.

3. The R&D director usually lacks a systematic methodology for assessing the innovative process. I am speaking not of technological capabilities, in which he clearly is well qualified, but of the application and diffusion of technology. The process of turning a scientific concept into economic reality involves far more than just capabilities. Economics, sociology, politics, and sometimes ecology affect the rate and significance of technological progress, as I shall demonstrate later.

Assaying the Future

There has been some progress lately in putting technological forecasting on a more systematic basis. In the last three years I have conducted seven seminars on the subject that were attended by more than 600 persons from industrial, academic, and governmental organizations in ten countries. I estimate that about one in four participating organizations has started a forecasting program.

There has also been a great deal of work in developing tools for better forecasting. One very promising new concept is the cross-impact matrices developed by the staff of the Institute for the Future.

But technological forecasting is still an infant science and art. It remains inadequate for some of management's needs because (1) any forecast is certain to embody some degree of imperfection as conditions change; and (2) forecasts of technical capabilities do not necessarily deal with their diffusion, input requirements, and impact.

So I suggest that another concept can be useful to management in anticipating and responding to technological progress. I call it monitoring the environment for impending technological change. I have been using it since 1961 in teaching at the Harvard Business School and the University of Texas and in consulting work with industry. Since use of the approach depends on an understanding of the process of technological innovation, let us first establish some findings from research in this field. Studies of several dozen post-World War II innovations by a number of researchers, including myself, show that certain factors are present:

1. A radical new technological advance is made visible to society first in written words, then in increasingly refined, enlarged, and more effective material forms, long before it achieves widespread usage.

2. The potential impact of the innovation is usually evident years before the new technology is in use on a scale great enough to affect existing societal conditions appreciably.

3. Social, political, and, now to an increasing degree, ecological changes may alter the speed and direction of the innovation's progress, as I indicated previously.

4. Innovation may be abruptly influenced by decisions of key individuals who control supporting resources or determine policies that affect their application.

5. Technological capabilities—for example, parameters such as speed, power, miniaturization, strength, and capacity—increase exponentially over time, once bottlenecks are broken, but will begin to level off if they encounter scientific, economic, or social barriers. (Failure to accept or accurately gauge this characteristic of acceleration happens to be a principal reason why ''expert opinion'' from very competent technologists, economists, and study groups so often proves to be fantastically conservative, if not totally wrong.)

There are, of course, occasional exceptions to these points. The atomic bomb project, for example, was kept a close secret from 1942 to 1945. When it did become ''visible'' to society, its capability was so obvious that it immediately altered military technology, strategy, and tactics, as well as international politics. Most technological innovations, however, are visible in theories, laboratories, and field trials long before they are operationally applied; and their effects are apparent before use becomes widespread.

To the extent that this is true, it should be possible to monitor the environment to detect the coming, the progress, and the consequences of significant technological advances. Monitoring, by my definition, includes four activities: (1) searching the environment for signals that may be forerunners of significant technological change; (2) identifying the possible consequences (assuming that these signals are not false and the trends that they suggest persist); (3) choosing the parameters, policies, events, and decisions that should be observed and followed to verify the true speed and direction of technology and effects of employing it; and (4) presenting the data from the foregoing steps in a timely and appropriate manner for management's use in decisions about the organization's reaction.

Note that monitoring includes much more than simply "scanning." It includes search, consideration of alternative possibilities and their effects, selection of critical parameters for observation, and a conclusion based on evaluation of progress and its implications. The feasibility of monitoring rests on the fact that it takes a long time for a technology to emerge from the minds of men into economic reality, with its resulting societal impacts.

There are always some identifiable points, events, relationships, and other types of "signals" along the way that can be used in an analytical framework. If a manager can detect these signals, he should be able to follow the progress of the innovation relative to time, cost, performance, obstacles, possible impacts, and other considerations. Then he will have two more important inputs to his decisions: (1) awareness of the new technology and its progress, and (2) some thoughtful speculation about its possible impact.

The traditional analytical procedures used by business and government evaluate only factors in the technical and economic environments. But often the key events—changing values and relationships that determine the ultimate significance of the technology and its timing—lie in social and political spheres. The transportation companies and public utilities, for instance, long have had to consider the political sphere. And it deserves re-emphasis that today ecological factors are becoming a stronger source of pressure for change.

Furthermore, the interaction of events between these environments can prove to be the significant force. The closing of the Suez Canal—a political move—affected the economics of supertankers, for instance. It follows that monitoring requires us to look for signals in all these environments.

Whither the Internal Combustion Engine?

The importance of multienvironment considerations is evident in current demands for new kinds of automobile engine power. The auto producer in the past has responded—and still responds—to demands for economy and power, which are both economic and social factors. He conscientiously studies the technical and economic facts of the internal combustion engine (ICE) and its competitors. He takes comfort from evidence that no other vehicle power plant can provide the performance and economy required of the U.S. family car. He knows, furthermore, that recent engineering refinement of the ICE has eliminated 70 to 80 percent of exhaust emissions.

But such an analysis neglects at least two potentially significant signals:

1. The congressional hearings on the electric car in 1967 indicated powerful potential economic support for other kinds of auto power plants—regardless of economics. This support could arise from the political environment in the form of arbitrary and mandatory government purchases of electric and steam cars, plus possible legislation restricting use of ICE cars.

2. The trend toward multicar family ownership clearly makes special-purpose vehicles feasible. In one study, a student of mine observed that the second and third cars in two out of three families which he studied each traveled on average less than nine miles per day, and in traffic that prohibited speeds of more than twenty-five miles an hour. Such power demand is well within the capability of today's electric-vehicle power plant—provided that the user accepts the costs and other complications.

Another student found that at least four couples (out of about 120) living in a Texas retirement-vacation resort had sold their second cars and were using their electric golf carts for local transportation! He later learned that this practice is widespread in some similar communities, such as Palm Springs, California.

The transportation requirements of persons in retirement communities and of many families in large urban areas are such that they do not necessarily need a second vehicle with the same power capability as the first.

When the industrialist begins to consider all possible influences, a plethora of questions can come up. For instance: what is the likelihood that utilities will offer special rates and locations for battery recharging? Is there any significant technical development under way in foreign countries? Are any government agencies supporting research in steam cars? What are the latest findings on air pollution?

The conclusion for the industrialist is obvious but still needs emphasis: conventional business wisdom—meaning economic and technical analysis only—can mislead you about the forces affecting technological progress.

Types of Signals

Within each environment many types of parameters and events serve as indicators of potential change.

In the Technological Environment

Time series of technical parameters and figures of merit (combinations of technical and economic parameters) are very suggestive when projected into the future. For example, the increase in the number of electrical circuits per unit of space or area in solid-state electronic systems points to a coming compression of system size to at least 1/100th of the size of 1960 circuitry. Meanwhile, circuit cost also is declining exponentially. Devices employing electronics—radio, radar, TV, computer, and military equipment—will become much smaller, more portable, cheaper, and more reliable, and hence will gain more widespread use. These devices will be available for use in many new situations.

Look at the curves in figure 4-1, showing a forecast by the U.S. Air Force Avionics Laboratory, which underwrote the development and the first application of integrated circuits. The forecast of technical capabilities, made several years ago, has proved to be reasonably accurate. These curves tell the electronic equipment manufacturer that:

1. Large–scale cost and size reductions in the equipment still lie ahead.

2. Electronic products in almost any present configuration will be rapidly and continuously made obsolete over the next five to ten years.

3. A new product in this field must be exploited very quickly, since its market life probably will be short.

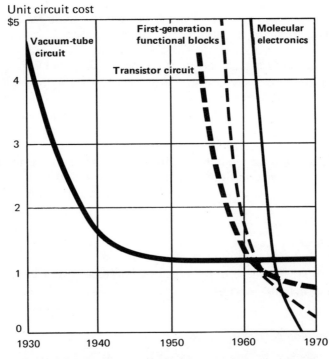

Figure 4-1. Projection of Cost Reduction in Electronic Circuitry to 1970, as Forecast in 1962

4. The wisdom of Solomon or the gambling instincts of an oil–well wildcatter will be needed, at times, to set production and marketing policy and tactics in this environment of rapid product change.

Reflections of interest in certain areas, problems, or phenomena also provide signals. A company may announce that it is establishing a laboratory to develop holography. An executive may state in a speech that his company sees opportunity in home entertainment centers. Or a professional society (such as the American Society of Mechanical Engineers) may expect 100 engineers at a conference on underwater technology, but 500 attend. Is this unusual response a signal of major progress and coming effort, or does it merely reflect wishful thinking or a "bandwagon" effect? We must monitor this technical activity to determine its true significance.

Demonstrations of new products, announcements of research progress, patent awards, and trade paper and professional society reports of materialization of new technology deserve scrutiny. An important example is Chester Carlson's first patent on xerography. The report of the patent award in the *New York Times* in 1940 was spotted by a young International Business Machines Corporation marketing man. During the next year and a half he tried to interest IBM in Carlson's invention. He failed, and so his company failed to capitalize on the potential of the new technology that public disclosure had placed in its hands. The signal was there, but the assessment of Carlson's first crude demonstration was inadequate.

In 1943 Eastman Kodak Company's technical publication, *Patent Abstracts,* published an abstract of Carlson's first patent. Kodak picked up the signal, but apparently no one monitored the progress of the technology, or management was not persuaded that it was significant.

In October 1948, the little Haloid Company held a major demonstration for the press in New York City. Company representatives not only showed, with laboratory–scale equipment, how xerography could be used to copy letters and other office paperwork, but demonstrated a camera that took and developed pictures in two minutes and showed a model printing press running 1,200 feet per minute. These and other potential applications were thoroughly discussed in the press ranging from *Business Week* and the *New York Times* to dozens of trade journals. Industry had its signal.

It is most important to note that two of these applications have not yet materialized for Xerox Corporation, Haloid's descendant, after twenty years, while copying, of course, has exploded in use. An appraisal of potentials made at that time could easily have been wrong. Progress should have been monitored to detect the ultimate true course.

In 1965 Xerox demonstrated its high–speed Model 2400 copier. Company announcements, speeches, and other reports, plus the growing speed of copying in previous model refinements, were evidence of accomplishment and an impending invasion of the duplicating field—of which no doubt the duplicating industry was well aware. In October 1969, Xerox advertisements described a new and higher-speed copier.

Now, what does xerography's growing capability imply for printing, either as a technical competitor of printing presses or as a device which reduces the need for printing? Those concerned should be monitoring this possible development. Monitors should, however, be wary of overoptimistic statements—no matter how sincere—about forthcoming technology. Recall the publicity about the Curtiss-Wright Aero-car and the Wankel engine in the mid-1950s, RCA's Ultrafax transmission-reproduction facsimile demonstration (almost simultaneous with Haloid's 1948 demonstration of xerography), and the Allis Chalmers fuel-cell-powered tractor. All were impressive demonstrations of new technology in use, but they have not yet become operational.

I do not mean to disparage these and other demonstrations. Some of these products fail for good technical or economic reasons. Others are displaced by superior technology. Still others, such as the Wankel engine (apparently), are merely delayed much longer than anyone would have imagined. My point is that demonstrations should be studied as signals. The Wright brother's first flight was 110 feet—a joke in performance. Now we know that the distance was irrelevant; the significance of the event lay in the nature of the accomplishment itself.

Performance data on technological improvements also must be scrutinized. These data are often mentioned in trade journals, professional society papers, technical reports of government agencies, and advertising literature. When related to earlier achievements in a time series, they reveal (possibly!) the state of the art, and they may suggest rates of technical progress.

One of the benefits of such reports is identification of problem areas and limitations, which helps to show what critical technical-economic factors must be monitored and where bottlenecks lie. A recent article in *Fortune* suggests that electronic typesetting and printing may become a threat to phototypesetting and conventional printing. The speed capability gain is enormous, but graphic arts quality is still low. What technological improvements have to be made to close this gap? This is a question of utmost importance to equipment manufacturers and users.

Usage and applications data, of course, provide information on the value and extent of adoption of a device with which to build estimates of technological needs and opportunities. The nature of usage can sometimes point the way to other technologies that must be created. Consider the growing use of plastics to replace metal. If plastics are to compete with cold-rolled steel sheet, vacuum-molding equipment must be developed to produce shapes of appropriate size and form for end-product applications. Have the plastic press manufacturers identified this signal and considered their alternative courses of action? Has anyone made exploratory designs of molding equipment large enough to handle auto parts? The signal is there, and the industrialists concerned should be monitoring further progress.

In the Economic Environment

Time series of costs point to relationships that are promising, or are intolerable. Time series of production, consumption, and sales activity point to volumes of production, and services which create new levels of facilities and material needs that cannot be satisfied without major changes.

Industrial and governmental financial commitments, budgets, and allocations indicate the support that will be given to a technology. Presumably this foreshadows its progress. Compare, for example, the federal commitment of millions of dollars for oceanography versus billions for the space effort.

There are, of course, many powerful signals emerging from economic trends. Since thousands of economists labor in this field, I will not presume to survey the possibilities. Suffice it to say that signals can be found in time series of costs, capacities, demand, available resources, rates of production, and consumption, among other data.

In the Social Environment

Population trends are a prime source of signals relevant to the ten-year to thirty-year horizon. Hindsight reviews of technological forecasts suggest that population figures are very neglected and unappreciated as criteria for assessing the economic significance of technical changes.

For instance, the Paley report (*Resources for Freedom*) on our needs for materials in 1975, published in 1952, was largely based on 1950 statistics. Because of erroneous population forecasts, the report greatly underestimated consumption of and demand for many materials (and, therefore, production facilities). Business and government should give much more consideration to the use of the most complete and recent demographic data in assessing the significance of new technology and in corporate planning.

Measures of activities, such as leisure time usage, education, occupational interests; measures of social conditions, such as the incidence of disease, poverty, crime, and air pollution; and measures of values, such as consumer attitudes, preferences, and interests, and political opinions—all these can provide useful parameters of social change. For instance, changing attitudes on overpopulation may give new impetus to birth control measures. We must also recognize the formation of special-interest groups, the delivery of speeches, the appearance of personalities capturing public attention, and the publication of books such as Ralph Nader's *Unsafe at Any Speed* and Rachel Carson's *Silent Spring*.

When assessing social attitudes, the manager or analyst must not apply his own value system. Though he may believe that Nader grossly misrepresents the facts of auto safety, that Rachel Carson exaggerates the effects of insecticides, or that antifluoridation groups are scientifically in error, he must keep in mind that their influence on technological progress stems from the attitudes they create, and not from the accuracy or completeness of their statements. The industrialist, secure in his technical–economic logic, can easily underestimate the force of public opinion when it differs from his perception of what is true.

In the Political Environment

Today it is the political environment in which many technological directions are initiated, resources are committed, and use is determined. So governmental actions that support technological development, underwrite development or finance utilization, or prohibit or limit applications must be watched very closely.

Early signals may be available, since formal government actions almost invariably are preceded by major committee reviews and recommendations, and by reports of debates about alternatives. Ronald Smelt, a vice president of Lockheed Aircraft Corporation, has pointed out the importance of the government committee review as a signal of impending technological progress in his industry:

> [A] current example is ... the growth of the surface effect ship. Work on support by an air bubble has been going on for many years, all over the world; a few years ago it grew into a specific program in England. In the United States the breakthrough occurred about three years ago when the Maritime Administration and the Navy together formed a special committee which recognized that the state of technology would not permit the development of a new class of vehicles, satisfying special needs for high-speed water transportation.

> [The] growth of science and technology is a relatively continuous process, with most technological advances casting shadows well ahead. (This is probably why the breakthrough seems to come in several countries at roughly the same time, even without conscious communication between the workers.) A definite stimulus is provided, in the majority of examples, by the formation of a government committee—probably the most effective method of bringing the technology face to face with the need.

Occasionally one can look beyond these public modes of decision making to their instigators. There may be a strong signal in the appointment of a certain person to a department or bureau from which he can influence the activity of a major agency. Identifying the interests, opinions, aims, and even obsessions of such individuals can help determine what technology is likely to be explored and supported.

A Hindsight Example: Missiles and Aircraft

To understand the monitoring concept and to clarify the analytical approach needed, let us look at a hindsight example. For a dramatic and quickly grasped case, consider the coming of the missile and its impact on the airplane manufacturing industry.

If somebody in that industry had been tracking events from the first extensive use of missiles in World War II, trying to determine their significance, and thinking about what further consequences to look for, his "journal" might have looked like table 4–1. His hypothetical analysis of the implications of each event would have been done, of course, at the time it was observed. He would have tried to establish those factors—figures of merit, effects, decisions, and so on—that were pertinent in the context of possible implications (the last column in table 4–1). No matter how our mythical observer might have interpreted these signals, with hindsight we know that the large manufacturers who had controlled aircraft production and design failed to recognize the technological revolution that was occurring and did not capitalize on the advent of the missile era.

The "journal" takes us up to the power struggle between the Army and Air Force for control of long–range missiles. Other straws in the wind in the 1950s included frequent discussion in print and speeches of "limited war" concepts, DOD and Air Force budget allocations for R&D and Sputnik.

That the industry had missed the signals was evident from a speech made in 1955 by Robert Gross, then president of Lockheed. As a trade magazine reported it:

> Of 22 major weapons systems now under development, only nine are controlled by airframe companies, Gross pointed out...."Shall we bend with the storm and see our industry splintered or face the wind and build more of the weapons systems ourselves?" he asked.

> He cited the growth of the guided missile field and technical advances such as new types of power plants and automatic flight as reasons for the situation now facing the industry.

As if to underscore what he said, in that year the Air Force first awarded a major missile development system contract to an unknown little newcomer, Ramo–Wooldridge Corporation. By 1960 the six largest aircraft manufacturers were suffering from reduced profitability, and the Department of Defense had formally recognized that the missile had replaced the manned bomber as the primary deterrent weapon.

A tremendous industrial upheaval and technological shakeout took

Table 4-1
Sample Journal of Technical Progress in Missile Development, from Aircraft Manufacturer's Point of View

Date	Event and Technical Economic Data	Possible Significance	Things to Consider
1944	V-1 used. 400 mph; 150-mile range. Can be deflected or shot down by interceptors and AA guns. Pilot less. Poor accuracy, small payload (2,200 lbs.) Different power plant (ram jet). Simple launch facilities. Cannot be recalled or redirected. Weather no limitation on use.	New method for delivering a warhead. Expendable and cheap; thousands might be used. Does not use conventional plane manufacturing skills or technology. Low-skill operating workforce. No present threat to bomber. Probably very low cost.	Accuracy, payload, range, and speed are poor. If each capability were improved, an alternative to the bomber? Counter-weapon available?
1945	V-2 used. 3,600 mph; 200-mile range. Pilotless. Rocket motor. Cannot be stopped by planes or guns. Poor accuracy, small payload. No warning. Germany launches about 1,300.	Conventional bomber defenses unable to stop this weapon. Uses chemical motor for propulsion; this technology not in airplane manufacturer's skills. V-1 speed limitation surmounted.	Launching facilities? Material? If accuracy, range, and payload improve, this is real threat. What are U.S. Army, Navy, Air Corps attitudes re future adoption?
1945	A-bomb. Explosive force is thousands of times greater than anything previously known. Can be delivered only by manned bomber because of weight and size. Expensive, scarce raw materials. Terrible effects and aftereffects.	Only a few bombers needed to deliver a given explosive force. Too heavy for use in a missile, but radius of damage makes need for accuracy less significant. Horror weapon, probably will have limited use. But what if explosive force were diminished or the device miniaturized?	What happens if size of bomb reduced to missile capacity? Availability of fission materials? Cost? Clean-up of after-effects? Reduction in power? National policy? International reaction to atomic warfare?
War ends, 1945	Russians and U.S. Army race to grab German rocket scientists. U.S. Army ships back 200 German missiles and establishes White Sands Missile Range.	Military badly want this technical knowledge. Army Ordnance deeply interested. Potential enemy deeply interested.	Air Corps still favors our products. But might the missile, in hands of Army artillery, reduce Air Corps missions, hence plane needs? Advances in missile accuracy, range, and payload?
1946	Regulus and Navajo missile contracts let by DOD. Range 5,000 miles. Nuclear warhead.	Real threat to bomber and SAC mission. Navy to obtain strategic defense role?	Technical success. Future funding. Response of Air Force to prototype performance.

1946	Electronic computer developed.	Computation speeded exponentially. Hence missiles can be guided and redirected to different targets more rapidly.	Effect on missile and guidance systems. Computation speed. On-target assignments.
1947–1948	Greek and Berlin crisis, crystallization of communist policy.	Russians intend to advance communism. Arms race to continue. Technical progress of all weapons systems will have priority.	Limitations in missile (and aircraft) performance will be gradually removed. Planes needed for what missions?
1948	Convair proposes ICBM.	Would turn into a major program affecting traditional bomber missions. Plane makers getting into missile business in big way?	Air Force response? What skills needed to make missiles? What mix of planes and missiles will be used?
1950	Korean War. Nuclear weapons not used. Missile-carrying planes, ground-to-air missiles appear.	Miniaturization of control. Reliability improvement. Both lead to missile guidance improvement.	What technical effect on missiles, planes, computers, and control systems?
1950	Electronic content of plane now up to 46% of cost.	Confirms that airplanes still are essential. Bombers remain necessary for tactical support.	Trends in plane and missile usage. Role of each? Further technical progress.
		Plane manufacturer's need for electronic skills and facilities probable, or else dependence on subcontracting.	R&D budget of Air Force. Cost of missiles and bombers? Skills and facilities needed.

place from 1957 (the year of the Sputnik) through the early 1960s. Signals of what was to come, however, had been evident in the decade following World War II.

Conclusion

Although precise technological forecasts obviously are desirable aids to management, inevitably they are only partially correct and cannot possibly be all-inclusive. Therefore we must monitor the environment to determine the ultimate course of technology, and its importance. The corporate management that ignores the warnings and opportunities in signals of impending technological change is trusting to luck, intuition, and the assumption that it will still have adequate freedom of action.

I suggest that a monitoring assignment be established in the corporate planning office and manned by the functional specialists—those in marketing, production, finance, and R&D—and even corporate planners themselves. An alternative is to establish this function under the vice president for research and engineering, provided he is given a strong marketing, economics, and sociology resource. In either case, the monitoring manager must train each of his specialists to take into account the political influences that might affect their respective areas.

A monitoring report should be presented to top management prior to the annual planning/budgeting meeting, with recommendations for further steps. Of course, conditions should be brought to top management's attention whenever there is a strong signal that implies a need for quick action.

Here are some thoughts to keep in mind when monitoring activity is going on:

1. Technology rarely achieves major economic impact until it is adopted on a significant scale, so there is ample warning. Production problems and the time needed for diffusion of radical new ideas delay the major economic impact for at least five and maybe even twenty years.

2. A signal usually has a number of possible implications, so all of them must be followed until it becomes clear which are the correct ones. But we tend to be too limited in our assessment of implications in that we consider only the state of technology at the moment of review. We should mentally extend the nature and degree of technical progress to be observed and then consider the implications.

3. There are many false and misleading signals in the environment, and it is hard to isolate the valid signals from the "noise." Since we lack the wisdom to be certain in our selection of relevant items, we must follow many possibilities with care. This is difficult, and the results will be imperfect, but it is not impossible to gain some guidance. After all, when Sputnik I was launched, it was rather late to conclude that rockets were here to stay.

4. At times the role of an individual is decisive; an able and determined man in a key position can dominate the direction or the timing of technology. President Kennedy's appointment of General Maxwell D. Taylor as Chairman of the Joint Chiefs of Staff in 1962 was a strong signal that the emphasis in military developments might shift from the old posture of massive retaliation to a more flexible response—that is, emphasis on technology other than bombers and missiles. Another signal, in turn, could be found in Taylor's 1960 book, *The Uncertain Trumpet,* which described the point of view that if the Army was to have "map of the earth" capability, the helicopter—representing the only available technology—was likely to receive greater government funding.

5. Many technological refinements are offered to solve some problems, and most never materialize in economic form. There are more contenders than winners. Therefore we must monitor many developments, realizing that only time will tell which is the truly significant technology.

5 Influencing the Effects of Technological Change

John S. Morgan

In his classic book, Managing Change, *John S. Morgan of the General Electric Company discusses and expands upon Professor Bright's theories in considerable detail. In the chapter republished here, Dr. Morgan presents one view of how to organize for technological forecasting.*

As we have already noted, it is not sufficient merely to understand the change that is going on now or that has occurred in the past. Dr. Morgan's work deals with the need for identifying and understanding the changes that are likely to take place in the future. Notwithstanding all the acknowledged defects and limitations of forecasting, he suggests a number of useful techniques for the intelligent identification of future technological change as a means for improving our control of the present. Going beyond the well-accepted premise that if you don't want to be overcome by change, you must learn to manage it, Morgan sensibly concludes that you must start by anticipating change—that is, by forecasting.

To master change, and not be mastered by it, we must "hasten the controlled, selective arrival of tomorrow's technologies," says Alvin Toffler in *Future Shock.*

Xerox's Dr. Myron Tribus states, "The key to the development of technology is managerial." Fundamental to such management is technological forecasting. Through the systematic use of an orderly technique, we can anticipate the major technological events that will affect our society significantly.

Only recently have managers realized the need to forecast technological change and its impact on their activities. We have long had economic forecasts, market forecasts, and financial forecasts. Why not technological? Dr. James R. Bright of the University of Texas estimates that only one in five organizations participating in seminars he has conducted over four years, attended by more than a thousand persons from industrial, academic, and governmental organizations, has started a forecasting effort, or even a continuous program.

As you consider the potentials of technological predictions, ask your-self such questions as these: What should be my goals in such forecasting? How do I perform this task? How should I organize for it? What are the pitfalls of forecasting? How can forecasts be better used?

What Are My Goals?

The year 2000 is closer to us than the depression, but many thinkers—economists, labor officials, and others—persist in thinking in terms of the 1930s. The past holds most of us like an anchor. Habit makes most of us look backward, not forward. One goal of forecasting is to change those habits. Another goal is to explode myths about technology. Aurelio Peccei, Italian economist and industrialist, predicts that U.S. and European research and development will reach $73 billion annually by 1980—but note that he includes European spending in that total.

Most Americans believe that their society is the unchallenged leader of the world when it comes to the development and utilization of things technical. This may once have been true, but no longer. Several things indicate that Americans are not as inventive, compared to the rest of the developed world, as the myths would have us believe.

Dr. Tribus tabulated patents per capita for a few nations of the world, normalized so that the figure for the United States is 100. Although the data are for 1963, the situation since has probably grown poorer, according to the United States Commissioner of Patents:

United States	100
United Kingdom	96
West Germany	175
Netherlands	181
Sweden	168
France	65
Belgium	65
Italy	31
Japan	12

The employment of technical personnel in R&D is another indicator of how well a society will do in technology in the future. Dr. Tribus constructed the following table by taking 10 percent of space and military R&D in the United States as applicable to the "civilian" economy, to show professional manpower during 1963 in civilian R&D (per unit of population, normalized to make the United States equal 100):

United States	100
United Kingdom	145
West Germany	95
Netherlands	157
Sweden	138
France	85
Belgium	82
Italy	33
Japan	125

All nations have shown an increase in technical effort since 1963 except the United States, which recently has shown a decline. The decline has occurred because of economic troubles and the disinclination of many American corporations to continue an expenditure such as R&D for which the payoff is ambiguous or far in the future.

Another goal of technological forecasting should be to minimize the ups and downs of R&D spending. IBM, with one of the best track records in research, spends between 5 and 8 percent of sales on R&D. But most managers agree that there are no rules about the best way to budget for it. President Mark Shepherd, Jr., of Texas Instruments admits that "some of it is just subjective as hell." Raymond H. Herzog, president of Minnesota Mining & Manufacturing, points out that the natural lag in the results of research (typically four years even in a short–range project) means that the money that might pull a company out of a slump has already been spent. Pumping new funds into research in a crash effort, he says, is neither necessary nor—in most cases—very wise.

Despite such demurrals, most managers of technical activities call for more stability in R&D spending. A forecasting program can help. Finally, the major purpose of technological forecasting is not necessarily to predict the actual form technology will take. As in other forecasts, the goal is to help evaluate the probability and significance of various possible future developments so that managers can make better decisions.

Technology is knowledge of physical relationships systematically applied to the useful arts. It can range from first intimations of how a basic phenomenon can be applied to solve a practical problem to an end product, device, or machine in an advanced operating system. Virtually any technology has a wide and relatively continuous range of characteristics in various applications over a period of time. This continuity makes technological forecasting possible.

While the forecaster cannot predict the exact nature and form the technology will take, except in a few immediate cases, he can cite probabilities about what performance characteristics a particular class of technology will provide by certain dates in the future. Furthermore, a good forecaster can analyze the implications of having these technical capacities ready in the future.

Consider technological forecasts as similar to market or economic forecasts. An experienced manager does not expect a market prediction to hit the mark to the actual dollar. Yet he wants his market forecaster to be approximately right.

Take the case of the electric auto. Electric vehicles are, of course, technically feasible. For a time in the early 1920s, the electric auto challenged the internal–combustion vehicle. The battery–operated unit still powers some city delivery conveyances, industrial trucks, golf carts, and other specialized vehicles. But the technological forecast for electric autos remains negative despite the advantage of virtually pollution–free operation. The problems are cost, weight, and power—too high in the first two instances and too low in the latter.

So technological forecasts thus far say "no" to the electric auto, but this may not remain the answer forever. Another goal for this activity is to keep monitoring the situation. Continuing change necessitates eternal vigilance.

How Should I Forecast?

There are many technological forecasting methods. For a summary of several, see *Technological Forecasting for Industry and Government* (Prentice–Hall, 1968), edited by James R. Bright. Dr. Bright believes that, with the exception of projects such as the development of the atom bomb, which was kept secret from 1942 to 1945 for security reasons, "it should be possible to monitor the environment to detect the coming, the progress, and the consequences of significant technological advances."

Here is a way to perform the technological forecasting task:

1. Inventory the important technological changes that you can see ahead; canvass others in the field for their opinions.

2. Arrange the list by relative importance; rearrange it according to probability of occurrence; then rearrange it according to time of occurrence if the events do take place.

3. For those listed events which have a strong combination of importance and probability, attempt to state the potential impact on society.

4. For every event, separate the possible consequences into those that hold potential positive and negative impacts.

5. Analyze the events and then plan how to maximize the positive and minimize the negative impacts.

6. Organize to put the plan into effect.

If you can make anticipation an intellectual discipline, some basics should begin to surface soon. For example: extrapolation may turn up as the first principle. Again and again, businesses or professions greatly affected by technology are caught by surprise by some development. The reason usually lies in a failure to extrapolate. Consider, again, the auto. The public and government show a growing concern about safety, air pollution, and traffic congestion. These concerns, together with technological developments, make it possible to extrapolate that future autos will be designed increasingly with problems of pollution, safety, traffic, and governmental pressures in mind in order to solve all four.

A second principle is the "imminent breakthrough." Take quantum electronics and the laser and maser. Now that technologists have learned to influence the energy states of atoms and molecules by radiation in new ways, and to withdraw stimulated and amplified emitted rays, we may expect to bring microminiaturization in electronics to new plateaus, including great decreases in size and weight and increases in the sophistication of the electrical effects that we can use. We may find new ways to use these processes to store, retrieve, and communicate information, and to extend man's vision and intellect and his ability to penetrate and affect matter.

The third principle of anticipation involves the "missing link." Often in considering technological possibilities, we encounter a step we cannot yet take. We see a final possibility on the horizon, but we do not know how to get there.

Here, we can at least write a description of what we need. We can tell a computer memory about the missing link, repeatedly telling it as science and technology advance. An example is the computer. Thirty years ago, scientists understood the basic principle of the computer. Early computers using mechanical or vacuum tubes were available. However, something to replace tubes was the missing link. The computer needed so many tubes that the heat from the filaments within the tubes made their use prohibitive in anything but an experimental apparatus. Furthermore, the tubes proved unreliable, expensive, and too large. Transistors and other semiconductors eventually came forth to provide the missing link with a cheaper, smaller, cooler, and more reliable replacement for the vacuum tube. The computer business today rests largely on the fact that the missing link was found.

With the electric car, the missing link remains an electrical source from something lighter than present batteries. Often the missing link in a technical development is nontechnological. For example, atomic power can dig canals and harbors, but the public will not as yet accept the nuclear explosion.

Sometimes the problem is an inadequate definition of the missing link. The supersonic transport (SST) was killed by Congress in the early 1970s, for instance, because of an almost total lack of such definition. Proponents failed to show the need for the plane and inadequately demonstrated how the SST would serve in the evolutionary development of future aircraft.

Technological forecasting may use a variety of techniques within the procedural framework suggested above. You must select the one or more that suit you best. One promising technique is demand assessment—the identification of important future needs which would be inadequately met by current technologies. Examples include traffic control systems for autos and aircraft in major population centers, a synthetic source for protein in our diets, a method to recover oil easily and inexpensively from shale, a way or ways to lower steadily rising hospital costs.

Another method, the theoretical limits test, pushes a known apparatus or phenomenon to its theoretical limits and tries to visualize potential implications—both good and bad. Consider the laser. The fact that light in a laser beam has a constant phase relationship has led to experiments to discover the implications of the phenomenon. One of the first technologies based on this marvel is hologram photography—creation of three–dimensional images. Such a development holds obvious importance to photographic concerns. By extrapolating the characteristics of holograms, you can also see applications in cryptography, devices to store and display multidimensional information, engineering design, communication techniques, and so on.

Parameter analysis, yet a different technique, goes to the heart of the forecasting process in predicting whether technical systems can reach or exceed key levels or parameters of performance by some future date. A celebrated example of a company that erred in parameter analysis is a successful maker of piston engines for aircraft. It ignored the jet field because it incorrectly reasoned that engine efficiency and fuel economy militated against jets ever replacing piston engines in commercial craft. Where it erred lay in the fact that jets can power bigger planes faster than piston engines, dramatically reducing the cost per ton mile and cost per seat mile.

Systems analysis can also help you to analyze technological futures, whereby the total environment is scrutinized. For example, an aerospace company entered the railroad–equipment business because its analysis showed that aerospace technology could be applied to the problems of rail passenger comfort, railroad speed, and economy.

Some forecasting techniques predict how competitors' technical actions will affect the company. When American Can Company acquired glass, paper, and plastics companies, competitors read that action as a shift from a "can company" to a "container company" concept, with profound technological implications.

Richard Rifenburgh, president of Mohawk Data Sciences Corporation, a maker of peripheral computer equipment, acknowledges that he follows the lead of competitors in research. "I want to trail a little to see on which frontier the volume is going to fall," he says. Nevertheless, the firm's line of ten devices in 1967 had expanded to more than sixty in 1971. Smaller companies, particularly, use this method, but all firms must watch the competition. They do it in marketing, finance, and many other areas. Why not in technology?

How Should I Organize for Technological Forecasting?

In general, the techniques you choose will influence your organization for technical predictions. Texas Instruments has an elaborate program called the OST system (objectives, strategies, tactics). The system is a formalized application of intuitive methods which proved successful when TI was much smaller, in the early years of the company's phenomenal growth. Size brought with it a need to disperse these methods widely throughout the company. OST principles do not differ significantly from those that govern other well-managed innovative firms. What is unusual is the degree to which TI's procedures are written, circulated, and later used in measurement.

Top management states objectives for the corporation and for eight distinct businesses in which it is engaged in detailed, measurable, quantitative terms. The goals demand courses of action that get spelled out as formal strategies. Each of the strategies is assigned to a manager who makes a ten-year forecast of opportunities, identifies areas of likely innovation, and sets up checkpoints to measure progress. Special forms must be filled out, describing in detail who in the company is expected to do what, by what date.

In some cases, a company may hire outside scientists, technologists, or consulting firms to do the job for it. The outside course is most feasible if you wish scientific surveys to determine a variety of scientific disciplines' activity, promise, and relevance to your company's interests.

Another approach is the "wild men" technique—the delegation of forecasting to one or a few highly imaginative and active individuals to stimulate really new thoughts about technological potentials.

The most common approach is the in-company staff. Staff planning or program evaluation groups, such as General Electric's TEMPO organization, have been established with full-time responsibility for evaluating various technological futures and advising corporate and division managers about perceived opportunities and threats. Long-range planning groups in other companies coordinate the development of technological forecasts in individual divisions.

Opportunity-seeking groups have been established in several chemical companies. They usually report either to top management or to the chief technical officer. They get in touch with current and potential customers to investigate how the company can help them solve technical problems and how some of the company's existing know-how can serve new applications.

The groups are supposed to coordinate with marketing, but they are purposely given independent status so that they can delve into long-range problems instead of the near-term ones that marketing generally involves itself with. Technical-information centers or commercial-intelligence units, another type of in-company staff, collect and evaluate data about technical trends.

What Are the Pitfalls of Technological Forecasting?

Technological predictions appear to be subject to four principal short-comings which should be kept in mind.

1. *Unexpected interactions.* The interaction of two or more technical gains may lead to the totally unexpected. Post-World War II decisions to emphasize manned bombers rather than missiles failed to anticipate the interactions of higher-powered atomic weapons, the increased reliability and reduced size of solid state devices, the capabilities of computers, and the development of new heat-resistant materials.

2. *Unprecedented demands.* An example of this is the computer. In the early 1950s experts estimated that only about thirty electronic computers would be needed to handle all the calculations then being made by every bookkeeper, scientist, and technologist in the United States. This apparent lack of demand kept many potential manufacturers out of the field. Actually, the computer made possible calculations and uses never before imagined. The dry-copying device is another example. The Xerox and other units did not merely take over the existing photocopying market; they created an entirely new market, changing typing practices, report distributions, use of published materials, and so on.

3. *Major discoveries.* Important developments—the transistor effect, superconductivity, lasers, steroid activity, to name a few—have opened totally unexpected technological opportunities. Both the shortcomings of imagination and the randomness of scientific discovery will undoubtedly keep forecasters' batting averages low in anticipating those major breakthroughs in entirely new phenomena.

4. *Inadequate data.* This is probably the factor that most limits technological forecasting. Fortunately, thanks to the computer, data supply is improving. However, forecasters often must develop some of their own figures before going on.

How Can Forecasts Be Better Used?

Herbert Hollomon of MIT, who spent fifteen years with General Electric before serving as Assistant Secretary of Commerce for Science and Technology under Presidents Kennedy and Johnson, believes that few companies are sufficiently receptive to the results of their own research. "They often set it aside," he says. "They never really decide what they would do if it were successful." While in Washington, Dr. Hollomon directed a study of the many small independent electronic firms that sprang up in the 1950s and 1960s along Route 128 outside Boston and concluded that many were started by frustrated scientists and engineers from bigger companies. Most of the small, specialized firms would not have existed but for the failure of larger corporations to exploit ideas and forecasts that were theirs for the using.

James Brian Quinn, business consultant and professor of business administration at Dartmouth College's Amos Tuck School, offers four suggestions for integrating decisions better with forecasts:

1. Forecasts should develop the pragmatic insights needed to make this year's decisions—not focus on esoteric problems of the year 2000. This does not mean that you should not look to or beyond 2000, but do it in the context of the decision you have to make this year.

2. Forecasters should place opportunities and threats in an appropriate order of priority. This will encourage action. It is easier to do something about one thing at a time. The human tendency is to do nothing when faced with unorganized opportunities and threats.

3. Forecasts should be fitted in with the company's regular cycles of executive decision. About 90 percent of most companies' expenditures are committed during periodic budget reviews, so this is the crucial time to submit technological forecasts.

4. Promising executives, wherever possible, should be exposed to planning and forecasting activities. Most management men today have had little meaningful background in technological affairs. With the world increasingly dominated by technology, they should remedy that gap in their background. Exposure to forecasting is one way.

In addition, nontechnical men may make excellent forecasters. It is a historical fact that highly qualified technical people rarely make good predictors of the future. Technical people who understand the problems are likely to assume that much time will be needed for the solution, while nontechnical people often exhibit childlike faith that the experts can solve almost any problem. Then the technical people sometimes go on to prove the nontechnical people correct.

Technological forecasting is relatively new. Like any new activity, it has its proponents and detractors. The question is not: should I do technological forecasting? It is: how should I do it? One chapter cannot do the subject full justice. For one of the best overviews on formal technological forecasting, see Robert U. Ayres's *Technological Forecasting and Long-Range Planning* (McGraw-Hill Book Company, 1969). You may not agree with his speculation: "It may be that science itself is to be the new religion of the world." But you do have to agree with him that technology is a powerful instrument of change.

If you wish to influence that change, you must start with forecasting.

Part II
Understanding Change

Understanding the characteristics of change is a far more complex task than identifying specific changes that may lie ahead. The articles in this section have been chosen to present a variety of perspectives on the process of change itself. By understanding what it is that we are attempting to change, or not attempting to change, we can better prepare to effect the changes we want and to obviate those that are not desirable.

The chapters in this section address themselves to the following aspects of understanding change:

1. Some assumptions about change that are generally true and some that are not;
2. Identification of techniques that are useful in effecting change, so as to better understand the things that create change;
3. Consideration of human reactions to change, so as to overcome and utilize invisible barriers;
4. Contemplation of a theory of organization which suggests a model of human behavior;
5. Evaluation of one approach to the problem of organizational change as a basis for understanding the dynamics of change on a group (as opposed to an individual) basis; and
6. Consideration of how to produce desired change.

Unfortunately, much of what is written about change and its characteristics describes carefully what it is not, or what must be done to achieve a desired result, rather than defining the phenomenon itself. This is probably because no one knows everything about change. In fact, so very little is really understood about change that it is necessary for us to draw upon a large number of examples and viewpoints to ensure a sufficiently high degree of comfort with the subject. Here we begin to explore the multidimensional characteristics of change: environmental, organizational, and human.

6

Preparing for Change

John S. Morgan

Like any other popular subject, the management of change has spawned a large progeny of myths, fallacies, and false assumptions. Returning to John Morgan's work, Managing Change, *we consider in this chapter twelve such myths about change and how they grew.*

Rather than simply being amused by Morgan's discussion, we should carefully consider the derivation of the myths he identifies and their likely impact on efforts to understand and manage change. Myths though they may be, these ideas and attitudes affect how people live and breathe and how they respond to the forces of change with which you are contending. In an age of "black holes" it is no longer safe to assume that certain physical forces, like gravity, will remain constant and behave predictably under all circumstances. Similarly, new insights in social theory effectively challenge many, perhaps most, of our old assumptions about change and how people prepare for change.

In 1927 the famed Hawthorne experiment was made among employees of Western Electric Company in its Illinois plant. Several attempts at change to improve production of telephones—with more money, more light, more space—had brought no startling results. Then a Harvard group under Elton Mayo came in. They isolated a few departments, introduced no dramatic changes, but emphasized that people were participating in the experiment. Output soared. Why?

Because the previous changes had sprung from fallacious assumptions. You cannot manage change successfully until you understand the fallacies and know how to avoid them. Among the many fallacies, the following twelve stand out:

1. All people resist change.
2. Only large or momentous changes are worthwhile.
3. Only large or momentous changes need serious attention.
4. Everything is changing overnight.
5. Change means improvement.

This chapter is based on chapter 3 in *Managing Change,* by John S. Morgan, edited by W. Hodson Mogan, Don A. Douglas, and Karen Kesti, and published by McGraw-Hill Book Company, New York. Copyright © 1972 by McGraw-Hill, Inc.; reprinted by permission. All rights reserved.

6. Change brings hardships for some.
7. Change brings rewards for the instigators.
8. Change is always unexpected.
9. No change is possible in a bureaucracy.
10. Technological change should and can be slowed.
11. Change usually comes by chance.
12. Man, infinitely adaptable, can stand any change.

Each of the dozen statements is misleading, deceptive, or false. Yet many managers believe some or all of them. Unwise actions stemming from such beliefs probably lie at the bottom of most mismanagements of change. Let us discuss each in detail.

All People Resist Change

This is nonsense. Some thrive on change; others do not. Your skill in managing change may hinge on your perceptions about your employees' tendencies.

Medical researchers report that man is equipped with an orientation response which gives him a neurological reaction to change. His senses quicken, his heartbeat speeds up when shifts in his work or other situations occur. He may enjoy the neurological reaction if it is moderate, or perhaps he cannot endure it even in moderate doses. That is for you as the manager to determine. With people who enjoy the neurological response, you have a different problem. Like those who have acquired a taste for caviar, they want some frequently. If the work proves too humdrum, the change lovers will leave or, worse, stir up some excitement on the job. At the bottom of much factory and office horseplay lies boredom.

The orientation response also includes a psychic reaction to change. It motivated the Hawthorne employees where better working conditions and even better pay had not, to any dramatic extent. In short, they responded better to higher psychic income than to higher monetary reward.

You will err seriously if you persist in thinking all people resist change. Such a fallacy has led to excuses for not inaugurating change, to wrong-headed preparations for change, or to wrong changes. The Hawthorne experiment particularly emphasizes this last point. While better lighting probably was desirable, it did not prove crucial. The Mayo psychologists found that the people injected with added "psychic serum" outproduced those who were not so inoculated, even when the psychic have–nots labored in excellent lighting while the psychic haves worked in lighting so poor that they could scarcely read a newspaper by it.

Only Large or Momentous Changes Are Worthwhile

This may also be expressed as "Change for the sake of change is bad." Implicit in both statements is the notion that if you must agonize over a change you might as well agonize over something momentous; make the trouble worthwhile. The fallacy here lies in the fact that most changes are small; yet in the aggregate they may add up to something significant. Change for the sake of change may prove useful, even though such shifts usually are minor. This kind of change may serve the valuable purpose of stirring up people by getting their neurological and psychic juices flowing.

A magazine editor had a regular policy of making modest shifts in editorial format from time to time. While he acknowledged that he was changing for the sake of change, he defended the practice as a "stimulus to readership." He added that "people need change now and then like a person needs a new suit of clothes." In effect, the editor was stimulating readers neurologically and psychically—appealing to their senses and egos.

Thousands of experiments in industrial change since Hawthorne have also demonstrated repeatedly the value of this. But the change for change's sake that omits the neurological and psychic factors in the equation is bound to fail. At best, it will do nothing. At worst, it can demoralize employees. It can leave buyers cold, too. For example, auto model changes that are mere face-liftings have met with less and less favor with the public in recent years. Yet changes providing some sort of neurological and psychic appeals have brought enthusiastic reaction. Ford's ill-fated Edsel failed because it was just another entry in a model range already well populated. By appealing to the buyer's eye, personal needs, or pocketbook, Ford's Mustang, Maverick, and Pinto have become textbook successes. Those three cars have stirred the buyers' juices, even though there were already other competitive entries to choose from.

Packaging experts say that a mere change in design may bring modestly good results, at best. But a change that brings even a slight touch of improved utility—such as easier opening—will prove a bonanza.

Only Large or Momentous Changes Need Serious Attention

This is not true. Most changes are small. Nevertheless, you will have to prepare for them as effectively as the big ones for several reasons: (1) the little changes serve as your proof of credibility in preparing for the big ones; (2) an accumulation of small changes poorly prepared can lead to large problems; and (3) a change which seems trivial to you may appear monumental to others.

One company moved its office hours ahead by half an hour during the summer. It noted the change in an employee newsletter, stating that the seasonal shift came "because of popular request, so that employees might have more time for recreation during the warm weather." Actually, three supervisors initiated the request so that they could reach the golf links earlier. They had checked it out with a few colleagues and had met favorable response.

But many other people objected. It conflicted with their tranportation and domestic arrangements. The uproar grew so loud that management had to rescind the seemingly minor change. Because it thought the shift in hours unimportant, management failed to prepare for it adequately. It reserved its concentrated efforts for more important matters. Yet the mistake went beyond the embarrassment of having to renege on a decision. It cost management even more seriously in lost credibility.

Everything Is Changing Overnight

Although change is coming faster, it is still not instantaneous. Copernicus devoted his entire adult life to changing then-prevailing notions about the sun and planetary motions. Darwin spent forty-four years in corroborating, explaining, and selling his change-generating theory of evolution by natural selection. Sir Lawrence Bragg shared a Nobel prize with his father for their joint work on analyzing crystal structures by means of x-rays—an enterprise in changing knowledge that took two lifetimes.

While city life changes, rural life continues at a slower pace. People who change frequently in one area—jobs, for example—may be stable in another, such as family relationships. People who lament too much about the speed of change are the hand wringers. The danger here lies in the possibility that the hand wringing will leave no time or energy for positive preparation for change.

Change Means Improvement

This is not automatically true. What is correct is the statement made by President Nixon in his State of the Union message in 1971: "Without change there can be no progress." The test is to select the type of change that will most likely lead to progress.

The wrong changes can mean regression. For instance, Sigmund Freud, the founder of psychoanalysis, also bears responsibility for helping to introduce the habit-forming drug cocaine. He saw it as a cure for neurasthenia, did not initially recognize its addictive properties, and fatefully published a paper about it, which he himself described as a "song of praise to this magical substance." The company that tried to adjust summer office hours thought it had introduced an improvement. It had introduced trouble instead. To support all change enthusiastically is naive. To support potentially productive change enthusiastically is wise.

Change Brings Hardships for Some

It need not. "Change is hard," as President Nixon also said in his 1971 State of the Union message, but it need not mean hardship. To accept the fallacy of universal hardship, as the hand wringers do, would be to stop most productive change. If you had stopped the industrial revolution (which probably would have been impossible), you probably would have avoided the exploitation of workers, especially women and children, but you would have kept the hardships of the farm life that demeaned or enslaved the bulk of the population before the industrial revolution. Change is always hard, but productive change lessens, not increases, hardship.

Change Brings Reward for the Instigators

Unfortunately, this is not always true, at least in the sense of rewards in recognition or money. Robert Mayer, codiscoverer of the principle of the conservation of energy, was driven out of his mind by lack of recognition for his work. Ignaz Semmelweiss, who in 1847 discovered that surgeons themselves infected patients with childbed fever, also went insane. His reward was to be hounded out of Vienna by the medical profession, who resented the suggestion that they might be carrying death on their hands. He went to Budapest, made little headway with his doctrine there, and died in a mental hospital.

In short, innovation often brings conflict—with upholders of the status quo, with jealous colleagues, or with those who claim they thought of the idea first. Elias Howe received a patent for the sewing machine in 1846, but his rights to the device were not established for another eight years, after much bitter litigation.

An inspector in an assembly plant suggested an automatic inspection device that changed him right out of a job. His employer found him another where he could—and was expected to—continue his activities for change. Some people would have said, "they don't pay me enough to make this kind of trouble for myself." Yet the inspector and others like him persist in their drive for change. No one knows exactly what motivates an innovator. Fortunately, most derive some form of psychic income from change, because they often win little else. The cynic may inhibit the acceptance of change by intimating that the innovator merely seeks his own personal material gain.

Change Is Always Unexpected

This is not true. Most literate, reasonably intelligent people know, in general, that change is coming. The danger in this fallacy lies in the assumption derived from it that the manager is absolved from the responsibility to inform people about future specific changes. On the contrary, he must avoid surprising people with specific changes. Even if an employee likes change, he probably dislikes surprises. Later we will have more to say about communication change. Now we can say categorically: if you have surprised someone with a change, you have failed to prepare for it.

No Change Is Possible in a Bureaucracy

It is more difficult to accomplish there, but it is still possible. To fail to attempt to effect change merely because you must work within a bureaucratic framework is to admit you are defeated without a fight.

One of the most celebrated examples in history of changes within a bureaucracy is Great Britain after her loss of the American colonies. One would have expected, after such a defeat, that the British empire would have perished in the early nineteenth century. On the contrary, the nineteenth century was Britain's and its empire's golden age, thanks to thoroughgoing reforms in law, administration, and concept.

And large companies are changing, too. In a recent 36-month period, 66 of 100 major American corporations announced significant organizational shake-ups. A substantial restructuring every two years in large companies is now probably average. When General Electric provided in 1970 for a new corporate executive staff, chairman Fred J. Borch explained it this way:

> There will be a much heavier focus on forward planning—not only at the corporate level, but at the individual business level as well. I can't overstress the need for this type of planning throughout the corporation to position it for the opportunities we see ahead. . . .
>
> We will continue to move forward in the further decentralization of authority to the managers of the various businesses. We want to cut down on the number of decisions which are now made at the corporate executive office and board of directors levels and push these down the line of the business managers. This will be a key factor as we move ahead.

Technological Change Should and Can Be Slowed

History suggests that technology cannot be stopped even if it were desirable to do so. French and Belgian peasants threw their wooden shoes (sabots, hence the word *saboteur*) into textile machinery which threatened their handicraft way of life. Ned Ludd and his fellow Luddites also attempted to stop technology's clock from ticking in England. None succeeded then; none are likely to succeed now. However, technology today is by and large uncontrolled. And there is a growing body of opinion that more control should be exercised. We are not proposing how government control such change. We are suggesting how you can control those factors subject to change which come within your purview.

We do not suffer from a lack of governmental planning—far from it. In a city like New York, reeling from near-disaster to near-disaster, a super-abundance of planning and earnest effort has surfaced. The trouble is that the plans and efforts cancel each other out. The problem when the technology fallacy and its related one about planning becomes accepted is that constructive change tends to get sidetracked. The issue is not that we have too much technology. It is that we do not have enough constructive and directed technology.

Change Comes By Chance

Only rarely does this prove true—as the result of an accident or of "serendipity" a word coined by Horace Walpole in 1754 to denote the faculty of happening upon or making fortunate discoveries when not in search of them. While trying to develop a new type of carbon paper, National Cash Register researchers happened upon a microscopic encapsulating process that today has changed photography, medicine, and electronics. Charles Goodyear accidentally discovered the process of vulcanizing rubber. In both cases, serendipity: the researchers were hunting, but not for what they found. Goodyear sought a method to make rubber usable at all temperatures. He happened upon the vulcanizing method; but the point is that he had for years been on the alert for an answer. So serendipity often proves to be more than blind chance. The beneficiaries of serendipity show themselves as people alert for change.

The miracle of change never comes solely by chance. On occasion, you may have observed something that becomes the germ of an idea. On a mundane level, for example, you may have grown exasperated at the way your secretary can never find anything quickly in the files. You mention the nagging problem to your wife at home. "You need a filing system like the one I use in keeping track of recipes," your wife remarks. "File by categories, with alphabetizing within each category. I don't file the recipe for apple pie under A; I put it under P for pies. Simple, really.''

And so it is. You speedily create a new filing system, borrowing the category idea from your wife. But was this chance? Only to the extent that you were looking for a new filing system. The chance occurred when your wife described her system. But eventually you would have found the trigger because you were looking for it.

The chance fallacy proves harmful when you never look for anything specific to change. Never will you find anything specific in that case, just vague observations that never pop into place in your mind to solve the problem that aches for a fresh, change-laden solution.

Man, Infinitely Adaptable, Can Stand Any Change

Measurable parameters limit the change that a man can absorb. Repeated stimulation of change can be physically damaging. Like a rubber band stretched too often, people lose their snap or, like a rubber band stretched too far, they break.

Psychological overstimulation is serious. Soldiers in prolonged combat conditions and victims of disaster have displayed these symptoms: (1) irritability and irascibility, (2) confusion and bewilderment, and (3) deadly apathy.

Psychological overstimulation can harm a man's ability to perceive and to think and to decide. Sufferers may deny that change is taking place, or specialize in a steadily narrowing field, or revert to obsolete panaceas, or become supersimplifiers who see one formula as the answer to all problems. Particularly, we must exorcise this delusion in preparing for change.

7

Change Agents, Change Programs, and Strategies

Warren G. Bennis

Although it may appear to some to be a largely academic exercise, many of us find it useful to identify conditions, people, or phenomena that function as change agents in our business environment. By identifying those things that cause change, we believe we can better control the changes that affect us.

In his book Changing Organizations, *Warren G. Bennis of the Alfred P. Sloan School of Management at MIT discusses change agents, change programs, and strategies. Although he deals only with certain types of change agents, his discussion is by no means as limited as might be supposed, and it should not be difficult for any reader to find recognizable counterparts of his change agents among those who hold comparable positions in other parts of our society (and even in our own business organizations). Dr. Bennis' analysis of the value systems of a modern organization is useful in thinking about those similar considerations that affect each of us on a day-to-day basis. If you wish to be a change agent yourself, it is helpful to be aware of the strategies employed by others who are agents for change in you own society.*

In the October 7, 1963 edition of the *New York Times,* a large classified ad was printed announcing a search for "change agents." It read:

> What's a Change Agent?
> A result-oriented individual able to accurately and quickly resolve complex tangible and intangible problems. Energy and ambition necessary for success....

Whatever doubts I had had up to this point about Madison Avenue's gifts for simplification and polish were lost. For I realized then and do now that any description of a change agent I would advance would have to include more factors than "energy and ambition," though these two are probably required.

The Change Agents

The change agents I have in mind are professionals, men and women who, for the most part, have been trained and hold doctorates in the behavioral sciences. Many of them hold university posts, and others work as full-time consultants, but they owe their professional allegiance to one of the behavioral science disciplines. While change agents are not a very homogeneous group, it may be useful to sketch out in broad terms some of their similarities.

Their Assumptions

They take for granted the centrality of work, in our culture, to men and women at work in highly organized, instrumental settings like industries, hospitals, and universities. They are concerned with organizational effectiveness, however intangibly defined or measured. So they are concerned with improvement, development, and enhancement. While their prescriptions vary, their diagnosis of organizational health pivots on interpersonal or group relationships and the implications of these on changes in technology, structure, and tasks. Although they are aware of these three nonpersonal factors and occasionally focus on them, their main preoccupation is with people and the processes of human interaction. Along these lines, it is important to point out that they are not interested in changing (or transferring) personnel but in the relationships, attitudes, perceptions, and values of the existing personnel.

Their Roles

They play a variety of roles as change agents: researchers, trainers, consultants, counselors, teachers, and, in some cases, line managers. Some specialize in one role, but for the most part they shift and switch from one to another. Frequently, change agents are not actual members of the client system; in other cases, they are. There are some who say that significant change depends on the impetus generated by an external agent. They argue that only a skilled outside consultant can provide the perspective, detachment, and energy so necessary to effect a true alteration of existing patterns. Advocates of the internal model take the opposite stand. They argue that the insider possesses the intimate knowledge of the client system (and the power to legitimize) that the external change agent lacks. In addition, the internal change agent does not generate the suspicion and mistrust that the outsider often does. His acceptance and credibility are guaranteed, it is argued, by his organizational status. Change agents tend to be self-conscious about their roles and their role changes vis-a-vis their clients. They go into instructive detail describing their interventions.

Their Interventions

Change agents intervene at different structural points in the organization (person, group, intergroup, and so on) and at different times. Blake and Mouton list nine major kinds of interventions which facilitate organizational development:

1. Discrepancy: calls attention to a contradiction in action or attitudes
2. Theory: research findings or conceptual understanding which helps the client system gain perspective
3. Procedural: a critique of existing methods of solving problems
4. Relationships: focuses attention on tensions growing out of group and interpersonal relationships
5. Experimentation: sets up comparisons and tests several actions before a decision is made
6. Dilemma: identifies significant choice points or exigencies in problem solving and attempts to understand assumptions and searches for alternatives, if necessary
7. Perspective: attempts to provide situational and historical understanding of problems through detached study
8. Organization structure: identifies source of problems as bound in the structure and organizational arrangements
9. Cultural: focuses on an examination of traditions.

Their Normative Goals

These are stated with varying clarity and specificity, but there is unmistakable evidence that their goals imply a particular vision of man and organization and a particular set of values which lay the base for this version.

To a large extent, these normative goals are aroused by dissatisfaction with the effectiveness of bureaucratic organizations. These objections were probably most cogently articulated and given the greatest force by the writings of McGregor, Likert, and Argyris.[1] These three books are often cited as evidence, and they are used by change agents as the foundation for various change programs.

Though each change agent has in mind a set of unique goals, based on his own theoretical position and competencies as well as on the needs of the client system, roughly speaking there are some general aims which most change agents would agree to. Argyris provides a graphic model which can serve as an example.[2] In figure 7-1 he shows (at the far left) the purported value system which dominates modern organizations—that is, bureaucratic values. These values, basically impersonal and task oriented and denying humanistic and democratic values, lead to poor, shallow, and mistrustful relationships between members of the organization. Argyris calls these "nonauthentic" relationships and says that they tend to be "phony," unhelpful, and basically incomplete; that is, they do not permit the natural and free expression of feelings which often must accompany task efforts. These nonauthentic relationships lead to a state which Argyris calls "decreased interpersonal competence," a result of the shallow and threatening state of the relationships. Finally, without effective interpersonal competence among the managerial class, the organization is a breeding ground for mistrust, intergroup conflict, rigidity, and so on, which in turn lead to a decrease in whatever criteria the organization is using to measure its effectiveness.

This is the paradigm: bureaucratic values tend to stress the rational, task aspects of the work and to ignore the basic human factors which relate to the task and which, if ignored, tend to reduce task competence. Managers brought up under this system of values are badly cast to play the intricate human roles now required of them. Their ineptitude and anxieties lead to systems of discord and defense which interfere with the problem-solving capacity of the organization.

Generally speaking, the normative goals of change agents derive in one way or another (explicitly or not) from this paradigm. Most commonly strived for are the following:

1. Improvement in interpersonal competence of managers.
2. A change in values so that human factors and feelings come to be considered legitimate.
3. Development of increased understanding between and within working groups in order to reduce tensions.
4. Development of more effective "team management" that is, the capacity for functional groups to work competently.
5. Development of better methods of "conflict resolution." Rather than the usual bureaucratic methods of conflict resolution, which include suppression, denial, and the use of naked and unprincipled power, more rational and open methods of conflict resolution are sought.
6. Development of organic systems. This normative goal, as outlined by Shepard and Blake,[3] is a strong reaction against the idea of organizations as mechanisms, which, they claim, has given rise to false conceptions (such as static equilibria and frictional concepts like resistance to

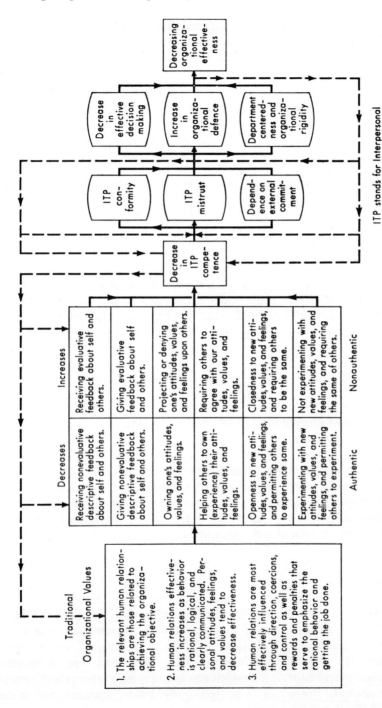

Source: C. Argyris, *Interpersonal Competence and Organizational Effectiveness* (Homewood, Ill.: Dorsey Press, 1962).

Figure 7-1. Predominant Value System in Modern Organizations

change) and, worse, to false notions of social engineering and change—for example, pushing social buttons or thinking of the organizations as a machine. Organic systems, as Shepard and Blake conceive them, differ from mechanical systems in the following ways:

Mechanical Systems	Organic Systems
Individual skills	Relationships between and within groups
Authority–obedience relationships	Mutual confidence and trust
Delegated and divided responsibility rigidly adhered to	Interdependencies and shared responsibility
Strict division of labor and hierarchical supervision	Multigroup membership and responsibility
Centralized decision making	Wide sharing of control and responsibility
Conflict resolution through suppression, arbitration, or warfare	Conflict resolution through bargaining or problem solving

Change agents conceptualize and discuss their normative goals in different ways; occasionally they work toward the same goal under different labels and for different goals under similar labels. But allowing for some exceptions, they would probably accept at face value the goals enumerated above. Where the differences among them come into sharper focus is in their choice of instruments or programs for implementing these normative goals.

Programs for Implementing Planned Organizational Change

The discussion here will focus on three broad types of change programs that seem to be most widely used: training, consulting, and research. Most frequently they are used in some combination depending on the needs of the client system and the particular skills of the change agent. For our purposes, we shall consider each of them separately.

Training

Training is an inadequate and possibly misleading word to use in this context as its dictionary meaning denotes drill, exercise, and the general notion of imparting skills through habit and rote learning. As the term is used here, it has a widely different meaning. It is used here to describe a particular variety of training which has been called "laboratory" training or education, or "sensitivity" or "group dynamics" training, and in most quarters "T-group training."

The T group emerged as one of the most important components of laboratory training and has evolved over the past eighteen years into one of the main instruments for organizational change. Bradford, as director of the National Training Laboratories, played a central role in the development of laboratory training; its growth was facilitated through the active participation of a number of university-based behavioral scientists and practitioners. Its main objective at first was personal change, or self-insight. Since the late 1950s or so, the emphasis has shifted away from personal growth to organizational development. As evidence of this shift, more and more laboratory training is conducted for specific organizations, using groups which follow organizational patterns rather then so-called stranger labs, where people come together from a variety of organizations and professions.

This is not the place to go deeply into the subject of laboratory training, but it might be useful to say a word or two more about it. It unfolds in an unstructured group setting where the participants examine their interpersonal relationships. The training process relies primarily and almost exclusively on the behavior experienced by the participants; that is, the group itself becomes the focus of inquiry. Conditions are promoted whereby group members, by examining data generated by themselves, attempt to understand the dynamics of group behavior—for example, decision processes, leadership and influence processes, norms, roles, communication distortions, and the effects of authority on a number of behavioral patterns, personality and coping mechanisms, and so on. In short, the participants learn to analyze and become more sensitive to the processes of human interaction and acquire concepts to order and control these phenomena.

T Groups are used in organizations today in the following ways:

Stranger Labs. Executives from organizations attend labs as "delegates" representing their organizations. The parent organization hopes to improve the organization this way by "seeding" a sufficient number of managers.

Cousin Labs. Organizations set up labs for individuals with similar organizational ranks but from different functional groups, for example, all first-line supervisors or all general foremen.

Diagonal Slices. T groups are composed of members from the same company but of different ranks and from different departments. No man is in the same group with anyone from his own work group.

Family or Functional Groups. These groups are identical to the intact group as indicated by the formal organization, for example, a particular supervisor would be with his work group.

   Decisions about the type of composition of T–group training are based on a variety of factors, for example, the stage of organizational development of the client system, particular exigencies facing the client system, and the competencies of the change agent. The extent to which laboratory training affects the organizational value system and structure is related to the T–group strategy utilized: the more it approaches the family group, the more the total organization system is affected.

Consulting

For every type and style of training there is an equivalent type of consulting. The type we shall be concerned with here is practiced by a number of change agents and is perhaps best exemplified by the work of the Tavistock Institute.[4]

   The change agent qua consultant operates very much like the practicing physician or psychoanalyst. "In undertaking my work," writes Sofer,[5] "I entered the same moral order as my respondents, helping them to maintain what was positive in their situation and to alter what was negative." So the consultant starts from the chief "presenting symptom" of the client, articulates it in such a way that the causal and underlying mechanisms of the problem are understood, and then takes remedial action.

   He employs an extensive repertory of instrumentation which he uses as flexibly as possible. Using himself most of all, he aims to detect and get close to the important data, to exploit every encounter he can in order to help the client system see "reality." He uses situations as they develop spontaneously to work through the tensions and resistances associated with them. Most of all, he uses himself as a role model. More important than the expertise and methodological help they contribute—and it is substantial—is the "...manner in which my colleagues and I defined and reconceptualized the problems. To the extent that this role model is emulated by the management group, change can occur."

   Heavy emphasis is placed on the strategy of role model because the main instrument is the change agent himself: his skills, insight, and expertise. Sofer reveals this when he suggests that psychotherapy or some form of clinical experience in a mental hospital is necessary preparation for the change agent.

   Argyris provides an interesting example of change agent qua consultant. He writes about two possible reactions clients have when their attempts to "seduce" him to give the "solutions" fail.[6] One is the expression by the executives of sorrow and dismay. Another reaction is their insistence that, since he is the "expert" consultant, he should provide some answers. Argyris writes:

Moreover, if their expectation of the researcher is that he should give some answers, because in the feedback situation he is the leader, what does this expectation imply concerning what they probably do to their subordinates? Perhaps this indicates that when they (as leaders) make a diagnosis, they feel they must make a prognosis. But if the above analysis is valid, what positive value is a unilateral prognosis? At best it gives their subordinates something to shoot at (just as they are behaving toward the researcher). But as they just experienced, if the leader (in this case, the researcher) is skilled enough to answer all their objections, he succeeds in making the diagnosis his and not theirs. Perhaps this also occurs when they succeed in answering all the questions of their subordinates when they, as superiors, are "selling" a new policy or practice.

So Argyris, as consultant, confronts the groups with their behavior toward him as an analog of their behavior vis-a-vis their own subordinates. He continually searches for experiential referents in the existential (here-and-now) encounters with his client system which can be used heuristically for the fuller understanding of the client.

If this description of the role of the consultant makes it sound more ambiguous and vague than the training process, this probably reflects reality, for in the consultant approach the processes of change and the change agent's interventions are less systematic and less programmed than in either the training or the applied-research programs.

Applied Research: The Utilization of Data
as Feedback Intervention

Almost all planned-change programs utilize research results in one way or another. The particular form of applied or action research I am referring to now is the one in which research results are used systematically as an intervention. This type of program was developed primarily by the researchers at the University of Michigan's Institute for Social Research, most particularly by Floyd Mann and his associates.[7] Here is the way it works. Survey data are collected and then reported back to the particular departments (subjects) in "feedback" meetings where the subjects become clients and have a chance to review the findings, test them against their own experiences, and even ask the researchers to test some of their hypotheses. Rather than the traditional uses of research, of a technocratic variety, where the findings are submitted in triplicate and probably ignored, this method strives for active participation of the subjects.

In other words, most methods of research application collect information and report it. There the relationship ends. In the survey-feedback approach, the collecting and reporting of results is only the beginning of the relationship. On the basis of the research results—and partly because of them—involvement and participation in the planning, collection, analysis, and interpretation of more data are activated. Objective information, knowledge of results, is the first step in planned change. But more than intellectual commitment is usually required. The survey-feedback approach is utilized in order to gain this extra commitment via active participation in the research process.

Richard Beckhard, too, utilizes data as the first step in his work as change agent, both as a way of diagnosing the initial state of the client system and as a way of using the data themselves as a springboard for discussions with the executive staff.[8] His procedure is very similar to that of Mann and his associates, except that the data are collected through informal, non-structured interviews which he then codes by themes about the managerial activities of the client. He then convenes a meeting with the particular subsystem on which the data were collected at an off-site location and uses the research headings as the basis for discussion. The following are examples of these themes:

1. Communications between president and line (or staff);
2. Line/staff communications;
3. Location of decision making;
4. Role clarification or confusion; and
5. Communications procedures.

I should reiterate that most planned-change inductions involve all three processes: training, consulting, and researching. In most cases, the change agent himself tries to utilize all their functions. Some change agents report, however, that they work in collaboration with others and that they divide their functions. For example, Argyris used L. Bradford as a trainer and Roger Harrison as a researcher. Sofer employed his colleagues at Tavistock to augment the services he could perform. It is also true that some change agents possess distinctive competencies which tend to direct their activities in certain channels.

What should be clear from the foregoing discussion are three points: (1) change agents play a variety of roles; (2) clients play a variety of roles— subject, initiator and planner, client, and participant-researcher; and (3) the final shape of change agents' roles is not as yet clear, and it is hazardous to describe exactly what they do on the basis of their reports.

Strategic Models Employed by Change Agents

In order to gain a deeper understanding of how these change programs are used in practice, it might be useful to sample some of the strategies employed by change agents. This turns out to be somewhat more difficult than one might think because quite often change agents fail to report their strategies or to make them explicit—even to themselves. However, two quite different strategic models are available to us: one developed by R.R. Blake in his "managerial grid" scheme and one through some work I was associated with at an oil refinery.[9]

Blake developed a change program based on his analytic framework of managerial styles. On the basis of this twofold analytic framework, it is possible to locate five types of managerial strategies. One dimension is "concern for people"; the other is "concern for production." As Blake points out, the term "concern for" represents the degree of concern for, not the actual production of, people's activities. Figure 7-2 shows the grid and the eight managerial styles. Blake and his colleagues attempt to change the organization in the 9,9 direction.

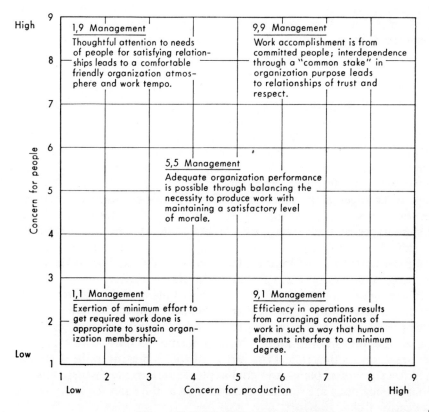

Figure 7-2 The Managerial Grid

In their strategic model employed to induce changes in the direction of "team management" (9,9) Blake and his colleagues specify six phases, which represent their most thorough and systematic work so far. Their strategy is based on experience with fifteen factories, ranging in size from 500 to 5,000 employees.

Phase 1 takes place away from the plant location; factory members are exposed to behavioral science theory (managerial grid and the like), take part in structural experiments, and participate in face-to-face feedback experiments and sessions of the T-group variety. All members of the managerial organization participate in the laboratory for a one-week or two-week session. Groups are composed on a "diagonal-slice" basis. It is believed that this diagonal-slice deployment is the most strategic at first. It allows organizational and interdepartmental issues to be aired more easily than they can be when the usual organizational constraints are present.

Phase 2 is also conducted off site and focuses on team training. Training groups are composed of a particular boss and his immediate subordinates, starting with the top team and reaching lower levels later on. Thus the unit of grouping is the actual "family" group, and actual conditions become the focus of analysis. This phase is based on the principle that if organizational change is to take place, it must be supported by the actual organizational groupings and must be exemplified and reinforced by top management.

Phase 3 is designed to achieve better integration between functional groups and between various organizational divisions, such as staff and line, technical and practical, sales and production, and so on. The normative goal of this horizontal linking is to create an organizational "culture" which can link relationships and articulate between departments in a more effective way than the bureaucratic model. In this phase, pairs of functional groups work together in order to solve the problems that exist between them. First they work as groups apart from each other, testing the image and stereotypes of their own group vis-a-vis the others and identifying obstacles to better integration. Then they get together and attempt to develop better methods of joint problem solving. This activity takes place, unlike that of the two previous phases, in the plant location.

Phase 4 gives real meaning to the concept of planned change, for it provides the mechanism for ensuring that the changes sought after are planned. In this phase, groups of from ten to twelve managers get together to set goals for the total organization. This composition is used at this stage in order to set targets that reflect the variety of forces present in the organization. After the issues, plans, and goal implementations are discussed by the various groups, they are summarized and used as the basis for an intensive organizational change effort.

Blake and his colleagues estimate that the time required for the first four phases—appreciation sessions, team training, horizontal linking, and setting of organizational goals—may be two years or longer. Implementing them may require an additional two years or so.

In phase 5 the change agent attempts to help the organization realize the goals established in phase 4. He deals with the organization much as a psychoanalyst would deal with a patient; in fact the program during this phase resembles the consulting approach discussed earlier.

Phase 6, the final one, is directed toward stabilizing the changes brought about during the prior phases. Blake estimates that this period lasts for a year. The role of the change agent is more passive during this period, and he is called upon for help less and less frequently. Rather than living with the client system, he is available upon request. The main effort during this phase is to ensure the maintenance of the present state of functioning.

Notes

1. C. Argyris, *Interpersonal Competence and Organizational Effectiveness* (Homewood, Ill.: Dorsey Press, 1962); R. Likert, *New Patterns of Management* (New York: McGraw–Hill, 1961); D. McGregor, *The Human Side of Enterprise* (New York: McGraw–Hill, 1960).

2. Argyris, *Interpersonal Competence,* p. 43.

3. H.A. Shepard, and R.R. Blake, "Changing Behavior through Cognitive Change," in R.J. Smith, ed., *Human Organization,* 1962, pp. 88–96.

4. See, particularly, the work of Jaques, Sofer, and Rice. E. Jaques, *The Changing Culture of a Factory* (London: Tavistock, 1963); C. Sofer, *The Organization from Within* (London: Tavistock, 1961); A.K. Rice, *The Enterprise and Its Environment* (London: Tavistock, 1963).

5. Sofer, *Organization from Within.*

6. Argyris, *Interpersonal Competence,* p. 104.

7. F. Mann, "Studying and Creating Change: A Means to Understanding Social Organization," *Research in Industrial Relations,* Industrial Relations Research Association Publication 17, 1957; F. Mann, and H. Baumgartel, *The Survey Feedback Experiment: An Evaluation of a Program for the Utilization of Survey Findings,*/Foundation for Research on Human Behavior, Ann Arbor, Mich., 1964; F. Mann and R. Likert, "The Need for Research on the Communication of Research Results," *Human Organization,* vol. 11, 1952, pp. 15–19.

8. R. Beckhard, "An Organization Improvement Program in a Decentralized Organized Organization," in D. Zand and P. Buchanan, eds., *Organization Development: Theory and Practice,* in press.

9. R.R. Blake, J.S. Mouton, L.B. Barnes, and L.E. Greiner, "A Managerial Grid Approach to Organization Development: The Theory and Some Research Findings," *Harvard Business Review,* vol. 42, 1964.

8

The Psychological Barriers to Management Effectiveness

Robert H. Schaffer

As noted in an earlier chapter, organizations as well as individuals have deep-seated psychological needs which often act as barriers to change—and to the effective management of change as well—when they frustrate needed change or cause unwanted change. In this chapter Robert H. Schaffer, president of Robert H. Schaffer and Associates of Stamford, Connecticut, discusses such psychological barriers and the use of various management strategies to overcome them. After identifying the psychological characteristics that play a part in creating barriers to change, he concludes that management strategy must use those characteristics rather than thwart them if it is to be effective.

The body of literature on the relationship between psychological factors and the achievement of organization results is large and still growing; a minimum, however, has been written about the issue that is probably the most pervasive and most expensive and that holds the greatest potential for change. The reason so little has been written about it is that, like the atmosphere, it is all around us yet invisible to the unaided eye.

"It," in this case, refers to the countless ways all of us subtly mold our jobs and our behavior on the job for what we believe to be rational, goal-oriented reasons, when actually we are being impelled by the pressure to satisfy psychological needs of which we are largely unaware. Sometimes these invisible or camouflaged mechanisms actually help the business, but often they drain energy from the enterprise or interfere seriously with its work. This article will try to make this ubiquitous phenomenon more visible and to suggest its far-reaching implications for strategies of management.

The Duality of Behavior

All human behavior is a fascinating blend of the rational and the irrational, the conscious and the unconscious. On the one hand, people are logical machines that perceive reality, make measured evaluations and judgments, and then respond with behavior calculated to achieve explicit objectives. At the same time, we attempt to satisfy psychological needs and minimize anxiety by methods of which we are largely unaware. This is an unending twenty–four–hour–a–day job: to avoid situations in which we feel anxious, threatened, or depressed, or appear to be incompetent, foolish, weak, and so forth. We steer toward situations (and try to manipulate the situations we are in) so that we feel accepted, respected, productive, and safe. The subtle (and usually unconscious) stratagems that we employ to succeed in this endeavor are known by the familiar term "defense mechanisms."

Rational goal–oriented behavior and unconscious defenses do not operate as two independent mechanisms. During a lifetime, defensive reactions become built into everything we do. Yet we tend to see our behavior as logical and rational, and thus have difficulty in distinguishing that part which is shaped by our need to minimize anxiety.

We are much more aware of the defense behavior of other people, though we may not diagnose it as such or understand what causes it. We are all well aware of the buck passer, the responsibility escaper, and the corporate underachiever, the man with ability who somehow always seems unable or unwilling to deliver. We know there is nothing rational behind examples of behavior like these that we see every day of our working lives:

1. A bright and able vice president of R&D has an assistant director who is regarded generally as rather incompetent. Yet for some reason, the boss is quite pleased with his assistant and has just given him a raise.

2. This president, whenever a crisis looms or a severe problem arises, calls a series of meetings involving everybody who might have something to contribute, and many who do not. These meetings are animated and lengthy. Rarely do they result in clear agreement on actions to be taken. Often the crises are settled in ways completely unrelated to the meetings. Nevertheless, whenever an emergency arises, all the officers prepare for meetings that last well into the night.

3. Mr. X is a prototype "authoritarian" manager. He never invites his people to participate in decisions; he always issues orders; and he often addresses his people in a tough tone of voice. An acute observer would see that, despite his manner, he rarely is explicit and clear–cut in his demands: thus, for all his toughness, they have a million ways to not do what he wants them to do.

Although written as humor, Parkinson's books come closer than much of the academic literature to capturing the mysterious ways in which men's hidden motivations lead organizations down pathways that are quite unrelated to where everyone says he wants to go. But the fact is that so far most of what has been perceived and written about is the noticeable, or even the offbeat and bizarre.

Before focusing on the interference between rational and defensive behavior in management, the point should be made that defense mechanisms often produce considerable successful managerial behavior. The forces that drive the most successful, able, and hardworking managers ahead, that encourage them to take risks, that inspire them to innovate and perform in many other unusual ways often stem from needs of which they are unaware. This positive side contains many clues for management strategy, once we better understand the other side of the picture, the rich variety of disguised behavior that managers use to satisfy their own psychological needs which are nonproductive for the enterprise.

The phenomena described here do not represent any psychological breakthrough by the author; rather, the effects of some well-known and thoroughly described psychological principles will be illuminated, effects which (like the "Emperor's New Clothes" in the children's story) are obvious but unrecognized.

Defeat without Trying: The Invisible Barriers

People try to minimize anxiety first by perceiving and interpreting the events around them, and then by acting in response to those perceptions, in ways that are most ego protective and reassuring. And both these mechanisms, perceptual and behavioral, can permit managers to achieve anxiety-reducing results at the great expense of organization achievement results.

Distortions in Managerial Perception

All of us wear colored glasses in order to see things in terms that are most fitting to our particular psychological needs and readiness. Thus while we share the same reality with others, we each tend to see that reality in our own terms.

For example, imagine that we are going to interview all the managers in a company, asking each two questions. What is it that keeps your enterprise from achieving much more than it is currently achieving? What will it take to get this enterprise moving more effectively? Although responses will vary a great deal from person to person, we can predict one result with considerable certainty. Virtually no one will attribute the shortcomings of the enterprise to shortcomings in his own managerial competence or behavior. Similarly, few will suggest that improvement in their own effectiveness might be a key to accelerating the organization's performance.

This predictable finding (test it if you doubt it) illustrates one of the most common and most limiting perceptive defense mechanisms of managers—the "doing all I can in these circumstances" illusion. Most managers place a definite boundary around their own scope for initiative. Within that boundary they see themselves as doing all they possibly can. When the boss is stuck, he can blame it on unmotivated, unqualified, or disloyal people; the people can blame it on their boss or various circumstances beyond their control. Needed improvements are always somebody else's job:

1. During the 1970–71 recession many managers were heard to rationalize almost every kind of disappointing performance in terms of the "state of the economy."

2. A team of managers in a large company was confronted with a demand for reduced costs. Although statistical evidence indicated that comparable companies were indeed performing at higher levels, most of these managers asserted that "their conditions were quite different," and that only by sacrificing quality or cutting maintenance could costs be reduced.

Thus, step by step, each manager whittles away huge areas of opportunity for initiative. We simply take them out of our line of vision. If they remain in sight, we have to confront each pathway of unexploited opportunity, and this could give rise to anxiety about our inability to respond. It is simpler to live in an environment that has been circumscribed so that it is controllable. Imagine how an enterprise would change if each of its managers perceived his current level of performance not as the ultimate of what could be achieved but as the mere beginning of a constantly expanding level of achievement. But this will not happen easily. These distortions in perception are extremely important to the people who hold them and, moreover, are completely believable to them and to almost everybody else.

Another form of defense by perception is denial. In the film "Never on Sunday" the heroine, Ilya, perceives the Greek tragedies as syrupy soap operas. While murder and mayhem occur before her eyes, she sees only love and happiness. This was a joke in the film, but similar behavior on the part of management is not uncommon. If the problem is too difficult to cope with, we may solve it by not seeing it:

1. Even though a possibly superior competitive product was already being market tested, managers of one company convinced themselves that their key customers, many of years' standing, would never be so disloyal as to leave them.

2. One company enjoyed an unusual spurt of growth and profits because of certain market conditions that were temporary in nature. In the resulting euphoria, however, all of its top management acted as if they had found the secret to a perpetual Christmas.

3. The head of a newly created, highly sophisticated central staff group assured his boss and his colleagues that the new function had been very well received throughout the organization. In fact he had aroused considerable suspicion and hostility, and few people would trust him with sensitive information.

Xenophobia describes a third form of defense by perceptive distortion. Man has a general tendency to differentiate between the good guys (with whom he identifies) and the bad guys. Thus the world is divided into heroes and villains, our team and their team, the "free world versus the Communists," and so on. There is this same tendency in enterprise to see our team—the idealized heroes—lined up against the villains. It takes many forms: production versus sales, headquarters versus the field, line versus staff, one product line versus another, and so forth:

1. During a major operations improvement effort in a large multiplant company, headquarters staff people complained that the managers in operations resisted new approaches to their jobs. Field people maintained, with equal vigor, that headquarters was presenting them with "academic" and impractical recommendations. These fervent accusations spared each group from focusing on its own need to change and improve.

2. In another company the president told a consultant, "We're just not getting enough good new products from R&D." The head of R&D told the consultant, "I can't set any directions for either our basic research or our product development because top management simply won't tell us where this company is supposed to be heading."

3. In a fast-moving, highly competitive industry, one company's marketers were convinced that their manufacturing division was incompetent because of increasing costs, poor quality, and poor service. The manufacturing people were equally convinced that unnecessary "catering to customer whims," an excessively large variety of sizes and custom options, and too many changes in instructions from production planning were undermining their ability to even hold their own, to say nothing of improving.

Of course, there is almost always some truth—often plenty of truth—in these allegations, which only makes it more difficult to see the psychological defense mechanisms at play. So long as one sees the major responsibility for change as resting with the other fellow, he need not feel a sense of responsibility for taking initiative. Thus management can blame the union and the union can blame management; planners can blame the operators for being "too focused on today" and the operators can blame the planners for being "too academic." This sort of distortion permits us to free ourselves, to a certain extent, of self-doubt. The nagging anxiety that might be aroused is masked as we get increasingly agitated about what the other fellow is not doing.

When Don Quixote dreams the impossible dream it is romantic, even inspiring. But when managers dream the impossible dream (another form of perceptual distortion) rather than come to grips with possible solutions, the enterprise suffers. This happens when a manager, to relieve his anxiety about a very tough goal, convinces himself that it is really beyond achievement. Once convinced, what more need he do? A variant of the impossible dream defense is to believe that the only way to reach an important goal is through some prior accomplishment which, at the moment, looks impossible. This too will relieve the manager of the pain and struggle of searching for approaches that might be within his power.

Here is an example. For years this consumer products company suffered from impossibly difficult union relationships. Plant productivity, abysmally low, reflected this state of affairs. Management felt that improvement depended on a shift in relations between management and the union, and a thaw on the part of the union with regard to work restrictions. Such a thaw would undoubtedly have opened the pathway to greater productivity, but it was highly unlikely to occur. Since the managers firmly believed, however, that this was the key to performance improvement, they were free to overlook many programs of action that were feasible even in their current situation.

The preceding examples illustrate how we organize our perceptions of the world to reassure ourselves and minimize personal anxiety and uneasiness. While this may be useful to us in one way, it often closes off the great number of alternatives and possibilities for realistic action that are open to us.

Behavioral Escapes

There are many different ways in which managers, by their actions as well as their perceptions, can unwittingly minimize their anxiety at the price of accomplishing the very goals they seek. Probably the most common escape is through busyness: The managers complain that they are too busy. They wish they had more time to think, to plan, and to view their jobs from a broader perspective. The assumption is that their busyness is a result of real job demands. The fact is, however, that many managers keep themselves comfortable by keeping busy. Quiet, unplanned time, empty desk tops, and silent telephones can provoke tremendous anxiety. Such pauses give them time to recognize many of their doubts about how things are going.

The large enterprise provides limitless opportunities for managers to keep busy. There are countless documents to be read and responses to be written (which will in turn generate new papers to be read); there are frequent meetings; telephone calls come in a random pattern. Any number of problems, emergencies, and crises cry out for management time. There are dependent subordinates who are happy to take up as much time as the executive cares to give, and company showmen who enjoy putting on presentations or meetings for anyone who will take the time to listen.

One of the greatest rationalizations of management is: "We've simply got to figure out how to get some time around here to do some thinking and planning." Considerable effort has been wasted in trying to redesign executive jobs, delegate routine tasks, shift the flow of paperwork, and so forth, in the hope that these steps will free the managers for planning and thinking. The fact is that, for most managers, this "freedom" is often very uncomfortable.

Consider this example. One director of a large manufacturing operation reorganized his job and his relationships with his associates so that they would carry more responsibility. Shortly thereafter, he went on a two-week vacation. When he returned, his in-basket contained only five or six items. In the past, there would have been enough material upon his return to fill two brief cases and an entire weekend at home. "To tell you the truth," he confided, "even though I designed this result myself, I can tell you that I feel damned uncomfortable and out of touch with things."

Managers are also able to keep themselves psychologically comfortable by escapes into structure and system. In order for large enterprises to work, human endeavor must be organized and institutionalized; there must be regular, understood procedures and routines. Thus every enterprise builds up its own pattern of operation at every leave, which makes it possible for everybody to understand how things should be done. At the same time, in order to survive and thrive, the enterprise must be able to change directions and policies; a balance is needed between routine and change. The problem here is that familiar routines are comforting and reassuring, while abandoning or restructuring institutionalized behavior can be disquieting. Thus, particularly in relatively stable organizations, it becomes increasingly difficult to distinguish clearly between those institutionalized practices that serve a real function and those that are merely vestigial.

Certain regular meetings are held, not necessarily because there are purposes to be served but because that is when that committee has always met. Reports are produced, not because somebody needs information but because somebody else has the responsibility of producing those reports. The executive committee meets every Monday morning, and its agenda tends to be made up in the same way each week. The methods of running the meeting—including what people feel free to bring up—tend to remain the same. But what is it that the committee is trying to accomplish? What do they want to do over the next six months or a year? Could they best accomplish these results by meeting five times a week, or once a month? What are the means by which they should attack their most important objectives? These are tough questions, and frequently it is more reassuring to simply carry on with the regular meetings in the regular way with the same faces.

Even those who protest most loudly about "too damn many meetings in this place" are often coconspirators in maintaining the schedule. Why? Frequently because a three-hour meeting on the schedule "takes care of" that chunk of time. The manager no longer has to consider how best to use those hours in the face of competing possibilities.

Management literature universally stresses the need to "manage by objectives," to have clear, well-defined goals and a method for measuring progress toward them. Most managers, however, are very skillful at escaping from commitment, avoiding unequivocal acceptance of exceptionally difficult goals. All sorts of escape hatches are built into the establishment of goals to allow for "conditions beyond control" in case of shortfalls (although most managers will not hesitate to take credit for achievement).

Financial vice president: "Sure we can go for a new issue now, but if you think we can get $25 a share in this market you're crazy."

Manufacturing manager: "Sure you can cut our maintenance budget, but you'll just pay for it in downtime and off-spec product."

School superintendent: "I agree it is important to measure and evaluate the results of educational programs. But the measures have to take into account some of the problems we have in this district that you don't find elsewhere."

How many progress reports have we read that say something like this: "While our achievements are up from last year, we feel that this is only a small fraction of what we should have been able to accomplish. We have therefore set our sights on..."

Our observations suggest that many managers become quite uncomfortable when they discover that their subordinates' view of a reasonable goal is significantly lower than their own. While the human relations literature, focusing on theories X and Y, stresses the inhibiting effect of the boss on the subordinate, the fact is that anticipation of a direct confrontation on the question of appropriate goals with one's subordinates can be traumatic to the boss. The manager wonders whether his people will rebel or, by one means or another, refuse to do the job or sabotage the goals. Will they be able to prove somehow that his goals are outrageous? Or might they quit?

To avoid these awful possibilities, managers frequently scale down the goal to a level that will be acceptable. They do not do this consciously, of course, and there are always enough "facts" to explain such a de-escalation, even to themselves. Sometimes a manager who has been forced to give ground will harbor an underlying sense of irritation. He may react by becoming overtly aggressive, hostile, or authoritarian, or engaging in other histrionics that reassure him as to his toughness.

The insidious nature of all these unconscious barriers to management effectiveness is perhaps best illustrated by cases in which managers, seeking to upgrade the effectiveness of the organization or overcome its problems, adopt programs which are in themselves forms of escape. When confronted with the consequences of inadequate performance, managers often prefer to see the fault clearly directed away from themselves. They also like to be able to look elsewhere for solutions, and are all too ready to believe that problems arise from faulty organization arrangements, the wrong management "style," inadequate information systems, lack of motivation on the part of others, or poor human relations or communications in the enterprise. They will carry out—or engage staff groups or consultants to carry out—all sorts of programs that are supposed to solve the problem. New management information systems will be installed. The enterprise will be reorganized. Managers will go off to examine their human relations.

These programs are often demanding, difficult, and time consuming. A manager deeply engrossed in them enjoys a number of self–defeating "benefits." He can comfort himself with the thought that he is vigorously attacking the issues. If he has brought in staff or consulting help, he can assure himself that experts are studying the situation. This permits him to overlook the things that he might be able to do differently to achieve better performance.

1. The president of one company could not bring himself to look his associates in the eye and reach agreement and commitment on some necessary tough performance goals. Instead, he went off with them to a human relations "confrontation" session in which many of his methods were subject to attack. After much open give–and–take, a variety of new ways of working were agreed upon. None of the discomfort of that meeting and the consequent shufflings around in company relationships and procedures, however, was as upsetting to him as forcing the issue on performance achievement would have been.

2. Another company whose profits were slipping downward went through a whole series of company reorganizations, each one designed to produce the "right" structure to manage the company effectively.

Four Important Principles

The illustrations in this article suggest the profound and pervasive ways by which anxiety–minimizing behavior becomes imperceptibly blended into the life of the enterprise through either unconscious or partly conscious means. These illustrations are merely samplings from a catalog that could easily outweigh Sears Roebuck's. We have focused on the "problem" side, but we must not forget that unconscious anxiety–reducing drives also impel us to behavior which can be highly productive.

How can a grasp of these ubiquitous forces help the leaders of enterprise? Four important principles underlie three strategic concepts which I believe are of universal importance to everybody concerned with establishing appropriate goals for an enterprise and mobilizing resources to achieve them.

Universality

Every human being, by one means or another, employs unconscious or partly conscious devices to keep from feeling uncomfortable. Some of these devices may help us achieve goals that we and our associates say we want to achieve. Others, as we have seen, are obstacles. Some may have no effect whatever on the achievement of goals.

Necessity

These forces are universal because they are essential to the maintenance of equilibrium. If one considers all of the real and imagined dangers to which man is exposed—including the fact that life is a temporary condition—it is obvious that worries and fears could easily overwhelm us. These defense mechanisms permit us to put worries out of our minds.

Individuality

Early in life we begin developing ways of dealing with difficult and trying events. These early patterns affect later ones, and gradually each person develops his own unique pattern of responses and defenses. This pattern of defensive reactions is built into all our behavior and becomes a major part of what we think of as each person's personality.

Stability

These patterns of reaction, gradually developing over a lifetime deep within the personality, tend to become fairly fixed in people by the time they reach adult life.

    Any strategy of management based on ignoring or thwarting the reality of these defense mechanisms is bound to fail, as is any based on the illusion that these fundamental patterns can be readily changed in an individual or a group. It seems to me that the major weakness of even the most creative work in human relations is its failure to come to terms with these facts. There seems to be a persistent belief that some universal ideal style for management can be defined (for example, theory Y). But the facts suggest that while theory Y may be great for some managers, others perform at their worst in ambiguous situations and at their best when they are told what to do. Similarly, the belief that a brief human relations training program can produce insights that permit people to successfully change their fundamental work patterns flies in the face of too much data.

Similar weaknesses underlie many other one-variable attacks on management effectiveness. When management tries to upgrade performance by reorganizing the company or a department, by introducing new management sciences approaches, or by increasing an R&D budget, it may be dealing with the manifest aspects of a problem while failing to come to grips with the latent aspects. Thus hidden barriers continue to undermine the new system or the new organization as effectively as the old.

Three Important Strategies

This leads to what I believe to be the three most important strategic implications for making the most of managerial potential and minimizing the inhibiting effect of the escape mechanisms. These are the use of multivariate strategies for change, the imposition of work disciplines on the job of management, and the maintenance of tough achievement goals.

Using Multivariate Strategies of Change

Any major effort to change the productivity or effectiveness of an enterprise must be designed so that, as new managerial methods, systems, and approaches are introduced, there are simultaneous efforts to help managers develop, grow, and become confident in operating in new ways. In considering any major change, it is important not only to discover what the objective facts suggest but also to determine the readiness for change in the enterprise. To design a change that goes beyond what people are able to deal with is to invite the mobilization of defenses against the success of the new organization, method, or approach.

If change projects are designed to match both what is objectively needed and what people are ready to do, the project can not only accomplish its immediate purposes but can also provide managers with new skills as well as the reassurance and positive reinforcement necessary to create readiness for more ambitious steps. In this kind of framework, major change, instead of becoming a series of disruptive crises and battles, becomes an accelerating, self-sustaining process involving many aspects of the organization's performance. Success at each level provides the foundation for next steps. As the enterprise changes, its managers grow, and as they grow they can handle more change.

Imposing Work Disciplines on Management

The production worker's job, the clerical job, and the first-line supervisory job can be defined in terms of specific behavior and specific results. The further up the line, the more difficult it becomes to describe precisely the goals and the steps to achieve them. Thus the more responsible the job, the greater the opportunities for managers to confuse their escape and defensive behavior with their result–producing behavior. To minimize this possibility, it is necessary for management to attempt to capture in writing as much of their jobs as possible in terms of commitment to definable (and quantifiable) goals; the strategies and work plans to be employed in achieving them; the timing of various steps; and the measures of progress along the way.

Each new decision area that management considers begins as ill–defined ideas. Only as management strives to shift more and more of the ambiguous and ill–defined into the orbit of specific control—where its work is defined, measured, and recorded in writing—can management protect itself from its own subtle and insidious escape mechanisms.

Maintaining Tough Goals

As the real demands for achievement in an organization diminish, the degree to which escape mechanisms dissipate energy increases geometrically. The organizations in which people seem to have the greatest morale and human relations problems, which have too many meetings, and whose executives are unavailable because they are so busy, are those organizations whose members have the lowest achievement goals (or, if their goals are high, the easiest means of escaping from failure to achieve the goals).

One of the classic errors of modern organization theory is the belief that in such cases the morale and human relations problems must be solved as a prerequisite to improving productivity. This view confuses cause and effect. Where the real demands for management performance are high, where tremendous energy and concentration are required, and where there may not be enough people to get the job done, the least energy is dissipated on off–target escapes. High standards and high productivity may be the key variables here.

In trying to employ these three strategies, of course, the manager must battle with his own escape desire, since each of the three strategies requires him to move into possibly uncomfortable and anxiety–provoking areas. But it can be done on a gradual step–by–step basis—if not alone, then with the help of staff or outside consultants—and the results are worth the fight.

9 Multilayered Management

Wilbur M. McFeely

An understanding of the management of change requires an understanding of organizational dynamics as well as of psychology. Putting the behavioral characteristics of a number of people together in a business organization creates not only a sum of their individual characteristics but a new, interactive multidimensional social organism with characteristics of its own. An organization is a system of responses to events, situations, policies, plans, and people (who in turn respond primarily to other people within the organization). While cultural patterns affect individual responses to a certain degree, they affect organization responses profoundly. And the larger the organization, the greater is the impact of this dynamic system of human interaction and cultural response.

In this chapter, Wilbur M. McFeely of the Conference Board's management research staff outlines a theory of the "three–ply organization" in which each of the plies is affected by individual responses within it, and all of the plies affect each of the others. Distorted perceptions as to where particular individuals, departments, or other elements of the organization appear in the "ply system" often frustrate the effective managment of change. Understanding this theory can help you to understand better the change that goes on—or that you want to go on—in your own organization.

Increasingly in large corporations the jargon of professional football is taking hold. The game plan is the strategy for achieving corporate objectives. The playbook contains the detailed plans and action programs, organization charts and manuals, and other data supporting the game plan.

The coaching of this team effort is characteristically designed to rationalize the team's performance. Thus major attention is given to:

1. Minimizing the incidence of individual or group behavior that is erratic or incompatible with the team's style of play.
2. Eliminating those tools, equipment, and materials that have poor performance records.
3. Setting performance standards, and establishing systems of measurement, evaluation, feedback, and correction.

4. Reducing the probabilities of making mistakes through various deci-
    sion–making techniques, and making improvisory techniques unneces-
    sary.
5. Selecting and training individual players to make them highly skilled,
    but nevertheless replaceable.
6. Lubricating human interactions to make them hit hard and effectively
    in ways designed to maximize the chances of the team's being able to
    achieve victory.

Suppose, now, that the team is not winning. Some things simply have to
be changed to get the team back into the running. The logic of the team's
underlying system indicates several possible approaches:

1. Restate the team's objectives and gain player commitment to them.
2. Change some of the coaching staff.
3. Shift some of the players into other positions, or put them into more
    logical groupings.
4. Bring in new players for various positions.
5. Try to retread other players to increase their effectiveness.
6. Adopt a new system of offense, and devise better defenses.
7. Enlarge the existing farm system and eliminate unprofitable franchises.

Current investigation into how companies plan and implement organizational changes indicates a reliance on these approaches. They seem to be
well grounded in conventional wisdom as being reasonable techniques for
bringing about change. Often they are effective in bringing about the
desired change, provided that the persons affected are also treated reasonably.

Managers also testify, however, that proposed changes are seldom, if
ever, accepted by the organization without qualification. There is almost
always some resistance to the planned change.

Evidently the greatest obstacle to change is inertia. And the prime inertial factors are existing traditions and attitudes: the habits and successes of
the past that are enshrined in the present. The inertial factors inherent in
every organization must be managed if significant change is to be achieved.

In examining these factors, it becomes readily apparent that no organization is homogeneous or monolithic. An organization, particularly a large
organization, tends to be multi–institutional in nature. Thus an analysis of
the problems of organizational change indicates that, within the management group which is most affected by change, there are at least three recognizable internal institutions.

To suggest that these internal institutions are like the plies of a laminate
would connote too rigid a stratification. Yet the analogy is useful as a

vehicle for examining the nature of the three internal institutions and the relationships among them. Thus an organization may be thought of as a laminate of three plastic plies—with emphasis on the use of the word plastic as an adjective. The bonding agent consists of immeasurable amounts of communication, work flow, authority, and patterns of mutual influence and support.

The key point of the analogy is the distinctive nature of each ply. Each has an idiom, a work focus, patterns of action and interaction, and other characteristics that are of the nature of discrete institutions.

At this time, insights concerning the distinctive nature of the three plies are quite tentative. Those who have examined the concept are not in full agreement that there are only three plies. Nor can they agree upon a label to characterize each ply. The labels are therefore for purposes of discussion only. Some alternate suggestions for the names of the plies are included in parentheses: (1) ideational (philosophical, ideological, perceptive), (2) synergistic (transactional, catalytic, enabling), and (3) process (technological, technocratic, operational).

Admittedly, the hypothesis of the three–ply nature of an organization has hierarchical overtones. But it is not simply another way of saying top management, middle management, and lower management. Differences among the plies flow from cultural characteristics rather than position. As one executive said: "I have the status and prerogatives of membership in the ideational ply but I am actually in the synergistic ply." Others attest similarly that the organization chart is not necessarily a reliable guide to membership in a ply. It is these cultural differences within the plies that inhibit or frustrate, foster or encourage, organizing for change.

Idiom

The differences among the three internal institutions are readily noticeable in the characteristic idiom of each ply.

Ideational Ply

The idiom reflects its orientation toward the long–range view, the big picture. Apparently it is also responsive to buzz words, trigger terms, and other style–setting expressions currently in vogue by thought leaders among corporate executives. This is evident from examples of the prevailing idiom—corporate objectives, long–range planning, management by objectives, market orientation, profit centers, free enterprise system, free market economy, decentralization, centralization, investment, divestment, diversification, liquidity, environmental influences, public affairs, company image (identity, character), stockholder reaction, governmental policy, international competition, result oriented, team–building.

This idiom is obviously very generalized in character and may have quite different shades of meaning in different companies. The idiom reflects broad concepts, ideas, notions, and prompting of policymaking managers.

Synergistic Ply

The idiom of this ply is quite varied and is sprinkled liberally with the jargon of specialists, with certain common–denominator words—system, study, analysis, policy statement, program, development, action goal, research.

These words come with a great variety of adjectival modifiers—financial, budgetary, cost, engineering, value, process, market, product, pricing, legal, personnel, organization, community, public, information, control.

The working language emphasizes also the experiment, the tentative approach, the provisional try, the contingency. What would happen if we tried this? Here is something that might be useful. What do we want to accomplish? What further data do we need? If this doesn't work, we won't lose much; where do we go, if this just doesn't work?

As the label of the ply suggests, the idiom reflects a variety of disciplines in both the arts and sciences. It is the language of the enabler, the catalyst, and of persons who are charged with fleshing out broad concepts, and making them operational.

Process Ply

The idiom of this ply reflects its concern with technology, processes, and mechanisms that in an economic or accounting sense result in value added to the product—schedules, methods and standards, standard costs, predetermined costs, over/underabsorption, raw material availability and quality, waste control, quality specifications and control, shipments, housekeeping, maintenance, job training, turnover, absenteeism, grievances, personnel practices, contract provisions, safety.

Some participants in this analysis have called this ply the "real gut world." It deals primarily with what is happening here and now. Clearly, however, it keeps its eye peeled for developments in processes and technology that may have future impact.

In terms of organization change, the implications of different idioms are fairly clear. There is nothing new in the thought that if people are to grasp an idea it must be expressed in a language they understand. The same idea may have to be couched in different terms to make it meaningful to different audiences. This truism is underlined in the three-ply concept of organization. The idiom that has clear meaning in one ply may have no operational counterpart in another. For example, an executive of a telephone company in reviewing efforts of his company to control operating costs within the traffic department states:

> The difficulty, in part, is that our top managers think and speak in terms of dollar budgets. At the operating level, however, the emphasis is on load. It is a problem of manning: How many persons are needed to provide adequate service at various load levels, on various holidays or days of the week? They think of dollars only peripherally. Their primary objective is to provide a level of service that will keep them out of trouble with both customers and top management. They are, of course, really managing dollar budgets but that is not how they think in terms of their jobs.

A junior officer in a bank puts it this way:

> Our senior officers talk about increasing the average return on the portfolio—but what does this mean to the small branch office manager? Does it mean that he should try to get another eighth of a percentage point on Mrs. Jones's loan?

From the standpoint of managing change, these varying idioms, reflecting as they do differences in work orientation, present more than a communications problem. More significantly, they may actually mask important considerations inherent in a change. As a result, hindsight shows some factors that should have been included in the planning for the change are not given sufficient consideration, or are completely overlooked. As an illustration, the chief executive of a metal processing company in reviewing the three-ply concept said:

> As you may suspect it touches several sensitive areas, and I see some things we overlooked in a recent problem area. We discussed with our key managers the changing nature of our markets. This means that in many of our product lines we must use alloys containing more exotic metals. But, although we must have these specialized products in our line, the orders for them are relatively small. At the process level, it means more setups and shorter manufacturing runs. I see now that in our product line planning we did not give enough consideration to its impact on manufacturing and, further, our incentive systems were not changed to reflect the new conditions so no one wants to run these exotic metal alloy products. We have spent many years trying to develop corporate incentive systems. My guess is that our standards people either did not see clearly the impact of these changes, or did not want to bring out how they impacted upon the corporate plan. We just did not make clear that these market changes would, of necessity, cause changes in our traditional manufacturing orientation and their support systems.

In this instance, the chief executive was thinking and acting in terms of market requirements. He assumed that when the manufacturing and systems managers saw the need for a new market orientation, they would understand the implications in terms of their functions and adjust to them. But inertia remained, apparently because many people—although they heard about the changes to come—tended to continue to think and act in terms of their own work focus.

Patterns of Interaction

The work focus of each ply as reflected in its idiom gives important clues as to what must be managed when change is contemplated. Of equal importance in planning and implementing change is some understanding of the bonding agent between the plies: the characteristic patterns of interaction and outlook. The ability of a management to effect change is influenced not only by the efficiency of its systems of communication but also by its capacity for managing the pressures that stem from the interaction among the three plies.

Obviously, the patterns of interaction or of response among the three plies of the organizational laminate are not fixed or rigid; the motive power of an organization is not transmitted through fixed gears, but by a fluid drive. But there are recognizable tendencies that cast additional light on the problems of managing change.

Within the ideational ply, for example, the most important characteristic is that its structure, work delegations, patterns of communication, and interaction tend to be a reflection of the chief executive officer. It reflects the "way he wants to go." It tends to be an extension, indeed, an expression of his management style.

This does not imply that the chief executive is free of the usual organizational restraints, or that he can ignore the historic cultural patterns in an organization. The chief executive is influenced by such constraints and evidently these do affect both the method and timing of organizational changes he may want to make. Nevertheless, his leadership style does tend to be dominant and to set the tone within the ply.

That there tends to be a high degree of compatibility of language and individual managing styles within this ply does not connote conformity. But executives who recognize themselves as part of this ply suggest, however, that one of its characteristics is relatively low tolerance for disagreement within the group. There is room for discussion and differences of opinion during strategic explorations, but no room for the heretic—and for most observers this is consistent with the concept of the final accountability of the chief executive.

People in the other two plies see it also as being highly peer oriented, both inside and outside the enterprise. "What the chief hears from another chief tends to be more credible than anything he hears from anyone on the inside," is a typical comment. Members of this ply often disagree at first with this perception of them, but on further reflection during interviews admit the tendency may be real.

Clearly, those who are part of this ideational ply see themselves as setting the pace, mood, and mode of corporate leadership. They want to project the image of a well-coordinated, smoothly functioning, aggressive, cohesive team. They are also highly conscious of their role of establishing and maintaining the "character" of the company, and they try hard to make this character pervasive throughout the organization, and to project the same identity to significant groups outside the enterprise—the community at large, financial institutions, government agencies, customers, and stockholders. This leadership role seems to underlie the great emphasis placed on teamwork.

These characteristics and outlooks are, of course, not confined exclusively to this ply. Each of the other two could be described, in part, in the same way. However, observers see these characteristics as being the more determinate elements that define the institutional nature of the ideational ply.

The other two plies in turn have a reciprocal influence on the ideational ply. And this system of mutual influence and support is constantly at work. This does not mean that the orientations of the three plies are congruent. At times they are, but at other times they may be quite different—even to the point of being in opposition. The characteristic attitudes and viewpoints of the synergistic and process plies make the reasons behind this apparent.

The synergistic ply—the inner ply of the organizational laminate—has certain cultural traits that are peculiarly its own. But the nature of its constant interaction with the other two plies clearly conditions its outlook. The members of this ply, at times, see themselves as being a part of the ideational ply because they are often involved in the management process of that ply. This participation is essential to the synergistic ply's role of taking broad ideas and concepts and translating them into operational realities. This involves a variety of transactions, catalytic roles, and some trade-offs.

But involvement with and membership in a ply are two different things. For after its involvement with the ideational ply in developing strategy, the synergistic ply is left with the difficult task of implementation. And "left with" is an apt term for what the synergistic ply sees as characteristic of its role. It sees itself as standing alone. There is often a feeling of being let down. The ideational ply may now be seen by members of the synergistic ply as not having a real depth of commitment, and as not giving its full support to the new strategy or program. As one organizational analyst puts it:

"They now feel they have been given inadequate support and unrealistic time schedules." And, evidently, this can go so far as to develop into a credibility gap.

Somewhat this same circle of moods seems to describe the relationships between this inner ply and the process ply. At times, the two plies embrace each other and tackle problems as though they were a single ply. At other times, however, those of the synergistic ply tend to feel rebuffed, and, as one executive put it: "During these periods, the reaction is often both thermal and sonic."

The synergistic ply is also the world of multiple loyalties. "I am bothered sometimes," says a personnel vice president, "that often I feel much more loyal to my profession than I do to the company." Much the same statement could come from the scientist, accountant, or computer technologist. At other times, these same persons exhibit an intense loyalty to their companies. Either of these loyalties may be accompanied by a kind of missionary zeal, as members of the ply see themselves as vital change agents. On the other hand, they are pictured by some as having "civil servant mentalities."

An inherent function of this ply is to be a channel of communication between the other two plies, to be a conduit for ideas and needs, to be an analyst and an interpreter of situations and events, and, at times, to be a buffer. Implicit in this function are potentially serious difficulties. Obviously, if this ply wishes to avoid any major unpleasantness or confrontation with either of the other two plies, its interpretive presentations may be highly filtered.

In a sense, the synergistic ply is somewhat amorphous. The multiplicity of its roles, and the nature of its involvement with other segments of the organization make it so. And it is this attribute that becomes an important consideration in the management of change.

The process ply tends to be somewhat rigid psychologically, which is a reflection of the ply's environment. Its world is very stable and resistant to change. Those within the process ply, for example, may participate in discussions, or receive memos concerning new strategies and plans, new concepts of management, and other forecasts of vital things to come, but their world does not seem to change. Tomorrow as today, they are under pressure to get out a given quantity of product, of a specified quality and at a predetermined cost. There is almost always a time lag between the formulation of new marketing or product development plans and their impact on the process ply. Further, some of the ideas for product development or market penetration never do come through, and consequently this ply remains relatively untouched.

Some managers report that this time lag or, more importantly, the fact that not all plans can be brought to fruition, tends to develop within the process ply a credibility gap toward the other plies. Typical of comments attributed to this ply: "We have seen them come and go." It tends to take much that it hears with the proverbial grain of salt.

This ply is reportedly highly ambivalent in its attitude toward the synergistic ply. This ambivalence appears to be at the root of many organizational problems. Thus the process ply embraces the synergistic ply when it is seen as a buffer between itself and the ideational ply, or when it is really needed to help solve a pressing problem. At other times, the efforts of the synergistic ply to be helpful may be resisted as meddling into the affairs of the process ply.

When others look at the process ply, they see a highly cohesive group with a relatively low level of tolerance for disagreement, and with a relatively long tenure that tends to foster institutional rigidities. Despite this psychological set, however, this ply retains an innovative thrust in the areas of technology and process techniques, and because of its vital economic role exerts a strong influence within the other plies of the organizational laminate.

Organization: A System of Response

This three-institution schema of organization does not negate the idea that orderly organizational changes can be made by following the concepts of teamwork and the logic of work. Rather, it underlines the notion that organization is a system of reponse—of people responding to events, situations, policies, plans, and other people—and that this response is heavily flavored by certain ingrained cultural patterns associated with each ply of the organization.

In formulating plans for change, most of the effort seems to be directed toward the outward or manifest aspect of change. The structure is changed, the positions are redefined, authority relationships are modified, and new management processes are initiated.

Many of the latent elements of change that may be of even more significance are either not understood or not given sufficient consideration. Some of the uneasiness people feel in the face of change is undoubtedly caused by the disruptions of latent functions, the existence of which are never fully perceived. To take an example: one company, in an effort to improve efficiency and to save time, substituted conference calls for the more tedious, time-consuming practice of calling meetings. At the manifest level, progress may have been made. But evidently the meetings also served certain valued latent functions. The meetings were a natural meeting place for the informal, casual conversations that every organization seems to need. These needs were no longer being met and something was lost in the translation.

Testimony indicates that when manifest changes are made without an equal awareness of the potential latent disruptions, strains may arise that even the organization itself may not fully understand. Often, apparently, these strains are projected in the form of extraneous or misleading issues that impede the management of change.

In that context, persons who have reviewed attempts at reorganization in terms of this three–ply model recognize in it a mechanism for anticipating problems. In effect, it provides something of a systems approach to reorganizing. It helps identify the intangible social or institutional networks.

Of course, inherent in any such "systems" approach are other implications. Are management development programs producing executives who can really manage change? At what points do what kinds of inputs have to be introduced to make a gross change in an organization? If the plies have to be modified significantly, how long does it take to effect a desired change? What needs to be done to the bonding agents?

Given the character of the possible answers to these questions, a key question emerges. Can there really be self–renewal in an organization?

10 An Interactive Approach to the Problem of Organizational Change

Robert C. Shirley

In earlier chapters we have considered the behavioral characteristics of the individual and certain elements of the behavioral characteristics of an organization. There is one more significant dimension in which organizational behavior must be considered. Visualize, if you will, individual behavioral characteristics as the "up-and-down" dimension of the multidimensional model we are building. Consider the organizational plies as the "side-to-side" dimension of the organization, and now consider the environmental, strategic, and programmatic dimension as the "back-to-front" dimension of the organization.

In this chapter, Robert C. Shirley, coordinator of academic planning for the University of Houston, "pulls it all together" in the multidimensional organizational structure described above. Although he describes the back-to-front dimension only briefly, it is helpful to consider this aspect of organizational change in the context of the organization as a whole. Dr. Shirley makes a case for integrating structural and human approaches to the management of organizational change. By creating your own structure for change and dealing purposefully with human characteristics and needs, you can increase the likelihood of your effectiveness by reducing or eliminating much of the ambiguity that would otherwise undermine the process of change management.

Organizational change is a term of many and various meanings. At one extreme of a continuum, the term is used to refer to very basic changes in individual beliefs, values, and attitudes within an organization. At the other extreme, it has been applied in a holistic sense to total organizational shifts in objectives, policies, and general modes of operation. In between the two extremes, the term has been applied to changes in almost all conceivable facets or dimensions of an organization. Consequently, the body of knowledge generally considered relevant to the managment of organizational change is extremely broad and ill-defined. The net result of this general state of ambiguity is confusion—confusion not only about what is meant by

This chapter is based on an article that originally appeared in *Human Resource Management,* Summer 1975. Copyright © 1975 by the Graduate School of Business Administration, University of Michigan; reprinted by permission. All rights reserved.

the term organizational change, but also about the purposes and areas of applicability of the numerous approaches to change which exist today. The purposes of this article are (1) to provide a perspective on change which will help to clarify its meaning and its systemic properties insofar as organizational activities are concerned and (2) to develop a framework to facilitate the management of change from a total firm perspective.

To gain a clear perspective on the notion of organizational change, it is helpful to first define the term "organization." Although there are at least as many definitions as there are writers on the subject, the prevailing orientation is that of a systems view. Regardless of precise wording, an organization is usually (and very abstractly) described as a complex system of mutually dependent parts. It follows that the term organizational change would logically refer to an alteration or modification of one or more parts of the system. This definition is not sufficient, however, insofar as operationalizing the notion of change in organizations. What is needed is an operational scheme of organization parts so that (1) the focus and direction of change sought may be clearly identified for any given situation and (2) the extended and interactive effects of a change in any one part of the system on the other parts may be anticipated and traced. The next few paragraphs present such a scheme as a necessary background for subsequent consideration of change causes, goals, targets, and techniques.

The Parts of an Organization

It is useful to view any organization as comprising six interdependent dimensions: environment, strategy, program, structure, behavior, and technology. These six dimensions in turn may be subdivided into their component parts to provide a comprehensive scheme for organizational analysis. Each major dimension is discussed more fully below.

The Environmental Dimension

The particular external conditions faced by any firm may be classified into one of the four major (although obviously interrelated) sectors of the environment: economic, social, technological, and political/legal. The economic sector includes phenomena such as characteristics and structure of the industry, competitor strengths and weaknesses, market trends, and other forces which are primarily economic in nature and have external origins. The social sector encompasses larger societal values, ethical customs, consumer psychology, minority group influences, demographic information of concern to the firm, and the like. The technological sector includes technological developments in the firm's industry or elsewhere which are relevant for new product development or improvement of production processes. Finally, the political/legal sector encompasses applicable legislation, regulatory agencies, court decisions, executive acts, foreign policy, and other forces which may present new opportunities to the firm or act as constraints on its operations. As is evident, the environmental dimension is viewed as a part of the organization itself, thus reflecting the open-system notion that organizational analysis solely confined to "internal parts" falls short of providing a complete understanding of the total system.

The Strategic Dimension

This strategy dimension of an organization refers to its basic product (service)/market scope, competitive emphasis, and objectives (performance criteria). Strategic decisions define the basic relationship of the organization to its environment and require determination of the following: product (or service) mix, customer mix, geographic limits of the markets to be served, competitive emphasis, and objectives related to profitability, growth, market share, and survival. Such decisions thus bridge the gap between the environment and the remaining organizational dimensions, providing a set of constraints to guide lower-order decisions concerning technology, programs (for example, production, marketing), structure, and behavioral requirements. Strategy decisions emerge from an iterative assessment of environmental opportunities and constraints in relation to internal resources, capabilities, and values; insofar as total system functioning is concerned, these decisions determine the overall requirements for inter-actions among the operational parts of the organization.

The Program Dimension

The program dimension of an organization comprises the major implementation programs developed by a firm to achieve its strategy. Included here would be technical plans developed for marketing (distribution, sales, promotion, market research), production (schedules, inventory management, quality control, operations), research and development, engineering, purchasing, personnel administration, and other major task areas of the firm. This dimension refers to the technical specifics of programs in terms of objectives, processes, and techniques utilized in each area to accomplish the overall strategy and objectives of the firm.

The Structural Dimension

The structural dimension of a firm refers to the formal arrangements which have been established to coordinate the total activities required to implement a given strategy. In a sense, this dimension reflects the "anatomy" of a firm via its focus on mechanisms and processes which link (both vertically and horizontally) the various parts of an organization. For purposes of analysis, it is useful to classify the major elements of organiztional structure as follows:

1. Distribution of functions throughout the organization (includes definition of functions to be performed, groupings of functions and the vertical and horizontal task relationships among functions).
2. Vertical and horizontal authority relationships (who has the authority to do what).
3. Communication/decision processes (the manner in which formal decisions are made and by whom, supporting informational inputs, and the information systems established to provide the inputs to decision makers).
4. Policies (the decision rules or guidelines established in finance, marketing, production, personnel, purchasing, research and development, and other areas; these guidelines serve to tie the performance of specific functions to the overall strategy and objectives of the firm).
5. Formal incentive systems (compensation plan characteristics, fringe benefits, incentive or bonus plans, promotion criteria, and other features of the formal reward system used by the organization).

Taken together, these five parts of the structural dimension establish the basic conditions under which organizational members perform their various roles.

The Behavioral Dimension

The behavioral dimension is composed of four major parts:

1. The individual (includes phenomena such as individual beliefs, values, attitudes, as well as overt behavior; also includes consideration of abilities, satisfaction, personalities, and other behavioral phenomena which are of an individualistic nature).
2. Interpersonal relationships (whereas the above focus was on the individual, the focus here is on interactions between two persons in accomplishing tasks).

3. Group behavior (this part refers to the group as a unit of analysis, including consideration of the presence or absence of group cohesiveness; informal group goals, leaders, and members; influence of the group over individuals; group norms; and other behavioral phenomena which are of a group nature).
4. Intergroup behavior (whereas the immediately preceding focus was on the single work group, this category relates to the interactions of two or more groups in accomplishing tasks).

The Technology Dimension

Finally, the technology dimension refers to the technology of production, plant and equipment, materials, and other physical parts of an organization.

Overview

Table 10–1 presents a summary overview of the dimensions and their component parts. This scheme serves to partially operationalize the earlier definition of organizational change. Thus organizational change occurs when one or more of the parts outlined in table 10–1 are altered or modified in some fashion. This is only a starting point, however. The utility of the scheme can be proved only by demonstrating how it can facilitate the management of change via systematic and orderly view of the process.

First Step: Recognizing the Need for Change

Organizations, of course, are constantly changing. Although the causes of change are many and varied, it is useful, for analytical purposes, to group them into two basic categories: external forces and internal forces. External forces creating the need for change in other parts of the total system emerge from the environmental dimension of the organization, in the form of extra–firm technological developments, changing societal values, changing market trends, competitors' actions, antipollution legislation, and the like. Although external forces impinge on all dimensions of the firm, the most frequent point of interface is with the strategy dimension. Strategy shifts (for example, in product or customer mix) in response to changing environmental forces then signal the need for further changes in the program, structure, technology, and behavior dimensions of the organization, creating an almost endless chain of reverberations throughout the system.

Table 10–1
Summary Listing of Organization Parts

I. Environmental	IV. Structure
A. Economic	A. Distribution of functions
B. Technological	B. Distribution of authority
C. Social	C. Reporting relationships
D. Political/legal	D. Communication/decision processes
II. Strategy	V. Behavior
A. Product mix	A. The individual
B. Customer mix	B. Interpersonal relationships
C. Geographic limits to market	C. The group
D. Competitive emphasis	D. Intergroup relationships
E. Objectives	
III. Programs	VI. Technology
A. Marketing	A. Technology of production
B. Production	B. Plant and equipment
C. Financial	C. Materials
D. R&D	D. Tools
E. Engineering	
F. Purchasing	
G. Personnel	
H. Other	

Note: Each of the major organization parts comprises numerous subparts which are not explicitly identified in this table. For example, the marketing program may be further subdivided into distribution, sales, promotion, and market research. In a similar vein, numerous subparts of the individual could be listed (his values, sentiments toward work, abilities, desires, overt behavior) to provide a more detailed focus for analytical purposes.

It is the function of various organizational elements to (1) identify external forces toward change and (2) analyze their implications for needed changes or adjustments in other parts of the organization. Market research, long–range planning, and R&D departments fall into this category. Yet what we often fail to recognize is that the responses made to external forces necessarily disturb the internal system equilibrium. This is in contrast to the case where internal forces themselves create the need for change. Internal forces may be generally considered synonymous with the term organizational stress—stress in sentiments, activities, interactions, or performance results. Such forces toward change thus represent conditions of equilibrium which are already upset within one or more parts of the organization. For example, a conflict in interactions may exist between R&D and production because of a disagreement over the proper tolerance levels required in precision manufacturing—such disagreement possibly emanating from the different goals, orientations, and values of the two departments. Or organizational stress may arise as a result of negative sentiments or feelings on the part of employees about their work. Many other familiar kinds of organizational stress could be cited. The essential point is that tension always exists in an organization undergoing change; however, the tension may be either consciously created by individuals or groups (in response to environmental forces) or it may itself create the need for change (in the form of organizational stress). Consequently, recognition of the source of the tension makes for a more informed assessment of probable reactions to change by those affected. If internal tension creates the need for change, then those affected should welcome relief; on the other hand, if the response to external forces disturbs some comfortable equilibrium internally, change is more likely to be resisted by the employees affected.

**Second Step: Responding to
the Need for Change**

Regardless of whether the forces creating the need for change in some part of the system are external in origin or internal, or both, the form of organizational response most commonly observed is that of analysis—however thorough or hasty. In the case of extra-firm technological developments, for example, analysis must be conducted to determine their feasibility of application to existing facilities and compatibility with existing skills. This analysis will then determine whether or not the formal change goal "to utilize new process A in the production of product X" can be established by the organization (explicitly or implicitly), with its associated implications for required structural and behavioral changes. In the case of perceived economic or market opportunities which may be achieved via alternative growth routes, the feasibility of merging with another organization might be analyzed in depth, as might the feasibility of growth through internal expansion or diversification. In the case of internal organizational stress, diagnostic analysis directed toward determining the causes of such stress would ideally be the first response by managers before any steps were taken to deal directly with the stress.

The scheme of organizational parts developed earlier can serve as a useful tool at this stage for the manager of change. Whether he alone is trying to develop some sort of action plan for responding to disturbing forces or whether he is evaluating analyses (written or verbal) prepared by others, the scheme provides a handy reference for truly systematizing the approach to the problem. A proposed change in the technology dimension (for example, utilization of some new equipment or process) may be subjected to an evaluation of its extended consequences for other parts of the system. What will be the effect of such a change on individual skill requirements or attitudes (see V. A in table 10-1)? What will be the effect on task interactions (see IV. A in the table)? What will be the effect on production scheduling (see III. and IV. B in the table)? What will be the effect on the current piece rate scheme (see III.F)? In general, what other parts of the total organizational system will be affected by this change in technology (see the entire table)? Have the costs and benefits of these extended effects of the proposed change been calculated?

Third Step: Establishing Change Goals

Once the manager has completed the analytic process described above and has become cognizant of the extended implications of any proposed change, he is ready to formally establish the goals of the proposed change. The analytic process of assessing consequences thus precedes goal setting in order to ensure feasibility of the goals. Illustrative goals include.

1. To diversify into product–markets X, Y, and Z (as a result of analysis of changing market opportunities or poor economic performance results in existing markets).
2. To merge (horizontally) with ABC Corporation (as a result of poor performance results perceived as being caused by lack of volume production necessary to achieve economies of scale in existing facilities).
3. To install specified antipollution devices on products D and E (as a result of a new legal constraint requiring such installation).
4. To move decision levels downward (as a result of organizational stress perceived as being caused by authoritarian decision making at the top levels of the organization).
5. To eliminate interdepartmental competition and foster collaboration (as a result of perceived stress in departmental interactions—for example, the production and R&D conflict noted earlier).
6. To change the structure of distribution channels currently being utilized (as a result of increased middleman costs which have contributed to poor performance results).

Although the illustrative goals obviously cover a broad spectrum of change situations, they (and all other possible change goals) generally have one thing in common: their successful accomplishment ultimately depends greatly on the extent to which necessary structural and behavioral changes are carefully implemented within the organization. Reflecting for a moment on the differences in the types of goals, however, it is possible to broadly classify them in a fashion consistent with the scheme of organizational parts developed in the table.

Strategic

Those change goals concerned with altering the relationship between the firm and its environment (for example, revised objectives, new product/market scope); examples of change goals of this type include 1 and 2 above.

Technological

Those goals directly related to changes in the technology of production, plant and equipment, and the like; an example of this type is goal 3 above.

Structural

Change goals which are concerned with alterations in reporting relationships, location of functions and authority, communication/decision processes, spans of control, formal incentive programs, and similar aspects of an organization's anatomy fall into this category. An example is goal 4 above. (Structural change is elaborated upon in the next major section below.)

Behavioral

Those goals which aim initially at changing values, attitudes, beliefs, norms, interpersonal relationships, group behavior, intergroup behavior, and similar humanistic phenomena; an example is goal 5 above. (Behavioral change is also elaborated upon in the next major section below.)

Program

Those change goals which focus on altering the objectives or structure of the technical implementation plans developed for marketing, production, R&D, and other task areas; an example is goal 6 above.

With respect to the above classification, it should be noted that the goal types are not mutually exclusive, as two or more types may be operative simultaneously. Changes in organizational structure and behavior may be pursued in and of themselves but, as noted above, changes in strategy and technology also necessitate changes in structure and behavior for their successful accomplishment. For example, the strategic change goal of "merger" will usually require structural change (consolidation of some administrative functions) and behavioral change (some transplanting of sole identification with one organization to that of a newly merged concern) for its successful accomplishment. On the other hand, structural change may be deemed appropriate given an unchanged strategy or technology in order to increase administrative efficiency or effectiveness. The above classification should permit the practicing manager to pinpoint just what type of change he is initially attempting to accomplish as well as its relationship to the other types.

A great deal of research on various change programs and situations has been conducted, the results of which are very useful to the manager who has diagnosed his firm's problems and formulated appropriate goals. Most of the work has been done in the area of behavioral change. The field of organizational development (OD) is an emerging discipline which focuses on educational strategies "employing experienced-based behavior in order to achieve a self-renewing organization." OD is based on behavioral science findings and theories and generally seeks to help employees to remove barriers which prevent the release of human potential within the organization. Some specific change goals sought with OD are: creating an open, problem-solving climate; building trust; reducing inappropriate competition and fostering collaboration; increasing self-control and self-direction for organizational members; and supplementing the authority of status with that of competence.

The field of corporate strategy is currently in its infancy insofar as the availability of useful research results is concerned. Several excellent conceptual schemes and guides are available for the top managers, however, most notably those developed by Ansoff, Katz, and Learned et al.[1] These schemes provide reference material on the various factors and influences involved in the changing of strategy as well as recommended processes for strategy formation. In the area of structural change, several excellent empirical studies are available, and a few classic studies focus on the impact of introducing technological change.

Fourth Step: Determining Change Targets and Techniques

As noted earlier, the initial adjustment or modification of any organizational part in response to external or internal forces creates reverberations throughout the total system. It was also noted that any of the types of change goals identified, when acted upon, eventually necessitate some subsequent change along the structural and behavioral dimensions. This partially explains why most of the literature labeled "organizational change" tends to focus on these two dimensions, particularly the latter. What is frequently overlooked, however, is that the ultimate results of a change effort are greatly influenced by which of the two (structure or behavior) is changed first in any given situation. The following paragraphs seek to clarify this notion for the manager, first by examining the two philosophies of target priority which now exist, and second by proposing a means for determining which area should receive initial attention.

The structural approach to change, as the name implies, is predicated on the assumption that one improves task performance by clarifying and defining the jobs of people and by setting up clearly defined job relationships, lines of authority, and accountability areas. Adherence to this philosophy implies that no matter what forces create the need for change, the initial change target will be one of the six major parts (or subparts thereof) of the structural dimension listed in the table. Thus, if the change goal is to encourage the practice of participative management (a behavioral goal), the change target would be the formal distribution of authority in the organization (a structural target) as opposed to, say, the authoritarian personalities of current power figures. This is not to say that the problem of authoritarian personalities would be ignored; rather, it is assumed by structuralists that the negative consequences of such personalities may be better alleviated via a restructuring process (formal realignment of personality change process), relying on behavioral modification to result in their subsequent voluntary delegation of authority.

The second philosophy, labeled the humanistic approach, is predicated on the assumption that one improves task performance ultimately by focusing on individual, interpersonal, group, and intergroup behavior. The organizational change discipline, as currently documented and practiced, subscribes primarily to this approach. Its difference from the structural approach may be clarified by considering, again, the behavioral change goal of encouraging participative management. The initial change target under the humanistic approach would be the authoritarian personality, with reliance placed on voluntary delegation of authority; no initial restructuring would be thought necessary to achieve a realignment of authority relationships within the organization. This approach comprises the field of organizational development and such well-known approaches as T groups, sensitivity training, and other variations of the general theme of laboratory training. These and similar educational approaches focus initially on one or more of the behavioral change targets listed in the table. Desirable changes in structure and performance are seen to follow behavioral change, with the implicit assumption being that a better atmosphere for problem solving (more cooperation, open acknowledgment and handling of conflict) will have been inculcated in organization members. A frequent criticism of this approach has been its relative neglect of structural and technological processes in organizations and its consequent overemphasis on behavioral processes.

Integration of the Approaches

The structural and humanistic approaches are frequently viewed as either/ or approaches. The major point to be made here is that both approaches are useful in a situational approach to change target selection. The key to integration of the approaches appears to lie in recognizing the uniqueness of particular change situations. Leavitt notes[2] that the differentiation of change approaches lies in "... (a) points of entry into the organization, (b) relative weightings, and (c) underlying values ..." To provide a means for integrating the two approaches, it should first be noted that the point of entry in a change situation will depend on whether or not accomplishment of a given change goal, as discussed above, involves changing both structure and behavior. It should be emphasized that any change in organizational structure will have ramifications for individual or group behavior, yet the reverse is not necessarily the case. The key point is that where structural change must occur, the associated behavioral change desired cannot be effectuated with direction until and unless the desired structural changes have been identified. Consider, for example, the case of a desired change in authority relationships between a superior and his subordinate. Until each knows his role, both within the organization and in relation to each other, it is difficult to meaningfully implement any techniques designed to change attitudes or interpersonal relationships. This is to be contrasted to the situation where changes in behavior are necessary to better perform an unchanged role within the organization. In the latter case, behavioral targets logically reflect the initial point of entry into an organization for purposes of change, whereas the former situation would call for a structural target (definition of authority relationships) as the initial focus.

It thus appears useful to classify behavioral targets as (1) those derivative of structural change targets and (2) those unrelated to structural change. If a change is desired in one of the six structural parts listed in the table, then that represents the initial point of entry in order to provide direction for subsequent attitudinal/behavioral change. If there is to be no structural change and the problem is purely attitudinal or behavioral in nature, the behavioral targets should constitute the initial points of entry.

In order to clarify the preceding notions, let us consider the case of merger (strategic change) as a final example. Both structural and behavioral changes are required as a result of merger. Structural changes emanate from an upsetting of the activities and interactions equilibrium, while behavioral changes are required to cope with the new structure and to achieve self-maintenance, growth, and social satisfactions. The key to determining which to attack first in accomplishing the "centralization of X, Y, and Z functions" lies in the fact that, for this particular situation, role content and relations must change—and this is initially a matter of structure. The behavioral change required to accomplish the new activities and interactions cannot be effectuated until the new activities and interactions have been identified—that is, unless the structural changes have been pinpointed and agreed upon. Therefore the structural approach logically reflects the initial point of entry in this particular situation, insofar as the target of change, while the humanistic approach (and its associated group of techniques) may be necessary to ensure that concomitant attitudinal/behavioral changes move in the desired direction—acceptance of new roles, role relations, and organizational identities.

That structural changes are necessary in a merger situation to provide some degree of coordinated effort is rather obvious. The fact that behavioral targets are derivative of structural targets is not so obvious, however, and deserves further explanation. It is generally the case that structural realignments resulting from a merger occur primarily at the managerial and supervisory levels. Necessary changes in formal authority distribution, differentiation and integration of administrative functions, and communication–decision processes may have little or no effect on the content and method of performance of lower–level operative and technical jobs; thus behavioral change strategies should be distinctly different between the managerial and operating employee classes, as the type and extent of behavioral changes necessary are *primarily a function of the extent of change in task performance methods and interactions.* The behavioral change targets might be segmented according to hierarchical level in this instance, as a greater degree of behavioral change will be required of those individuals experiencing role (structural) changes. Of course, there may be instances in a merger situation where behavioral changes unrelated to structural changes are also necessary. For example, there may be a perceived need to shift (at least partially) organizational identities and loyalties to the parent organization surviving the merger. No structural changes may be called for in this particular case, and behavioral targets logically constitute the appropriate initial focus insofar as change is concerned.

The relative weightings assigned to the structural and humanistic approaches and techniques should also be greatly influenced by the dictates of the situation. It is entirely plausible, for example, that structural change will have such tremendous and far–reaching consequences for human behavior that much emphasis should be placed on humanistic approaches and techniques. This is a question of method or technique, however, and not a question of targets. The two are frequently confused. The "attacking" of structural targets does not automatically mean that an authoritarian or unilateral "decree" approach is utilized without consideration for the individual(s) affected. Thus structural change targets can be acted upon under conditions of mutual goal setting, deliberation, and equal power distributions (as developed by Warren Bennis) or via a shared approach (as noted by Larry Greiner) to better assure identification with change outcomes. The philosophies underlying methods or techniques of change are well developed by Bennis and Greiner.[3]

Bennis' typology of change processes is often erroneously associated only with humanistic approaches to change (probably because of his leanings in that direction); it can more properly be viewed, however, as a philosophy of implementation rather than a philosophy of target selection. His paradigm of change processes provides several key considerations related to the implementation of change, primarily via its emphasis on the nature of goal setting (mutual versus nonmutual), power ratio between the parties involved in change, and the extent of deliberation involved in change processes. Greiner takes an approach similar to Bennis' as he views various approaches to change in terms of their position along a "power distribution" continuum. At one extreme are those approaches which rely on unilateral authority; more toward the middle of the continuum are the shared approaches, and, finally, at the opposite extreme are the delegated approaches. Greiner arrives at an interesting conclusion when he notes that "we need to reduce our fond attachment for both unilateral and delegated approaches to change." His reasoning concerning the predicted failure of completely delegated approaches to change is that such an approach removes the power structure from direct involvement in a process that calls for its strong guidance; it appears that a completely unstructured approach to change and the associated ambiguities involved lead to feelings of anxiety on the part of affected employees and thus impede the process of implementing change.

Conclusion

This article has attempted to clarify the notion of organizational change and its systemic properties. A paradigm of organizational parts was presented to aid the manager in tracing the interactive and extended effects of any change goal contemplated for the organization. Particular attention was devoted to the interactive nature of structural and behavioral change—two primary target areas which are always affected no matter what type of change goal is at work. As a final note, it should be recognized that the intent of this article was to present a framework for structuring one's thinking about change causes, goals, targets, and interactive effects. Issues such as "how to overcome resistance to change" and "the best methods for effecting change" purposefully were not addressed; numerous (and useful) articles exist on these subjects. Yet the fact is that change is both a highly situational and complex phenomenon which is always characterized by process ambiguities—that is, individual differences and unforeseen events always crop up to distort our best-laid plans for implementing change. The attitudinal thesis of this article is that it is better to initially approach such an ambiguous process with some structure for analysis of causes, goals, and targets than with none at all. Perhaps the best we can hope for is structured ambiguity rather than ambiguous ambiguity in our approach to change— the former at least holds the promise of our being able to anticipate and identify the forces underlying and causing the ambiguity. The paradigm presented herein has hopefully provided a means for anticipation and identification of such forces by utilizing a systems approach to the problem.

Notes

1. H.I. Ansoff, *Corporate Strategy* (New York: McGraw-Hill, 1965); R.L. Katz, *Cases and Concepts in Corporate Strategy* (Englewood Cliffs, N.J.: Prentice Hall, 1970); E.P. Learned et al., *Business Policy: Text and Cases* (Homewood, Ill.: Richard D. Irwin, 1969).

2. D.L. Keegan, "Organizational Development: Description, Issues, and Research Results, *Academy of Management Journal,* December 1971, p. 456. For an additional summary of techniques and issues in this area, see A.P. Raia, "Organizational Development—Some Issues and Challenges," *California Management Review,* Summer 1972, pp. 13-20.

3. W.B. Bennis, "A Typology of Change Processes," in W.G. Bennis et al., eds., *The Planning of Change* (New York: Holt, Rinehart & Winston, 1961); L. Greiner, "Patterns of Organization Change," *Harvard Business Review,* May-June 1967, pp. 119-122.

11 Change by Design, Not by Default

Robert R. Blake and
Jane Srygley Mouton

While much of the discussion in previous chapters has as an underlying assumption that the would-be manager of change (the change agent) is in full control and intends to effect certain changes to his own benefit, the reality is that most individual and organizational change takes place without any control at all. It is useful to consider a philosophy of "causing change" as distinguished from merely manipulating the evolutionary process through which most individual and organizational change actually occurs.

In this chapter, Dr. Robert R. Blake and Dr. Jane S. Mouton, president and vice president, respectively, of Scientific Methods, Inc., of Austin, Texas, suggest that revolution can be avoided by causing rational change in a controlled manner. The alternative to evolution or revolution, according to this theory, is the identification of an ideal which can then be worked toward. From a practical standpoint, of course, it is often not realistic to pursue ideals, however desirable they may be. Yet even if you substitute pragmatic goals for ideal objectives, the idea of establishing an objective, appraising the starting point, and proceeding on a step-by-step basis is worth considering.

Those who have studied organization processes over the past ten years have shuffled and shifted the labels applied to their subject. Not only scholars but industrial men as well began in the late fifties to study and discuss what now has emerged as a science in itself. They first referred to it merely as organization change, then organization improvement, and eventually organization development.

What they seem to have been seeking and what has finally emerged may more appropriately be described as "systematic development." This title reflects the fact that much has been learned about changing, improving, and developing an organization. The dynamics of change are now far better understood than ever before.

Men can at last act deliberately to take systematic steps to achieve specifically planned change within their organizations. There are proven ways to

This chapter is based on an article that originally appeared in *S.A.M. Advanced Management Journal*, April 1970. Copyright © 1970 by the Society for Advancement of Management; reprinted by permission. All rights reserved.

move an organization from where it stands to where it should stand to be a model organization. This suggests the surface meaning of systematic development, but it is far deeper and more meaningful for the businessman of the future. What underlies systematic development?

The Dilemma of Change

Change is thought of in various ways. This poses a major dilemma. It may be that processes of change are limited to evolutionary modifications or revolutionary churnings. Or change may be a process which can be engineered according to specifications of systematic development. If one thinks in an evolutionary or revolutionary way, his strategy and tactics of change are quite different from those he would have if he thought according to a systematic development approach.

Creeping Change by Evolution

Evolutionary adjustments occur when change is small and within broader status quo expectations. Evolutionary accommodation rarely violates the traditions or customary practices of those involved in it or affected by it. An underlying assumption is that progress is possible if each problem is dealt with as it arises. Changes are usually piecemeal, taking place one by one. Because they are adjustments within the status quo, they seldom promote great enthusiasm, arouse deep resistance, or have dramatic results. Solutions that prove sound are repeated and reinforced. Those that are unsound simply disappear. Such evolutionary adjustments are based on the belief that, beyond survival, growth and development are most probably for the company that is most successful at finding solutions to each specific problem as it arises, situation by situation.

Acceptance of evolutionary concepts is widespread by many managers and scholars of behavioral science for several reasons. The changes often represent forward progress. They rarely constitute significant departures from past practices. They are reasonably easy to understand and accept. They are unlikely to provoke resistance.

But there are limitations to expecting significant change or development from evolutionary ways. Only those problems that force themselves into the limelight are likely to be solved, and these are not necessarily the most important for the good of the organization. The very fact that an evolutionary approach accepts the status quo arrangements of the system as a whole poses what may be the real barriers to progress. Prevailing values often constitute rigidities which prevent deeper problems from being seen, or, if a brief awareness does occur, organization norms make the problem harder to tackle.

Evolutionary processes are likely to be so slow that even though change is occurring, its tempo does not prevent the organization from falling ever farther behind. They may be little more than accommodations, adjustments, and compromises involving matters of style and technique only, not the deeper and more significant aspects of the organization. The evolutionary approach on the whole and despite its limitations is highly characteristic of American corporate life.

Revolutionary Upheaval

Processes of change can be viewed as revolutionary when the shift results in overturning status quo arrangements. Revolutionary change causes violations, rejections, or suppression of old expectations. It compels acceptance of new ones. Revolutionary changes are more likely to be effected through the exercise of power and authority which can compel compliance.

Revolutionary change rarely is resorted to except where situations have become so intolerable that evolutionary modifications are seen as insufficient and if there are other possibilities, they go unrecognized. Revolutionary change is likely to be championed by those who feel deeply frustrated by the status quo, although the same status quo is resented just as much by those adhering to it.

Another motivation to revolutionary methods is the desire for speedy change. When traditional assumptions and rules of conduct are overthrown, revolution brings about a new situation very rapidly. The underlying tensions may extend back over a long period of suffering, and the relief gained from taking a new action is often better than either the standing still or pursuing an evolutionary course, despite the risks that are involved in revolution.

These changes may have dramatic results, and they may be either positive or negative. Long-standing problems may be fundamentally resolved one way or another. Negative side effects are often produced, such as underground resistance, a building up of resentment, and sabotage as opposed to involvement, commitment, or dedication—particularly among those from whom compliance is extracted.

Both evolutionary and revolutionary methods are as old as history. Both are deeply ingrained in the assumptions by which men are guided. This, however, does not mean that they are sound approaches to change.

**Systematic Development: The New
Scientific Way to Change**

Systematic development is a new alternative to evolution or revolution. It starts neither with acceptance nor with rejection of the status quo. Rather it begins with an intellectual model of what might be ideal, or what "should be." The properties of the model are specified according to theory, logic, and fact. The model is pretested against probable circumstances, projected over defined periods of time. The model is a blueprint, not of what is, but of what should be.

The use of such a strategic model is not the same as planning or as management by objectives. Both of these methods are undertaken within the status quo constraints and often entail little more than extrapolations from the past projected into the future, rarely improving an active process of learning to reject the outmoded properties of the status quo. Both planning and management by objectives, however, are invaluable conceptual tools in implementation of such a model. Here are the important specifications for an approach based on systematic development.

Designing a Model of What Should Be

Clear-cut objectives are a prerequisite to the kind of development that takes place under the systematic approach. An ideal model specifies what the results should be at a designated time. To be systematic, the model must be based on theory, fact, and logic, uncontaminated either by assumptions embedded in the status quo or by extrapolations from the past.

The model must be understood to represent the ideal, not the idealistic. Ideal thinking can identify what is possible according to theory, logic, and fact. Ideal thinking can be tested against objective criteria to assess its practicality. Idealistic thinking, on the other hand, would have an unreal quality, probably rooted in self-deception and expressing what is desired or what is wanted without having been tested against theory, logic, or fact.

Idealistic thinking is subjective and is based on criteria having little or nothing to do with the facts of the situation. Ideal thinking has sometimes been suspect and rejected as idealistic. Yet through history, some of what might qualify as among the world's greatest change projects—the Magna Charta, the Constitution of the United States—have probably come about through ideal-type formulations.

Objective Appraisal of the "As Is" Situation

The status quo cannot be taken for granted. It is as necessary to learn what the status quo is as to describe what it should be. The "as is" is formulated in a way which permits point-by-point paralleling between what is and what should be, to be implemented under the ideal model. Weaknesses and strengths of the present situation can become clearer.

When the ideal is used as a spotlight to see the actual, objectivity about what is can more readily be attained. Without an ideal model of comparison, rationalization, self-deception, and ingrained habits operate to obscure the true properties of the situation. To change a situation, then, those responsible for operating it must learn to reject it. This is not "unlearning." It is new learning through which insight is acquired into the deficiencies of arrangements that exist. From a technical point of view, it is a strategy of escape from corporate ethnocentrism.

This step of learning to reject the status quo is most difficult. It is a fact usually left undone. As an ideal model, the Constitution was insufficient because it did not reflect active learning to reject the status quo which contained deep injustices in the American cultural scheme. Amendments and court interpretations attest to this. We continue to identify and reject some of these deep lying contradictions.

Discrepancies between Actual and Ideal

The gaps between actual and ideal are motivators. Closing gaps gives organization development and changes its direction. When conditions that should be rejected and replaced are identified, steps of development can then be planned and programmed for implementation.

A deeper significance than appears on the surface comes sharply into focus when development is built upon producing and closing gaps as a method of motivating change. There are two concepts of motivation here: tension reduction and financial and status rewards. Much industrial thinking is based on acceptance of the idea that financial and status rewards are important motivators. But these alone appear insufficient to provoke the tensions that motivate men to search for solutions to problems. They may in fact even do precisely the opposite.

Many organizations give salary increases and promotions to those who best fit into an outmoded status quo. Here the reward system is unlikely to motivate actions to change. But there are psychological factors in all problem situations that appear to be important for stimulating creativity and innovative problem solving. When men recognize a clear-cut discrepancy between what is and what should be, tensions arise that focus their thoughts, efforts, and feelings on how to resolve the matter to eliminate the contradiction.

Such tensions provide a motivational force that compels men to solve those problems that pose barriers to corporate performance. They may arise independently of financial or status rewards, and they appear to be highly critical in the achievement of the solutions to problems. Through understanding the force of these tensions, leaders can make deliberate use of them, harnessing energy toward orderly production of change. This energy is only partially tapped in the conduct of industry today.

The contrast of motivational forces of tension reduction with those of financial and status rewards is clear. But this should not imply that they work in opposition, though they can do so. Money and status do contribute to a person's feeling fairly and justly renumerated and accepted by the organization. When such feelings are present, men tend to become involved in the organization and committed to its objectives, thereby experiencing the kinds that are associated with discrepancies and call forth action.

Complete Ideal Model and
Organization Subsystems

The ideal model is complete only when it takes into consideration all identifiable forces bearing on each subsystem of the corporation. This includes not only the forces that are directly controlled by the organization but also the outside environment within which the organization is embedded and under the influence of which it must operate.

Steering, Correction, and Control Mechanisms

Merely setting processes in motion does not necessarily ensure that the action needed for converting from the actual to the ideal will take place. Steering, correction, and control mechanisms and retrolearning techniques are indispensable for guiding development. Ideally, the situation should be measured before development is initiated, at various points during the development activity, and at the end of it. Then information is available to steer action as well as to determine results. The organization can identify factors in the situation impeding progress and unsuspected weaknesses or limitations in the model. Signs of drag and drift can be anticipated and corrected.

Systematic development has several advantages. One is that it relies upon theory, logic, and facts. It therefore arouses enthusiasm for bringing about change rather than resistance to it. There is only one real limit on the magnitude of change that is possible through systematic development and that is the capacity of men to reason and analyze their problems. Risk is reduced because the changes which are projected can be tested beforehand for their probable consequences before implementation is started.

There are also disadvantages. The depth of intellectual endeavor calls for rigorous thinking which is most demanding and time consuming. Many managers prefer the excitement of fire fighting to the conceptual activity and brainwork that systematic development calls for.

These three possible methods of change underlie understanding of how it occurs. Evolution and revolution take place "naturally." They have emerged through history. Systematic development, by comparison, has properties in common with the scientific methods that are used in designing experiments and verifying results. Systematic development as an alternative to evolution and revolution is an example of the wider movement of society from a prescientific to a scientific age.

Tomorrow's Changes

What is this scientific approach to change going to mean for organizations of the future? What implications does it have for industry?

Many new steps and increasingly more rapid progress can be expected through the deliberate design and management of change for the future. A look at the past readily suggests simple examples of the kinds of change involved.

Imagine a group of railroad men at the turn of the century and what might have happened had they recognized their business as the transportation business instead of railroading, set growth and financial objectives for an ideal transportation business of the future, set the model for achieving these objectives, then concentrated their energies on systematically implementing the model rather than "saving" the railroad.

Imagine the strides that might have been made by unions of working men for their memberships had their leaders, back in the days when they were embroiled in pushing for various sections of the Wagner Act or fighting Taft-Hartley, designed specific models of ideal union/management relationships, and had their management counterparts recognized the soundness of the ideal model approach. Something far better and more valuable for working men might well have been achieved than has been through revolutionary strike tactics or the chipping away at "management prerogatives" through grievance procedures.

The possibilities of progress through the systematic design of change are bounded only by the imagination—progress not only for industrial and other organizations but even for world society as a whole.

12 Is Opposition to Social Intervention Resistance or Coping?

Joseph Zacker

In considering social change we can learn techniques that are applicable to change in other contexts as well. One interesting aspect of the question of how to interpret opposition to change has to do not with the nature of the opposition itself but with the reasons that caused or allowed the opposition to arise. As described in this chapter, change agents (or innovators) sometimes are so preoccupied with the "plan" that they give the message to those whose views or behavior it is intended to change that there is no way but outward conflict to cause modification or improvement in the process of change.

Although the subject of this chapter by Joseph Zacker of the Department of Psychology, City College, City University of New York, is a training program for policemen, the elements of that program are applicable to all types of change management. Substitute yourself for the psychologist in the described situation and you will find many useful analogies to your own environment.

As psychologists respond to shifting societal needs, they more often find themselves working in new settings and with unfamiliar groups. An extensive body of empirical knowledge or experience is often wanting in such novel situations; without these guides, our actions are more likely to reflect deep-rooted values that may conflict with our professional values. It then becomes crucial that we clarify what these values are, or what we think they ought to be.

Events that took place during an innovative training program for police officers, a group largely unknown to most professionals, dramatically illustrate how a social intervener's values may be put to the test. Further, they bring into focus potential disadvantages of trying to explain novel events in terms of familiar theories derived from other groups.

This chapter is based on an article that originally appeared in *Professional Psychology,* May 1974. Copyright © 1974 by the American Psychological Association; reprinted by permission. All rights reserved.

**Atypical Clientele: Training
Program for Policemen**

A community-oriented, police service delivery strategy has been emerging in the last few years. Known as the neighborhood police team (Team) structure, it is designed to increase police officers' initiative, responsibility, and Team member cooperation, in no small part because of increased communication between Team officers and community residents.

Implementing Team operations requires a period of training to orient personnel who are accustomed to operating along conventional lines. Psychologists can have a meaningful role in facilitating such organizational changes, taking part in the conceptualization process, the training, or its evaluation. As we become more aware of organizational effects on the worker and his efforts, and especially as we learn that such service systems as the police have enormous potential for harm or for benefit to society, opportunities for psychologists as social interveners in such systems assume greater urgency.

To facilitate the shift from traditional to Team operations in the police department of the New York City Housing Authority, the following program was designed. During four consecutive weeks, groups of about thirty-two experienced police officers each gathered for one week of training at the Psychological Center of the City College, City University of New York. The training program was designed with a number of assumptions: (1) the civilian staff (the author and two advanced doctoral students in clinical psychology, Mona Munoz and Elliot Rutter) were not competent to advise upon "correct" police functioning; (2) the staff should provide an atmosphere conducive to participatory learning about matters of Team functioning; and (3) training should be designed to enhance those very qualities seen as essential for effective Team functioning: initiative, responsibility, interdependence among Team members, and active decision making.

The training curriculum incorporated the following primary elements, all of which are innovative training experiences for most police officers.

Self-directed Inquiry Subgroups

The entire group would periodically form three subgroups, each composed of about ten officers. Each subgroup would be presented with a different, but related, topic for discussion. During these discussions, the staff would serve solely as facilitators of goal-directed activity and not as group leaders or experts. The officers themselves were to be responsible for the discussion's content, which would subsequently be orally summarized by a subgroup member to the entire group. As such, members of each inquiry subgroup could teach and learn from their peers in *all* subgroups.

Practice Interventions in Human Crises

Police everywhere are frequently called on at times of personal crisis. Yet policemen rarely get feedback as to their effect on the outcomes of such situations. They never have the opportunity to observe the effects of several different interventions in the *identical* crisis situation. During practice interventions the roles of people in crisis were portrayed by the psychologists or officer volunteers. These "actors" portrayed their civilian roles, as scripted, up to a certain point. At this time two officers would enter the scene (unaware of what had preceded their entry) and attempt to manage the situation. For each run-through of each script, several pairs of officers intervened at the same point, and on each occasion the actors improvised according to their reaction to the trainees' intervention. The audience of officers, observing the action behind one-way mirrors, could see how different behaviors by their intervening peers affected the outcomes.

Simulated Community Meeting Workshops

A three-hour workshop saw each officer assume the role of a participant at a community meeting (tenant, Team policeman, housing administrator, and so on).

Daily Feedback Session

To facilitate communication and integration of the previous day's experiences, Days 2-5 began with feedback sessions during which the psychologists and officer-trainees could voice impressions and reactions.

The Problem: Immediate Opposition

Prior experience with policemen led the staff to anticipate that there would be some initial resistance to the training because the staff members were psychologists. Policemen seem to expect psychologists to criticize them, encourage universal and indiscriminate nurturance, condemn the use of force in any form—to expect, in short, psychologists to be neither realistic nor practical in their views of police work and policemen. It was expected that this source of resistance would dissolve as the staff became known by the officers.

Each week, however, the level of opposition manifested by the policemen was much higher than had originally been anticipated. There were similarities in each group. Suspicion of the psychologists was quite apparent, and hostility was intense and openly expressed. On several occasions, thinly veiled threats against the staff occurred.

One common form of opposition was as follows: "They" (police department and Housing Authority administrators) were accused of having unfairly manipulated and denigrated these officers in the past; there was intense and prolonged griping about various incidents. A repeated theme was that no one had listened to their grievances. The psychologists were equated with "them" as also wanting to get something from the officers without giving anything back, and we were expected to report back to the administrators about the officers' "personalities." Whereas the officers expressed impotence about effecting changes regarding their administrative superiors, however, they were angrily defiant in proclaiming that we would *not succeed* in manipulating them.

Other forms of opposition included provocatively challenging us to "admit" our true intentions (to brainwash us or to use us as guinea pigs) and our views (why don't you tell us how you *really* feel about cops?), and treating us as if we were authorities, despite our clear self-perception and explanations to the contrary. For example, in the first inquiry groups each week the officers would usually sit facing the facilitator (despite the chairs having been arranged to form a circle), speaking *to him,* waiting for *his* comments, refraining from using police "lingo" or common four-letter words, and explaining *to him* things they were all familiar with.

Whereas we more or less expected the *kind* of opposition we met, one may question our surprise at its *intensity.* Indeed, one may well ask if our surprise was an expression of our own resistance to the police officers. We were not simply naive, though, since we all had prior experience with police officers and administrators of that same police department. In retrospect, our astonishment seems primarily due to our not having met earlier with those policemen who would later be the trainees. We compounded that error by then expecting these men to react as others had.

Staff Response to the Opposition

Not surprisingly, the staff experienced a good deal of tension, especially since so much of the officers' anger was directed at them. Repeated expo-sure to four weeks of periodically concentrated suspicion and vehemence by armed clientele is an unusual test of the psychologist. The social intervener's response to the stress engendered by such direct opposition will reflect the depth of his commitment to his stated goals and values.

Consistent with our goal of recognizing the officers' autonomy and since ventilation and sharing of grievances were their immediate concerns, we did not press for adherence to the curriculum. Rather, we reflected the nature of the complaints against other authorities ("you don't like being treated that way") and against ourselves ("you think we also want to manipulate you" or "you think we are taking orders and that we report back to them").

Despite initial and periodic bewilderment at the intensity of feelings manifested by the officers, we usually answered questions openly and honestly and acted so as to enhance their recognition that the outcome of training rested primarily with them. When the patrolmen treated us as leaders during the inquiry groups, for example, we stated that they were not there to teach us and, if they persisted, we simply left the group.

Outcome: Collaboration

A consistent and remarkable phenomenon occurred each training week sometime between the end of Day 2 and the start of Day 4—a sudden diminution of group opposition. Typically, several of the men who had been among the most outspoken would resume their griping, only this time to be "put down" by their fellow officers ("C'mon, we've wasted enough time on that already" or "Let's get down to work and stop the bullshit").

If a few men still preferred to complain, their voices were drowned out as the tide within the group turned toward concentration on the curricular tasks presented. The remainder of the training week was for each group exhilarating and marked by a high degree of involvement and mutual cooperation. In one instance, for example, a group asked us to schedule an extra workshop so they could get a second look at some of the interactions. At another time, an officer was being roundly criticized by his peers for the manner in which he had intervened in a practice crisis simulation. A heated debate was raging, but when a psychologist tried to tone down the criticisms, the officer in question loudly objected. "No, let it go on, this is the best part of the whole training." It went on.

When the patrolmen completed anonymous, open–ended questionnaires at the conclusion of their training week, a number of them wrote about the first two days. About one-third of these noted that the griping had lasted too long, some adding that we should have cut it short. Another third, however, saw these events as either unavoidable ("there is a need to devise a method by which the complaint sessions which we had on Monday and Tuesday could be shortened without causing hard feelings"), or as constructive: "(It) got the group to think together and familiarize each patrolman with one another; the men had a chance to express themselves, how they really felt; it installed a very good feeling of brotherhood, spirit, and unity."

Discussion

It is to be expected that when psychologists encounter opposition, they will tend to interpret it according to concepts with which they are most familiar. At a time when theories of psychodynamics (especially psychoanalysis) have reigned as the organizing principles for most American mental health professionals, for many of us our perception of institutional opposition will be affected by the psychoanalytic concept of *resistance*.

A Psychoanalytic Explanation of the Resistance

Unlike Sullivan who considered that resistance might simply be "something that opposes what was presumed to be helpful," conventional psychoanalytic theory requires that the oppositional behavior should not be considered true resistance unless one infers that unconscious impulses are being defended against.[1] Regarding the patrolmen, one could argue, as did Freud in explaining opposition to psychoanalysis by physicians and philosophers, that the very intensity of their opposition during the first few days suggests "that resistances other than purely intellectual ones were stirred up and that powerful emotional forces were aroused."[2]

    Searching for an explanation of events in terms of a familiar theory will almost certainly lead one to find what he seeks. A psychologist oriented primarily toward psychoanalytic theory might infer that the "emotional forces" aroused in the police officers centered on conflicts about dependent impulses. Most of the officers were from minority groups and of low or lower-middle socioeconomic background. Both of these factors are associated with overly punitive or distant parental (especially paternal) behavior. Dependent impulses in such children are likely to be one sporadically gratified, enchancing anxious repression and the erection of defenses against their later arousal, awareness, or expression. This line of conceptualizing might even lead one to speculate that the choice of police work in itself may reflect an unconscious conflict—identifying with the aggressor, perhaps, by becoming a distant and punitive authority, or manifesting a repetition-compulsion by joining an organization in which there are once again superriors who (like one's parents) are seen as distant, uncaring, and punitive. In such psychoanalytic terms the officers' behavior toward us could be understood as transference.

    By our refusing to accept the roles of either "good" or "bad" authorities, or the role of psychotherapist, and by fostering instead interdependence on fellow officers, while simultaneously noting that each was an "authority" in his own right, anxiety about dependence and transference reactions were minimized.

While further elaboration could be presented, the foregoing should suffice to present a psychoanalytic explanation of the opposition–resistance and its reduction.

Some Shortcomings of the
Psychoanalytic Explanation

The psychoanalytic model of resistance stresses intrapsychic conflict and ambivalence about change. Perhaps there is unwarranted pessimism about human nature in this view, and as seen also in comments such as Rice's "Individuals and groups of individuals *always* behave in ways that are not wholly explicable in terms of their rational and overt intensions."[3] Or in Menninger's interpretation of resistance as forces that lead each person "to defend himself against any change in his life adjustment."[4] In the same vein, Bion saw *all* members of new groups as initially reacting with various defensive behaviors.[5] In some fashion, these comments from proponents of the analytic model have not moved far from Freud's implication that there is a side to human nature that is antithetical to growth and insight.

The foregoing psychoanalytic formulation is not considered an adequate explanation of what occurred during training, although it may have validity for some of the officers. In the program, one could not simply dismiss as distortions many of the reported instances in which administrative superiors treated the officers callously or with indifference. If but half of their complaints were justified, then their initial reactions to the staff could not be taken solely as resistance to the awareness of dependent, or other, repressed impulses.

Whatever our orientation, opposition may tempt us to overconceptualize and defensively apply familiar concepts from the office (classroom, lab, or hospital) to situations where they are inappropriate. One could certainly describe the events during training in terms of other conceptual systems. While a psychoanalytic explanation has been presented here, the comments regarding the danger of clinging to the familiar would seem to apply regardless of one's particular orientation.

Overinvestment in Our Programs

Klein noted that in self-designed programs the innovator is likely to resist both prolonged explanation of the planning process with newcomers and serious consideration of proposed modifications, a common outcome being "that opposition to the recommended change hardens and even grows as the ultimate clients sense that their reactions will not materially influence the outcome in any way short of defeating the plan in open conflict."[6]

Before training began, we had discussed the possibility that the curriculum might be rejected by the patrolmen. In that event we were prepared to offer aid to the officers in any appropriate way to implement their own alternate plan. Had they wanted no training at all, we were even prepared to withdraw any curriculum. In having such a minimum of "vested interest,"[7] the opposition may have been neutralized, allowing dormant forces for motivation and self-involvment to be expressed. In not *insisting* that these officers change, the present program stands apart from those that fit a behaviorist model, wherein the most important objective is changed behavior in the client.

An Alternate View of Opposition

In decades past, resistances to innovations were likely to be judged as entirely negative, as roadblocks in the way of progress that had to be dealt with or lived with. There was little question but that the innovator was in the right, the resisters in the wrong. More recently, some social scientists have come to see resisters as serving such positive purposes as maintaining integrity by raising issues that require consideration and forestalling the sometimes impulsive actions of overeager innovators. What we are proposing here is that opposition to our programs can be more than merely an effort to maintain individual or organizational integrity. Rather, opposition may also represent efforts to constructively *increase* integrity.

In the present program, the *active* nature of the opposition may have in itself been a constructive change in behavior in officers whose apparently low morale may have signaled the presence of *passive* resistance in their work performance. Their active opposition at the start of training may well have demonstrated their trust in the psychologists; that is, they felt safe enough to complain freely. When they were responded to with acceptance and respect, it is not surprising that actualization of motivation and commitment took place.

If one is being manipulated and ignored, it seems appropriate to do what these officers did: to complain about it, to ask to be heard, and to oppose that which appeared to be a manipulation. In reality, the police officers had not been part of the planning for either the organizational change or the training program. To that extent, the program was prepared *for* them by other people. In this light, the opposition appears as an adaptive response, as an expression of autonomous behavior.

By actively voicing their complaints, the officers brought up direct issues. How much more adaptive this seems than if they had passively accepted what was offered with halfhearted involvement. Middle-class upbringing tends to engender discomfort in the face of clear and direct opposition and the open expression of anger. This "open" style seems more conducive to rapid, intense involvement, however, than does our middle-class "professional" style, which is so often intellectualized and controlled. Can this style engender a form of culture shock that has led us to avoid intensive work with people who have more direct (confrontational) styles than our own?

A Proposed Philosophy for Social Interveners

As agents of social intervention in the classroom, laboratory, institution, or community, psychologists may be alerted to situations in which unexpected opposition from clients leads them to act in such disrespectful ways as attacking those who oppose, or withdrawing in anger or depression at, the "inadequacies" of their clients, or themselves.

The facilitative or consultative process, of which psychoanalysis is but one form, calls for respectful and realistic recognition of the circumstances with which the client must cope. What seems ideal, though clearly difficult to achieve, is a respect for the client that borders on humility, a recognition that factors may well exist in the client's life that he has not chosen to reveal or that he cannot then articulate, and of which we have little or no awareness.

A true respect for the client who opposes our efforts would seem to require two interrelated attitudes in the psychologist: (1) "Since he is not behaving as I expected him to or as I think I would, then *I have been in error,* for surely he must be influenced by something I am not aware of" (the reader may recognize here an assumption similar to that recommended by Alfred Adler for the psychotherapist: *the* criterion for full understanding is the ability to accurately *predict* the other's behavior); and (2) "If he cannot or will not let me know what accounts for his opposition to what seems a sensible path, *have I the right or obligation to coerce him?"*

Notes

1. H.S. Sullivan, *The Psychiatric Interview* (New York: Norton, 1954).
2. S. Freud, "The Resistances to Psychoanalysis" (1925), in J. Strachey, ed., *Sigmund Freud: Collected Papers,* vol. 5 (New York: Basic Books, 1959).
3. A.K. Rice, *Learning for Leadership* (London: Tavistock, 1965).
4. K. Menninger, *Theory of Psychoanalytic Technique* (New York: Basic Books, 1958).

5. W.R. Bion, *Experience in Groups* (New York: Basic Books, 1961).

6. D. Klein, "Some Notes on the Dynamics of Resistance to Change: The Defender Role," in W.G. Bennis, K.D. Benne, and R. Chin, eds., *The Planning of Change,* 2d ed. (New York: Holt, Rinehart & Winston, 1969).

7. G. Watson, "Resistance to Change," in W.G. Bennis, K.D. Benne, and R. Chin, eds., *The Planning of Change,* 2d ed. (New York: Holt, Rinehart & Winston, 1969).

Part III
Creating Change

We have considered the identification of change, its causes and likely prospects, and we have considered how to achieve a better understanding of change in business organizations and in human society generally. In this section we address the act of creating change within the business organization.

For the purposes of this discussion, the term "business organization" also embraces large social-service institutions, governmental and military organizations, and human aggregations of all kinds. If you can change a business organization through the application of certain principles, it is reasonable to assume that those same principles can be used to change other kinds of organizations as well.

A thread of theory has emerged in the chapters preceding this section— theory, however, which is supported by many years of actual practice in effecting change in business organizations. Basically, to effect change on a rational and controlled basis, the following elements are needed: (1) organization, (2) participation, and (3) creativity.

The chapters in this section are organized generally according to this three-point outline. They are intended to add to your understanding of the techniques necessary for the effective management of change. Although very little has been written on the development of creative attitudes conducive to change, the section concludes with a particularly interesting chapter on that subject.

13 A Systematic Approach to Managing Change

Ronald J. Soltis

There are many valid ways to develop an organized approach to the management of change. No one approach is appropriate in every circumstance. It remains for the change agent himself to evaluate his own situation and develop the best way of managing it.

Ronald J. Soltis was director of general consulting for Westinghouse Tele–Computer Systems Corporation at the time he wrote this chapter. The methods he describes are especially useful in large organizations, where change must often be initiated and controlled within one or more discrete organizational units.

Much of Soltis' approach is derived from his experience in project management, and thus it includes the familiar elements of "define, design, and implement" common to most project or systems proposals. An interesting aspect of Soltis' approach is the combination of these utilitarian techniques with a change agent whose principal purpose is to goad, motivate, catalyze, and coordinate the work being done by the normal project organization. He tells how to integrate the concepts of participation, people development, project control, and creativity into your approach to managing change.

Managers are constantly having to cope with change—in their own jobs, in their departments, in their companies. Some of this change is revolutionary, some evolutionary, some recognizable, some not. Internal and external forces are causing managers to act and react in introducing changes into their immediate business environments.

Like other companies, Westinghouse Electric Corporation felt the pressing need to improve and accelerate the change process in its organization. The problem had been especially apparent in the area of management information and control systems, where the rate of progress in some divisions was noticeably faster than that in others.

So in October 1967, the company decided to investigate the causes and nature of change in the hope of finding ways to make the process more effective. Led by a key executive, a group of fourteen peer–level operating

This chapter is based on an article that originally appeared in *Management Review*, September 1970. Copyright © 1970 by American Management Association, Inc.; reprinted by permission. All rights reserved.

and staff managers with highly diverse backgrounds, plus a consulting psychologist, was formed to undertake the investigation.

The group's task was to record and analyze the process by which business change is most effectively accomplished. Specifically, the group was concerned with change in connection with management systems. It was recognized from the outset that the effective use of modern information systems technology has been hampered by the difficulty of communications between operation personnel and systems experts on the one hand and by interdepartmental barriers on the other.

Objectives

Some of the objectives established for the group were to: (1) study the basic psychological elements involved in the process of change; (2) devise a means of improving communications among the line and staff functions of the company; and (3) develop a plan of action and techniques to aid in the effective accomplishment of change involving information systems.

Because the Westinghouse project was aimed at the field of management systems, it may be useful to define the term at this point. A management system consists of three basic elements: (1) organization (the people physically involved in an operation); (2) facilities (buildings, machines, tools, inventory, cash—all the tangible assets of the operation); and (3) information (the bond that allows the organization and its people to effectively use the facilities at their disposal). These elements work together to achieve business objectives or goals of the organization.

Unless these business objectives are established, understood, and commitment to them achieved, less than optimum utilization of the three elements will occur—no matter how effective each element is singly.

Thus some of the key subject areas studied by the group during this project included the roles of line and staff, the relative merits of edicted versus evolved changes, acceptance of risk, information feedback and its importance during the change process, and implementation timing. Implied in these are: (1) definition of individual roles that each player has to perform in the change process; (2) stakes involved; and (3) perceived risks and associated rewards or penalties to all participants, if objectives are met or missed.

Also implicit in the group's considerations was recognition of the well-known NIH factor (not invented here), which usually should be called the NUH factor (not understood here), as a barrier to change imposed from outside the organization.

Conclusions

Many sessions were held by this group, and extensive research was conducted into the fundamental problems associated with change. At the same time, the practical experience of the participants was brought to bear upon the somewhat theoretical findings of the research study. Among the conclusions reached by the group were:

1. Barriers to change arise primarily from the perceptions of people and relationships among and between them.

2. Genuinely common goals can be established only by a participative negotiation process—no matter what the authority structure suggests to the contrary.

3. An independent change agent, a properly qualified person acting as a catalyst or linking pin in a group, can effectively stimulate productive change. Acting as a catalyst, the change agent has no personal bias or involvement in any specific portion of the problem.

As a result of the study, Westinghouse developed a business change technique and accompanying organizational approach that has been used successfully by client organizations both within and outside the company.

Managed Change Technique

The technique and organizational approach is called Managed Change Technique (MCT), a name that Westinghouse has copyrighted. MCT is concerned with obtaining involvement, commitment, and measurement of management effectiveness in making change and, specifically, in effective improvement of management systems. It also instructs managers on the structure and rationale behind change. MCT has three basic elements:

1. A well-documented, highly structured logic approach to business analysis. This establishes short-term and long-term objectives, project direction, and priorities. In this approach, managers draw on proven management techniques for problem identification, objective setting, planning, problem solving, and project management. A top management team directs this function and periodically reviews the objectives, reevaluates them, and possibly introduces new ones—thus perpetuating the process.

2. A task force organization. This element is the most complex of the three because it requires the complete involvement of users in the application of the technique. It involves the creation of a temporary pseudo-organization with a manager and project managers who direct assigned responsibilities of various work groups. It consists of client people at all

levels of line management, including professional people. The functional work groups receive guidance in making plans and in using such techniques as decision-tree analysis, gap analysis, or more complex approaches as required by the task at hand to establish individual objectives, while giving support to one another in achieving overall business objectives.

3. A change agent. A catalyst and coordinator, this person trains, assists, and motivates the task force team to apply the MCT logic technique to its own business problems and to help eliminate communication barriers, both between levels of the line organization and among functions on the same level. The catalyst also trains the users to use MCT themselves after he has left. The MCT logic and the organizational role requirements of the technique are documented in a step-by-step operations manual. The general consulting staff of Westinghouse Tele-Computer Systems Corporation developed the 600-page MCT Operations Manual to be used as a communications tool by the MCT specialists to describe the systems logic and to maintain control.

In essence, the manual is a general work plan followed on all projects. It outlines the concept of MCT and present processes that are adaptable to a wide range of different situations. The techniques used are worked out in detail—from those used by management in assessing overall business objectives and goals to those used by the highly specialized work groups.

Effect on Authority

The classical authority/responsibility pyramid that exists in business organizations is familiar to managers. Most of these pyramids are characterized by invisible vertical and horizontal gaps. These gaps tend to represent communication barriers, both between levels of the line organization and, perhaps even more importantly as indicated by the vertical gaps, among functions on the same level. The Managed Change Technique has caused a compression and, in many cases, an elimination of these gaps, thus allowing free interchange of the information required to accomplish the goals of the business.

As a management development tool, MCT works to create islands of authority and responsibility, at times altering the pyramid chain of command to a more functional horizontal structure. When required, this allows authority and responsibility to be directed to those levels below top management where the job is to be carried out.

Results

The results achieved with MCT have been outstanding. One user completely reshaped its business. This organization more than doubled its sales volume and expected profitability, while revamping almost its entire product line. The final number of end products was boosted to fifty products—forty-five of them new, with only eight of an original forty-eight remaining. Since applying MCT, the organization pushed sales from $38 million in 1967 to $80 million in 1970, while maintaining a constant work force of about 1,600.

One of the goals set for the MCT project was a 5 percent increase in profitability for each major product line. Actually, six product lines increased profits by 16 to 26 percent. Another objective achieved in the program was the shortening of manufacturing cycle time. In the case of one major product, cycle time was reduced from 2.5 years to forty weeks. In a second case, it was reduced from four months to two months; in a third case, from three weeks to three days.

How MCT Is Applied

Now that the conceptual basis and organizational approach to MCT have been described, let us turn our attention to how this change logic technique is actually applied.

The vehicle that applies the change logic technique is the client task force organization, as shown in figure 13-1. Each box on the chart has a prescribed role to play in the process. The steering committee is made up from the top management of the user organization. Its responsibilities include setting broad objectives and goals, establishing priorities, coordinating activities, and reviewing final results. The task force manager, designated by the steering committee, has overall responsibility for execution of all projects, while the project managers have responsibility only for the work groups assigned to them.

The user's key functional managers constitute an advisory committee that coordinates the design and installation of overall systems and is responsible for obtaining the operational benefits identified. The work groups perform necessary analyses and establish detailed objectives for specific areas. They are responsible for doing the work required to develop and install the new or changed systems that will satisfy the established business goals.

At the beginning of a new project, the change agent, who is a specially trained consultant, may assume the role of task force manager, but one of his first assignments is to teach the client organization's designated manager to assume active leadership as rapidly as possible.

All the people shown on the chart are members of the user organization, with the exception of the external resources, such as technical or business specialists who are brought in temporarily to advise on specific problems.

The unusual aspect of the Managed Change Technique can be perceived by examining the basic differences between it and the customary consulting

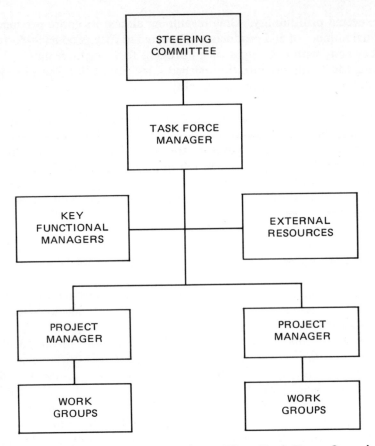

Figure 13–1. Managed Change Technique: Client Task Force Organization

approach. Typically, consultants examine the organizational environment on a relatively short–commitment basis, determine what changes are required, and complete their assignment with a report to the client management. The responsibility for obtaining results based on this report is left to the client management. Often the results are not what the consultant anticipated or are temporary because the people who conceived and thoroughly understood the proposed new systems have been removed. When they leave, parts or all of the organization often tend to revert to their previous state.

In the MCT approach, the change agent acts principally as a catalyst and coordinator who trains the client people in the use of step–by–step logic to develop among themselves the changes required. New systems are developed by the people who will use them and the understanding, the desire, and the commitment required for successful implementation are "built in." When the outside agent leaves, the forces of change, developed within, remain behind.

Logic Change Approach

The following is a general description of the phases of the step-by-step logic that is applied to accomplish effective functional involvement in the change development. Within the general repetitive cycle of planning, action, and review are five time-and-event-related phases. The MCT general work plan consists of these five phases:

Phase I: Business analysis. A systematic analysis of a total business environment is made in a relatively short time so that top management can formulate meaningful short-term and long-term objectives recognizing existing capability, competition, and other constraints.

Phase II: General design. The task force takes the output of the first phase—short-range and long-range goals and their priorities—and develops thorough plans to achieve these goals by improving the existing management system or developing a new one.

Phase III: Detail design. The conceptual plan developed in phase II, along with the detailed goals and information needs, is converted into design specifications for the new system. Also, flow charts, decision tables, logic description, and desired arrangement of input and output information are developed.

Phase IV: Implementation. The design specifications are converted to specific action programs, including computer programs; the new programs and systems are thoroughly tested; the entire system is developed in its operational environment by the people who must use it; and it is placed into its full operational mode.

Phase V: Appraisal. After the new system is fully operational, an extensive evaluation is made of original objectives, benefits, efficiencies, competence, and control. Necessary changes and future needs are then determined. It is a rare system that does not require changes after installation to make it work effectively in an operating environment.

As work progresses from phase to phase, the task force organization, as described in the previous section, is modified, in respect to both the number of people and the skills involved, to meet current needs of the project.

The five-phase process is flexibly designed to pick up currently operative business change plans at the time the MCT is initially applied. In addition, the MCT process can apply with minor modification to business change needs outside the normal scope of the management information system.

The fringe benefits of this five-phase process can be just as important as the final system that results. For instance, the analyses made in phases I and II usually uncover new problem areas or ineffective or unnecessary processes that can be corrected immediately and independently of the major project.

Detail Logic

Each of the five phases described above is further divided into the steps necessary to complete that phase. For example, phase II, general design, includes the following five steps:

Step 1: Initiate the general design.

Step 2: Collect and document data on the present systems.

Step 3: Analyze the present systems.

Step 4: Define and establish objectives and information needs.

Step 5: Prepare justification.

Each step for each phase is further broken down into all of the tasks necessary to perform these steps. These tasks are properly sequenced to guide the people involved in performing the project through the logic required to complete the step. As an example, step 2 of phase II, collect and document data on present systems, requires the performance of eleven different tasks. Some of these are:

Task A: Obtain department or section organization data.

Task B: Obtain or prepare a statement of department or section functions and objectives.

Task C: Identify subsystems that carry out the department functions, responsibilities, and objectives.

Task D: Identify and obtain copies of inputs and outputs.

Task E: Prepare general or process flow charts for subsystems.

Project Control

Perhaps one of the most important benefits, besides consistency and under-standability, that have been obtained from this level of detail is the ability to schedule, measure, and control work done by the people assigned to these projects at this finite level. On the basis of the experience gained through application of this technique, time for each task's completion is estimated and scheduled in the Task Progress Report. The man working on each task simply indicates what has been completed or the percentage of completion of the task he is on.

Project control is vital to maintain project costs within budget and to identify specific areas requiring immediate action to maintain schedules.

Also, detailed schedules for each level of activity help direct and control the development and implementation effort and provide these additional benefits: (1) effort is concentrated on priority jobs; (2) responsibility for accomplishment is assigned; (3) duplication of effort is eliminated; and (4) false starts are reduced.

As a result of this forecasting and control technique, projects have been accomplished within plus or minus 5 percent of the time originally estimated.

Benefits of MCT

A number of benefits have been experienced by organizations that have applied the Managed Change Technique. Among them:

1. The organization's key people are directly involved. They study, plan, and implement their own program and make the required decisions, with the guidance and assistance of Westinghouse consultants. Therefore the resulting change is understood and accepted. Experienced client functional managers (in manufacturing, purchasing, engineering, and so on) intimately familiar with their own operations, work closely with experienced MCT specialists skilled in applying the technique to management problems. This interaction provides a team effort that gains the greatest improvements in profit and customer service and contributes most to the attainment of other user goals.

2. An objective and natural outgrowth of MCT is the develpment of key personnel within the user organization for positions of great authority and responsibility. The in-depth exposure to the overall business purpose and the relationship of various functions to that purpose is in itself a broadening experience. When people with this background are given the responsibility for planning, installing, and operating a new management system or changing an existing system, an atmosphere for rapid growth is usually created.

In addition, as client people work closely with MCT consultants on every step of every project and are exposed to tailored educational programs, they themselves become proficient in the techniques of goal setting, objective problem solving, and other aspects of the Managed Change Tecnique. This provides a cadre of experts within the organization who can plan, develp, and carry out future programs.

4. The Managed Change Technique Operations Manual is available for client use and includes all the basic information on organization needs to maintain an ongoing change program.

Some of the specific goals achieved through application of MCT include improved profit, improved customer service, reduced inventories, reduced manufacturing cycle time, and motivation of management. Other benefits

are the accomplishment of changes in the shortest practical time; the mini-
mization of failure in effecting necessary change; the organization of
departments and operations to provide improved control of business and
improved sensitivity to markets; the tailoring of systems to meet the user's
needs and environment; the development of an organization's capabilities
for using new tools and techniques in management and functional areas;
and the development of an organization's ability to perceive, evaluate, plan,
develop, and manage future changes.

The MCT approach provides an organization's top executives with a
fresh and objective insight into their own business that helps them define
the need for and direction of changes in their management systems.

14 A Way to Manage Change

Harry J. Moore, Jr.

Another approach to effecting change in a large organization is described in this chapter by Harry J. Moore, Jr., director of manufacturing services for IBM Corporation. His basic perception is that managing change requires a fine coordination of people and systems. Such coordination, however, can be difficult to achieve, especially in large organizations where communication and control are complex and sensitive.

The approach to managing change described here entails the development of more effective two–way communication to attain certain specific objectives. It is intended to help line and staff people see such objectives as their own objectives and deals with change in the sense of better work or more work, rather than adaptation to new ideas or the creation of new ideas for the organization as a whole.

Even though this chapter describes a patent-type approach to integrating communications into the process of change management, you will note certain marked similarities to the other change management approaches described in this section. Such similarities characterize most viable systematic approaches to the management of change.

The faster the operating environment's pace of change accelerates, the harder it is for organizations to pinpoint the internal changes that are needed, and the harder it is to implement these changes. Managing change requires a fine coordination of people and systems. Such coordination can be particularly difficult in large organizations where communication and control are both complex and sensitive.

In a hierarchically structured organization, where communications travel up and down through different levels without skipping any, the communication process can take too long; in addition, the more people there are in the chain, the more chance there is for misinterpretation. When an organization is divided into segments that operate more or less autonomously, the communication process has fewer vertical levels, but management has another problem: that of tying all those segments together so as to optimize corporate objectives. What is needed is an effective process for taking an overview of the entire operation; defining a variety of desired results in terms of the organization's overall goals; zeroing in on particular activities that must be instituted, eliminated, or revised; and making sure these changes occur, with the desired results.

Every organization has some way of approaching this momentous task. One popular approach is the "staff activity." The staff, usually organized according to function (marketing, engineering, manufacturing, and so forth), can be defined as an extended arm of top management, by virtue of this authority. It can at times cause actions to take place without line management above the point of action being aware of or playing a part in the decision. (This, of course, is not always palatable to line management.)

There are several types of staff activity. One is the military type, in which the staff person provides input to the "general" regarding a particular problem the general wants to make a decision about. A second type of staff activity might be described as "supportive": basically, its function is to perform research in a certain area (determined by top management), such as what kind of manufacturing processes or materials might be available for future products, and then to communicate this information to the line. Then there is the "control" type, which measures how the line operators are performing against the objectives set by top management. Finally, there is the "service" type, which performs specialized work for the line organization, such as recruiting personnel or handling legal matters.

All these variations have limitations. Even when two or more types are combined, the staff person usually has no spelled-out procedure to follow, and no clearly defined authority; so the inevitable result is conflict between line and staff. Line managers—the people who are directly involved with producing results within a particular function—begin to complain that the staff is looking over their shoulders and diluting their authority. To the staff, it appears that line management is resistant to change. In more than one case that I know of, line management has raised such cries of anguish that top management has responded by pulling the staff entirely out of the picture.

How, then, can top management achieve effective performance in the organization with a minimum amount of bureaucracy? To my mind, the solution lies not in a radically new concept of organizational structure or control but in a better application of the staff concept. In IBM's products divisions, we have been employing a staff technique—which we call Functional Staff Management, or FSM—for a number of years, with significant success. FSM has two principal advantages: (1) its line and staff responsibilities are clearly defined, thus minimizing conflict, and (2) it focuses on things that need to be changed and applies various resources to managing the changes.

Two-way Communication

Before describing how FSM operates, let me elaborate on that second point. Line people know a great deal about the work they are doing that is frequently not communicated to higher management or staff. If these people can contribute their knowledge to a specific process that they know is designed to achieve specific results for the entire organization, they will be motivated to perform better. The "unresponsiveness to change" of which they are sometimes accused may be only natural. As Einstein explained in discussing his theory of relativity, a man riding in a train cannot determine his speed or position unless he has another point outside the train against which he can relate himself. Without such an outside point of reference, he cannot determine when to change speed or direction in order to reach his objective. FSM's overview approach provides the outside point of reference to the man (line personnel) in the train (the organization) via top management and staff.

The objective of FSM is to ensure the performance capability (that is, capability to produce desired results) of the organization. This capability can exist only when the functions within the organization have been provided with the necessary information, resources, and services, and are using them effectively. Since communication between line and staff must therefore be two-way, FSM groups are composed of both line and staff people. Their interaction is what mitigates line/staff conflict.

A typical FSM group is headed by a corporate staff person who is usually the director of one entire manufacturing functional area, such as manufacturing, engineering, purchasing, or production control. For him, FSM is a full-time job; he may even have one or more consultants or assistants. The other members of the group are functional coordinators—line people who have been appointed by the heads of their divisions to represent those divisions in the FSM group. While the staff head is responsible for overseeing the entire area and making sure the activities decided upon by the group are related to desired results, the functional (or line) coordinators are responsible for assuring effective performance.

Since FSM is an ongoing program, it cannot be said that it "begins" anywhere. My description of it, however, will begin with the annual planning session, a two-to-three-day meeting that forms the core of the FSM program. Here the staff head and line coordinators determine the capabilities required to operate at the desired performance level, find out what capabilities are currently missing (we call that "identifying voids"), and sometimes propose projects and research assignments to eliminate the voids.

In order to determine capabilities, it is first necessary to know what results you want. Too often, people who are performing one function in an organizational context tend to look at that function from the bottom up. They take the various parts of the function as currently being performed, say that those parts represent the function, and then come up with a group of "results" that are the output of those parts. That is an upside–down approach, unlikely to identify the changes required.

The correct point of view is from the top—that is, from a desired–results standpoint; from here one can determine the activities that must be performed to achieve the results. Taking this viewpoint is often a hard task for people who have grown up within a conventional functional climate. FSM is designed to change their orientation, but sometimes the old view-point is so deeply ingrained that it is never really altered.

What Capabilities Do We Have?

The FSM group must agree on the primary end results that the company expects the function to produce, and on the factors, inside or outside the company, that affect that function and its ability to produce. These factors are the key points that require overview. We call them "areas of capabil-ity," and they may be broken down into several subareas. Suppose, for example, that "people" is a major area (which it is for most functions); subareas might include recruiting, training, motivation, and so forth.

The input the staff head brings to the annual planning session is crucial to the analysis of capability areas. He must communicate (1) an analysis of the feedback he has been receiving from the line during the year; (2) his awareness of what is going on outside the company—in universities, other companies, and professional associations; and (3) his evaluation of what is going to be happening in the company and its environment during the coming year.

This staff input, combined with information provided by the line coor-dinators as to the existing situation in their various locations, forms the basis for the next task of the planning session: determining the level of desired performance for each subarea. A good way of deciding on "desired" performance, we have found, is to first look at and attempt to define excellent performance. When excellence is not attainable because of a lack of resources, a lower or "desired" level of performance is agreed upon. The lower level of performance must, however, be acceptable in light of the company's overall objectives.

For instance, in the area "people," subarea "training," excellence in terms of the functional goals could be achieved by setting up a school at a central geographic location, staffing it with experts, and having all person-nel brought to the school. Because of travel costs, operating workloads, and other limitations placed upon the line organization, excellence is not an acceptable objective. A desired level, however, might be achieved by sending a small group of company training people to the school and then having them return to the line location and set up local schools to train others.

After the FSM group arrives at a desired capability level for each sub-area, the staff head and line coordinators together evaluate the existing levels. The differences between the desired levels and the existing levels are the capability voids.

Getting Rid of the Voids

After the planning session, the staff head pulls together all the information generated, including any suggestions that have been made by the line coordinators. In a month or so he goes back to the coordinators with a series of specific proposals for eliminating the voids. It is the coordinators' responsibility to determine how important each proposal is to their area of the business function and to set priorities. The proposals can result in either improvement projects or research assignments; these are carried out by a person or persons within the line organization and coordinated by the staff head.

For example, suppose that in a planning session in the purchasing area a void is discovered—the need to increase ability to negotiate engineering contracts. The staff head might then recommend that an improvement project be set up to determine how to teach this ability to the buyers in the line. This project, he suggests, could be handled by two people: someone with experience in engineering contracts and someone with training experience. The coordinators agree on the need for such a project and assign it a high priority. They then provide, from the line, the two people who carry out the project by determining what techniques must be taught and developing a curriculum.

The responsibility for the results produced by this project lies with the staff head. The line has, in a sense, lent him resources to produce a result for the benefit of the entire corporation. He must keep track of the project and also see that it does not conflict with the line people's regular responsibilities.

In some cases the void cannot be eliminated via a short–term improvement project, so a research assignment is set up instead. For instance, the FSM group may decide that training programs must be continuous over an extended period of time. In this case, a permanent group of functional and training experts would be assigned to conduct research; as specific training needs were identified, they would be assigned to this group as projects.

It is the staff man's responsibility to see that both projects and research assignments are closed out when the void has been eliminated, so that resources can become available for other projects and assignments.

The Feedback System

In order to keep track of each project, meetings are held on a planned periodic basis. These are conducted by the staff head and attended by the line coordinators and the person(s) whose project or research assignment is scheduled for review. Besides the project and assignment reviews, there are what we call Functional Staff Management reviews to determine how close each capability is to the desired level within the line organization. The FSM reviews are scheduled every eighteen to twenty-four months at major locations and every twenty-four to thirty-six months at smaller locations (where there is less potential for getting into problems without recognizing them). They are conducted by the line coordinators and attended by the line personnel at that particular location. The staff person attends these meetings on a selective basis.

The staff head also receives feedback from audits conducted by the corporate audit department regarding procedural activities, and from his contacts outside the organization. He shares this information with the line coordinators. If it becomes evident during the year between major planning sessions that capabilities have changed, project or research assignments may be started or stopped at any time.

As a result of this overview system, the staff head is able to identify problems that are common to various divisions and recommend solutions that can be adapted from one to another. For example, recently we wanted to institute a minority: supplier program in every IBM purchasing department within the United States. The staff head was able to present the general objectives of the program to the line coordinators—so they could see it from a corporate "results" point of view—and to share with them the discoveries that were being made at other locations during the implementation process.

The staff head is also responsible for the interaction of his particular area with other functional areas. Suppose, for instance, that the quality engineering department discovers a problem in the quality of a product, and this deficiency turns out to be the result of vibrations that occur when the product is shipped. Packaging, then, has to come into the quality engineering picture. It is the staff person's responsibility to make sure the necessary communication takes place. Each staff head also presents a review of his activities every quarter at a meeting attended by other staff heads.

Flexibility and the Change Process

Our experience in applying FSM to a number of manufacturing areas has shown that the implementation must differ according to the maturity of the

function. For example, production control is what we call a mature manufacturing function—it has maintained the same structure for some time
without major problems, and there is much top management awareness of
all its aspects. The focus of FSM for this function is on the future operational environment. Projects are few in number, although the ones that are
proposed are generally larger and more significant than for a less mature
function. It is not necessary to go through the entire process of determining
desired capability levels on a yearly basis at the planning session, and the
FSM review covers only those major changes that the group has focused on.

On the other hand, our distribution function has recently undergone a
regrouping of various activities (traffic, packaging, distribution engineering, and so forth). It now must be looked at from the top, which means the
complete FSM process of defining desired results and the activities that
affect these results.

The key word in the term Functional Staff Management is the last one.
Management of the process of change is, I believe, what distinguishes our
system from other types of staff activity. Both staff and line people have
clearly delineated responsibilities, and every activity is directed toward finding out what needs to be changed and toward managing that change—in
other words, determining where we need to go and how to get there. Feedback is constant and systematic.

We have found that by directly involving the line people in the overview
process, we can get along with a smaller staff than is common in other organizations. Much duplication of effort is avoided, and the line people are
required to stretch their perception of their own jobs to include the objectives of the entire company.

While FSM is particularly applicable to the large company that has
become divisionalized, it could be employed in small organizations as well.
Determining voids in capabilities and pinpointing the projects needed to
eliminate those voids are useful procedures for organizations of any size.

15 Management by Objectives in Marketing: Philosophy, Process and Problems

Michael J. Etzel and
John M. Ivancevich

An interesting phenomenon of our business culture recently has been the emergence of a technique called management by objectives, or MBO. Unfortunately, over the past few years, almost every program designed to move people or organizations to new achievements has been tagged with that label. And, inevitably, many constructive programs which do embody MBO techniques have been tagged with other labels to avoid the stigma that has become attached to MBO as a result of its overuse. The simple fact is, however, that MBO can be quite useful in effecting change within organizations, and the technique should be considered in any study of the management of change.

In this chapter, Professor Michael J. Etzel of the College of Business and Economics, University of Kentucky [Lexington], and Professor John M. Ivancevich of the College of Business Administration, University of Houston, provide a good summary of MBO which, while concerned specifically with marketing, can be extended by analogy to virtually any aspect of management—especially if you add to this description the important participation benefits of MBO which, though not emphasized in this discussion, can be especially valuable in efforts to manage change.

In recent years, management by objectives (MBO) has been one of the most striking developments of management in various organizational units such as marketing, production, and research and development. The widespread acceptance and use of MBO as a process for managing marketing units makes it an important technique that marketing executives should understand.

This article will focus on MBO issues and practices for marketing units. The objectives of the article are fourfold. First, the evolution of MBO and its basic operational tenets are presented. Second, the MBO process applied to a marketing example is described. Third, implementation considerations for the marketing executive are outlined. Finally, some problems regarding the use of MBO in a marketing setting are discussed.

The Evolution of MBO: A Review

Drucker and McGregor were two of the earliest advocates of the use of MBO.[1] Drucker, who acted as the catalyst that set the stage for MBO's current popularity, expressed the importance for management of balancing needs and goals to get results. McGregor, on the other hand, advocated the use of MBO to optimize the superior/subordinate relationship by emphasizing performance, participation, and commitment rather than personality, and stressing future action rather than past behavior. These two modern viewpoints on MBO stress a number of important factors. First, a significant feature of managing an organization is the ability to achieve results. These results must be evaluated by comparing them to some previously established standard. Second, MBO recognizes the desire of many managers to assume responsibility and exercise a high degree of self-control in job performance. Third, an underlying assumption of MBO is to involve managers directly in the planning, organization, and control of their jobs. The idea is that involvement leads to commitment and if a person is committed, he will be motivated to perform in a manner that contributes to his objectives. Finally, MBO develops a systematic framework for participation between a superior and his subordinates. It is much more than a one-shot participative experience. It is a continuous effort that stimulates, encourages, and rewards the participants.

The Tenets of MBO

The majority of MBO writings focus on the production manager's use of the approach. It is the production manager who is thought to have the most measurable or quantifiable output units. Surprisingly, the marketing executive who is selling these units of production is often neglected as a potential adopter of MBO. There are many issues already researched and discussed in the production management literature that have specific applicability to the use of MBO in marketing.

In reviewing the evolution of MBO and current thinking about the approach, there appear to be four basic tenets for the marketing executive. These are: objectives, time, participation, and motivation.[2]

Objectives

The objectives are clear, concise statements of anticipated accomplishments that are planned and expected to happen. They are job-related results. For example, an objective may be to increase the sales of product A by 10 percent within the next six months in the Chicago sales region, to increase customer inquiries from 5,000 to 7,500 per year in the western geographical region, or to reduce controllable selling expenses from 20 to 15 percent of sales by December 31, 197-.

Objectives can also be less quantitative and more personal development oriented. For example, a marketing research manager may present an objective concerning his return to school within the next year to update his knowledge of sampling designs. Most organizations encourage developing both quantitative and personal development objectives in their MBO programs.

Time

The time ingredient provides the marketing MBO participant with a schedule for reaching various levels of accomplishment. The time frame may be six months, one year, or even five years. In essence, the time factor is an effort to encourage the manager—whether in advertising, sales, or some other marketing activity—to accomplish specific objectives within a formal, designated period of time.

Participation

It appears that for a subordinate to fully accept an objective, he must play a significant role in designing it.[3] Although participation at one time was considered a managerial panacea, the results of more recent empirical research are inconclusive reagrding the importance of participation. It has been found, for example, that clear, specific objectives are more important to performance than a sense of participation.[4] However, it has also been established that participation results in greater subordinate acceptance of decisions.[5] A possible explanation for this apparent conflict is suggested by Carroll and Tosi in their description of legitimate participation. If an individual perceives that he has some control over both the way objectives are set and the means of reaching them, he views his participation as legitimate and responds favorably.[6]

Motivation

MBO can be considered a motivational process, since individual commitments and achievement of results can lead to a high level of intrinsic job satisfaction. It is assumed that the manager who is knowledgeable about and participating in the MBO process is motivated. Likewise, a salesman who is involved in developing his travel routes and makes a commitment with his superior to follow the routes has a reason to be motivated. He has had a role in planning this part of his job.

In many ways, then, MBO is a philosophy, a process, an organizational change approach, and more. The most significant point is that it is results oriented and can certainly be used in many different ways in marketing departments. Scrutinizing the intent of such originators of MBO as Drucker and McGregor and the four operational tenets, a number of potential benefits logically emerge. These are:

1. Concrete objectives can direct performance, reduce uncertainty, and serve as an instrument of communication.

2. MBO can point out where greater coordination between managers is required. For example, one marketing unit may have to cut down its request for budget money because another unit needs the money more.

3. MBO can remove performance appraisal from the realm of a superior acting as a judge evaluating subordinates to a role of counseling and encouraging.

4. MBO can provide subordinates with the latitude and freedom to reach decisions without always checking for approval.

5. MBO can lead to improved planning since the manager knows what his objectives and his superiors' expectations are.

6. MBO can produce a shift from control over people to control over operations. The manager is evaluated on how well he manages the operation.

7. MBO can generate a more immediate response to deviations from standards because the manager knows his objectives and their priorities.

Any marketing executive who is attempting to build a team and weld individual subordinate activities into a common effort should at least examine MBO. Improved marketing effectiveness requires that each job be directed toward the objectives of the whole organization. Any determination of the success of the executive and his subordinates requires some measurement of their contribution. This is basically what MBO is about—concentrating on results so that the organization can adapt, grow, and survive.

The MBO Process

Basically, the MBO process consists of three generally accepted steps: (1) meaningful organization objectives are developed by top management; (2) superiors and subordinates jointly develop objectives for the subordinate that are consistent with the organizational objectives; and (3) superiors and subordinates at some later specified time assess the subordinates' performance.

The process—with some minor refinements—is presented in figure 15-1 and illustrated with a marketing example below. In the example, it is assumed that MBO is being applied to a marketing organization that includes a marketing vice president, a divisional sales manager, and a territory manager. To facilitate the explanation, the remainder of the marketing organization and the other areas of the firm will not be considered.

Setting Organizational Objectives

Because objectives are critical to the operation of an organization, the top management of virtually every organization makes some attempt at formulating them (figure 15-1, step 1). However, research has established that the process often stops there.[7] The organizational objectives become distorted and never filter down the operating levels to the advertising manager or salesman in the field. Simply stated, there is a breakdown in the system between what the organization intended to do and actual performance, because a process for directing and monitoring objective-based activities does not exist. One function of MBO is to prevent this from happening.

*Converting Organizational Objectives
into Marketing Objectives*

Once organizational objectives are specified, they can be converted or reduced into objectives for the marketing division. For example, if one

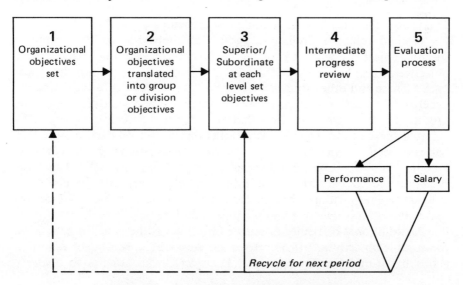

Figure 15-1. The Generalized MBO Process

organizational objective is to achieve and maintain industry leadership by obtaining a total market share of 30 percent, the marketing vice president may have as one objective that of increasing market share by 2 percent per year for five years. The divisional sales manager, in consultation with his immediate supervisor, the vice president, might establish the development of a formerly ignored geographic area as one of his objectives. Finally, at the next level, the territory manager, working with the division head, plans to increase the salescall ratio through increased sales training for his salesmen.

Three things should be noted in this example. First, as objective setting moves down in the organization, the objectives continue to become more specific, but they all emanate from the organizational objective. Second, only one objective at each level was mentioned, but in actuality there are likely to be several objectives at each level and a single objective at one level may produce two or three objectives at the next lower level. Finally, in the example the division and territory managers' objectives were stated in general terms. At each level in the marketing unit, the set of objectives should be formally recorded and assigned priorities. The problem of measurable objectives will be discussed shortly.

Objective Setting by Marketing Managers

The actual process of setting objectives at each level in the organization involves a superior and subordinate working together and jointly translating the objective that has filtered down from the level immediately above into anticipated accomplishments for the subordinate (figure 15-1, step 3). This is both the most important and most difficult aspect of MBO.

Limited research findings suggest that the existence of acceptable specific objectives leads to higher performance[8] and that participative objective setting has a greater individual effect on performance that feedback.[9] These and other studies have provided some evidence regarding the benefits of objective setting. However, there are potential pitfalls in this process. For example, objectives that an individual perceives as very difficult to achieve can lead to decreased rather than increased performance.[10] It has also been shown that, to be effective, organizational objectives must take into consideration an individual's personal objectives.[11] When these factors are combined with the realization that objectives differ in their difficulty of achievement and that the time frame for accomplishing objectives varies, the process quickly becomes quite complex.

An additional difficulty in setting objectives is the value of producing measurable objectives.[12] If objectives are measurable, success or failure in achieving them is readily apparent. However, in an attempt to quantify objectives two problems can occur. First, proxy measures that fail to adequately measure performance may be used (for example, conducting a sales training program does not necessarily indicate that an objective of improved selling skills has been accomplished). Second, less measurable objectives such as the professional development of subordinates may be overlooked. Particularly in marketing where measures are plentiful—sales, market share, brand awareness, number of accounts, advertising exposure, sales expense—such things as the development of managerial skills may not be adequately emphasized.

Each organization must develop tailor-made MBO forms to list objectives, record progress, and plan future activity. These forms are an agreement on expected performance between the superior and the subordinate. Each retains a copy of the form, which becomes the focal point of the intermediate progress review and evaluation sessions. A concise example of such a form is presented in table 15-1. The objectives, projections, and plans to achieve the objectives are worked out by the superior and subordinate. At each periodic review (in this example, there are three), actual performance is filled in and any changes in the plans are briefly described. This form becomes a permanent record of expectation and performance. A more elaborate form might include space for evaluation in each periodic review and a method for calculating overall perfomance for the individual.

Intermediate Progress Reviews

Once individual objectives have been established, formal periodic reviews should be conducted to evaluate progress, reconsider unrealistic objectives, and make adjustments for unanticipated organizational or environmental developments (figure 15-1, step 4). If the MBO program is set up on a one-year cycle, these intermediate sessions are generally scheduled every three to four months.

In the table the divisional sales manager has fallen below the stated objective for expansion in the southwestern region in each review. Since both he and his superior are aware of this, corrective action can be taken. On the other hand, he is exceeding objective 2; possible some resources that are being used here could be transferred to objective 1.

It is suggested that the supervisor perform two roles in the intermediate reviews. First, he should listen to and evaluate the subordinate's remarks concerning progress toward objective attainment. If an upward or downward revision in the objective(s) appears appropriate, the superior must decide if the subordinate is realistically assessing the situation. Second, the superior should provide the subordinate with pertinent information, such as

Table 15–1
Sample Planning and Performance Evaluation Form

Performance and Action Plan for John Smith—Divisional Sales Manager

Objective Statment	3 Months Projected	3 Months Actual	Plan	6 Months Projected	6 Months Actual	Plan	9 Months Projected	9 Months Actual	Plan	1 Year Projected	1 Year Actual
1. Expand in SW region and achieve 10% market penetration	1%	.5%	Temporary transfer of salesmen to SW territory	.4%	3.5%	Increase advertising expenditure 10%	7%	5.5%	Develop sales promotion to counter competition	10%	
2. Increase profit on product line A by 7% over 2 years	.25%	.25%	Continue rate and type of promotion, continue expense reduction	.5%	.6%	Watch other product lines for losses at the expense of this increase	1.5%	2.1%	Consider readjusting goal if performance continues	3%	
3. Select 2 salesmen for territorial sales management positions out of 20 initial candidates	2%	20	Rotate candidates with most potential in district manager's office	2	11	Allow each candidate to participate in significant "people" decisions	2	5	Allow each candidate to participate in significant "strategy" decisions	2	

organizational changes or activity of competitors, that may affect his objective achievement. These sessions should be supportive and serve as positive reinforcement for subordinates while also acting as a checkup to catch potential problems or dysfunctional behavior before it can seriously interfere with progress toward the total objectives.

Evaluation Process

The final step in the MBO process is the performance evaluation (figure 15-1, step 5). This is the final meeting, during which performance over the entire period is evaluated. Performance reviews are often divided into two separate activities: (1) an evaluation of the objectives achieved and relation of these accomplishments to such reward systems as salary increments or promotion considerations, and (2) an evaluation of performance intended to aid the subordinate in self-development and set the stage for the next period.

The final review, which often follows several intermediate reviews, should not contain surprises for either of the parties involved. If the subordinate has been performing unsatisfactorily, both he and his superior should be aware of it. Given such a situation, it may appear that both objectives mentioned above could be accomplished in one session. However, salary discussions are frequently fraught with emotion, and people tend to engage in self-deception or rationalization to justify their behavior. As a result, the subordinate who has potentially the most to gain from a discussion on improving his performance may learn very little if salary must also be discussed. By separating these sessions by two or three weeks, the opportunity for growth could by improved.

Thus the final evaluation process consists of two sessions. In the first, the subordinate's performance is reviewed, with an emphasis on the results achieved. For example, assume that the divisional sales manager is able to produce only one qualified territorial sales manager (table 15-1, objective 3) by the end of the year. He has failed to meet his objective. Unless some force beyond his control prevented its accomplishment, this failure should be reflected in his bonus or other annual reward. The second session is future oriented. Conducted in a supportive, constructive atmosphere, the strengths and weaknesses of the subordinate are discussed and a program for growth is designed. It should be clear to both parties that this session is intended to improve the individual, not to find fault or criticize. The thrust is to examine how and why some objectives were not accomplished and whether objectives that were accomplished resulted from systematic effort rather than by chance. Past accomplishments based on systematic effort can serve as the basis for future efforts to achieve objectives. In the case of developing territorial sales managers, the vice president may find in the final review with the divisional sales manager that training is not his strong point and he avoids it. If that is the case, the divisional sales manager must be made to realize the importance of developing a capable group of subordinates.

Recycling

The final performance evaluation session leads directly into setting objectives for the next period. If necessary, the organization's objectives are reviewed and revised (indicated by the dotted line in figure 15-1. This would be somewhat unusual, since organizational objectives generally have a degree of permanence. More normally, divisional or group objectives are determined, individual objective–setting sessions are held, and the MBO process repeats as described above.

MBO Implementation Considerations
for the Marketing Executive

After the marketing executive understands the four tenets and the MBO process, it is then necessary to begin work on developing an implementation strategy. Once executives become familiar with the process, implementation often appears to be an easy task. It has been found, however, that proper implementation is fraught with difficulties.[13]

To implement MBO, an integrated, tailor–made, systematic program should be developed. Like any major organizational change effort instituted from the top of the organization, MBO must be clearly understood by the marketing participants. In addition, the participants must be motivated to use MBO and have a fundamental knowledge base concerning the necessary implementation steps and anticipated results. The marketing executive who fails to carefully prepare for potential implementation problems and the resulting consequences often becomes disenchanted with the entire MBO effort.

The implementation effort involves three phases: learning the MBO process, actual implementation, and evaluation and modification. Whether MBO is being used in sales units, advertising, distribution center, or marketing research teams, these three phases should be considered.

The Learning Phase

Before a marketing executive even attempts to implement MBO he must appreciate the necessity of learning the process. Failure to properly train participants in setting objectives, performing intermediate progress reviews, and conducting the final evaluation can lead to a misinformed and frustrated marketing unit. The learning phase typically involves formal training in the various steps of the MBO process. The training program can prepare MBO participants via formal firsthand experience in the concepts of objective setting, superior/subordinate objective discussions, participation, and feedback.

In the training segment it is recommended that actual marketing examples serve as the participation reference anchors. This realism improves the learning impact of the training segment. In addition, it is possible to show how the marketing unit must integrate its MBO effort with other organizational activities such as performance evaluation, salary decisions, and promotional review. The limited research available suggests that MBO has a better chance of improving effectiveness if it is carefully integrated with formalized procedures such as salary reviews.[14]

Each marketing unit must develop its own job-related program for the learning phase. The literature indicates that marketing participants can develop MBO skills best in a formal training setting.   The emphasis in these programs is on transmitting information and knowledge, performing each of the MBO process steps in the classroom, reflecting on the training experience, and discussing the on-the-job sequence of events. There is no research that shows the optimum amount of training necessary. Each marketing unit must determine this in accordance with its particular needs.

Actual Implementation

Despite in-depth training experiences and encouragement by top management, many MBO programs flounder immediately after the training experience.[16] This is in part due to the shock that sets in when a trainee attempts to implement what he learned in the hypothetical training situation. Talking about such objectives as improving the frequency and size of sales orders in a training program is much easier than discussing specific percentages and time periods with a superior or subordinate in an actual objective-setting session.

An item of top priority in the implementation phase is the development of a guideline manual or operating procedure that sets forth the procedures, time frames, and other relevant MBO-related processes that will be followed by the marketing unit participants. One large fast-food company attempted to implement MBO in its marketing department but failed to utilize any guideline manual. The marketing managers, though knowledgeable about MBO, became so frustrated with the lack of procedures to follow that they failed to meet any of the time deadlines for each of the steps in the process. Active resistance and rebellion were so widespread that the program was discarded a mere nine months after the MBO training program. This kind of frustration with and discarding of MBO is a common occurrence.

Another implementation issue that often creates controversy involves deciding which unit or executive will be responsible for MBO—that is, who should be responsible for initiating and overseeing the program. Some suggest initiating the process at the lowest managerial level—for example, having the salesmen set objectives that are passed up the organization to the next level.[17] It has also been suggested that the personnel department begin the process by issuing corporate objectives to lower levels in the hierarchy; the personnel unit then oversees, in a staff capacity, the entire program.[18] The most widely used implementation strategy is to start the process from the president's office.[19] Research indicates that exactly who initiates and oversees the program is not the major issue.[20] Instead, the marketing executives involved in MBO should be concerned with the total commitment and active participation of their entire team or unit. A marketing unit that has a passively interested vice president or company president will have difficulty convincing subordinates of the importance of the MBO program. The apathy of top-level MBO participants appears to filter down quickly to the lower management levels, with the result being a lack of interest in the program.[21]

Evaluation and Modification

After twenty years of MBO, one would probably assume that there are numerous evaluative studies that indicate how management by objectives has led to improvements in effectiveness such as greater levels of sales, more effective expenditures of advertising dollars, or more thorough marketing research efforts. The sad fact is that evaluation and modification plans are lacking. Only the works of Raid,[22] Tosi and Carroll,[23] Mayer, Kay, and French,[24] and Ivancevich [25] have looked at these issues. This is a poor record of evaluation in light of the fact that thousands of organizations in industry, government, education, and health care have experimented with MBO.

Can the marketing department or any unit, for that matter, afford to spend thousands of dollars and innumerable man-hours on a seldom-evaluated concept? It seems apparent that a marketing unit implementing MBO would be well advised to evaluate its efforts regularly and make necessary modifications in the original programs. Such things as the attitudes of participants over time, the various effectiveness measures used in the unit, and the actual activities engaged in by participants during the various steps in the MBO process should be evaluated. Of course, this type of monitoring is time consuming, but those companies with even the slightest record of success with MBO had to make necessary modifications in their programs that stemmed from some kind of scientifically based evaluation. In addition to these three crucial aspects of the MBO implementation phase, a number of other problem areas must be seriously considered by prospective MBO adopters and users in marketing departments.

Notes

1. P.F. Drucker, *The Practice of Management* (New York: Harper & Row, 1954), 60; D. McGregor, "An Uneasy Look at Performance Appraisal," *Harvard Business Review,* vol. 35 (May-June 1957), pp. 89-94.

2. This blending overview is succinctly presented by Paul Mali, *Managing by Objectives* (New York: Wiley, 1972).

3. W.J. Reddin, *Effective Management by Objectives: The 3-D Method of MBO* (New York: McGraw-Hill, 1971) p. 18

4. G.H. Varney, "Management by Objectives: Making It Work," *Supervisory Mangement,* vol. 40 (January 1972), pp. 24-30.

5. N.R. Maier, "The Quality of Group Decision as Influenced by the Discussion Leader," *Human Relations,* vol. 3 (June 1950), pp. 155-174.

6. S.J. Carroll and H.L. Tosi, *Management by Objectives* (New York: Macmillan, 1973), p. 7

7 D.D. McConkey, "Implementation—The Guts of MBO," *S.A.M. Advanced Management Journal,* vol. 21 (July 1972), pp. 13-18.

8. E.A. Locke, "Toward a Theory of Task Motivation and Incentives," *Organizational Performance and Human Behavior,* Vol. 3 (February 1968), pp. 157-189.

9. E.A. Locke and J.F. Bryan, "Performance Goals as Determinants of Level of Performance and Boredom," *Journal of Applied Psychology,* vol. 51 (April 1967), pp. 120-130.

10. A.C. Stedry and E. Kay, "The Effect of Goal Difficulty on Performance: A Field Experiment," *Behavioral Science,* vol. 11 (November 1966), pp. 459-470.

11. H. Levinson "Management by Whose Objectives?" *Harvard Business Review,* vol. 18 (July-August 1970), pp. 125-134.

12. A.P. Raia, "A Second Look at Management Goals and Controls," *California Management Review,* vol. 8 (Summer 1966), pp. 49-58.

13. N.J. Horgan and R.P. Floyd, Jr., "An MBO Approach to Prevent Technical Obsolescence," *Personnel Journal,* vol. 50 (September 1971), pp. 687-693; D.D. McConkey, "MBO—Twenty Years Later, Where Do We Stand," *Business Horizons,* vol. 16 (August 1973), pp. 25-36.

14. Carroll and Tosi, *Management by Objectives.*

15. John Douglas et al., "A Progression Training Model for MBO," *Training and Development Journal,* vol. 27 (September 1973), pp. 24–33.

16. For some reasons for failure see D.D. McConkey, "20 Ways to Kill Management by Objectives," *Management Review,* vol. 61 (October 1962), pp. 4–13.

17. S. Kerr, "Some Modifications in MBO as an OD Strategy," in V.F. Mitchell, R.T. Barth, and F.H. Mitchell, eds., *Academy of Management Proceedings,* Academy of Management, Minneapolis, August 13–16, 1972, pp. 39–42.

18. J.M. Ivancevich, "A Longitudinal Assessment of Management by Objectives," *Administrative Science Quarterly,* vol. 17 (March 1972), pp. 126–138.

19. D.D. McConkey, *How to Manage by Results* (New York: AMA 1967).

20. H.L. Tosi and S.J. Carroll, "Some Structural Factors Related to Goal Influence in the Management by Objectives Process. *Business Topics,* vol. 20 (Spring 1969), pp. 45–50; Ivancevich, "Management by Objectives."

21. H.L. Tosi, J.R. Rizzo, and S.J. Carroll, "Setting Goals in Management by Objectives," *California Management Review,* vol. 12 (Summer 1970), pp. 70–78.

22. A.P. Raia, "Goal Setting and Self-Control: An Empirical Study," *Journal of Management Studies,* vol. 2 (February 1965), pp. 34–53; idem, "Management Goals and Controls."

23. H.L. Tosi and S.J. Carroll, Jr., "Managerial Reaction to Management by Objectives," *Academy of Management,* vol. 11 (December 1968), pp. 415–426.

24. H.H. Mayer, E. Kay, and J.R. French, "Split Roles in Performance Appraisal," *Harvard Business Review,* vol. 43 (January–February 1965), pp. 123–139.

25. Ivancevich, "Management by Objectives."

16 Before You Try to Make a Change

W. Calvin Moore

The immediately preceding chapters have described various systematic approaches to creating change. They are essentially "outward-looking."

In this chapter, W. Calvin Moore, vice president and director of engineering and research in the York Division of Borg-Warner Corporation, presents a good "inward-looking" summary of things to think about before preparing to implement change.

In considering any planned change it is well to inventory all the social and personal elements as well as the atmosphere in which the desired change must take place. People often fail to recognize that the environment interacts with the human dimension. Thus an assessment of his own beliefs and values is an important part of the change manager's inventory. It is entirely possible that there will be enough positive environmental and human values to make this particular change management task a simple thing. Sometimes a mere push is all that is needed where, lacking that understanding, a shove might have seemed necessary.

The chapter reminds us that in seeking to bring about change, you need to recognize that your own beliefs may not be shared by some or all of the people who will be affected by the change.

A new office manager, on the job for only six months, came up with a realignment of tasks and a new system for work flow among his subordinates. The new procedures represented a great improvement in efficiency: waiting time for supplies would be cut in half, peaks and valleys in the volume of mimeographing would be ironed out, each subordinate's job would be covered during his vacation—in short, service would be improved and everybody's job would be easier.

But when he tried to put the procedures into effect, his subordinates created an uproar. A month later, the new procedures still were not working properly because some subordinates were sulking, snapping at each other over matters of status, and generally dragging their feet. What went wrong?

It is perfectly normal for people to resist change. Change of any sort means that those affected will have to learn new habit patterns, and the

This chapter is based on an article that originally appeared in *Supervisory Management*, August 1971. Copyright © 1971 by American Management Association, Inc.; reprinted by permission. All rights reserved.

prospect of this learning process induces anxiety. Furthermore, not all change represents progress or improvement in some circumstances: where no improvement is foreseen, the change will be resisted. Thus what those trying to bring about the change may see as stubbornness or lack of cooperation may be looked at by those affected as self-protection.

Some Ground Rules

The findings of psychologists and social workers who have tried to introduce technical changes into primitive cultures point to several ground rules that are helpful in introducing new procedures or work patterns.

1. The manager seeking to bring about a change should recognize that his own beliefs may not be shared by his subordinates and his attitudes may not meet with their approval.

2. The beliefs and attitudes of his subordinates should be seen as having a functional utility. They are habit patterns that have helped the subordinates perform without stress or anxiety under the old way of doing things.

3. Any change should be looked at from the point of view of those who will have to use the new system or procedure. This will help to anticipate difficulties in getting acceptance and help in devising ways to make the transition more acceptable.

4. Sweeping changes are disruptive, and should not be introduced without considering carefully all the consequences. It is usually better to bring about changes gradually, one step at a time.

5. Any significant change triggers emotional tension—either because old behavior is found to be inadequate or because new behavior must be acquired. The dissipation of these tensions may take a considerable period of time. A clear incentive to change helps those affected to do so.

6. The severity and duration of the frustrations caused by the change will determine whether subsequent problems arise.

Making Change Acceptable

To make changes acceptable, the following techniques have been used successfully:

1. Make the change rewarding at an early time.
2. Make adherence to the old ways unrewarding, but be careful not to generate resentment.

3.   Get acceptance of the change by leaders of the group affected.

4.   Relate the change to existing routines. Tie the new to the old and familiar.

5.   Introduce all changes with the fullest possible consent and participation of those who will be affected by them. In other words, spring no surprises.

17 Organizing for Adaptation: The Case for a Behavioral View

George H. Labovitz

The larger and more complex an organization becomes, the more complex must be the change agent's techniques for managing change. Or so at least goes the conventional wisdom. There is, however, an alternative view which holds that organizational growth can be effectively planned and controlled by focusing on the behavioral mechanisms which allow structure to evolve and not on the structure itself. This view contrasts the organizational characteristics required for success in a changing environment with those required for success in a stable environment.

In this chapter Professor George H. Labovitz of Boston University presents a well-framed behavioral view of organizing for adaptation to change. An understanding of the organizational characteristics he describes should be helpful to the change agent in both large and small organizations. Of necessity, very small organizations may require some compromise in the organizational considerations discussed here, but you will find that the underlying principles are valid in organizations of any size.

Survival in the modern marketplace dictates constant growth, and one of the most difficult and persistent problems facing modern organizations is planning this growth. Management consultants are usually asked to describe how an organization should develop and to answer the question—what will we look like? There seems to be a tendency to assume that the future organizational design is out there, somewhere. With a good consultant or a medium, we can discover it or, if nothing else, we will trip over it in time. A crucial point is that nothing is going to evolve "out there" in the middle of a five-year plan unless action is taken now. The state of any particular organization in the future is directly contingent upon actions taken in the present.

Veterinarians and pediatricians sometimes find themselves comforting owners of puppies and babies when the infants appear to be growing disproportionately. One week the head seems too large, then the legs too long, and so on. Assuming the subject is healthy and normal, it is a small matter to assure that in time overall growth will balance out any disparities and that the infant will evolve naturally to its maximum potential. Underlying this simple assurance is the scientific fact that babies and puppies—indeed, all living things—are, in a sense, programmed for growth. Organic systems contain a complex chemical code which predetermines or plans their development.

Unfortunately, corporations cannot always make the same claim. Without a specific plan or code for growth, neither babies, puppies, nor companies can achieve balanced development. Outmoded strategies, poor communication, and improper delegation have the same effect on organizational expansion as the twist in a rubber balloon. They serve as constraints to overall natural growth and cause areas of the organism to grow at disproportionate rates. This condition results in inefficiency, frustration, and pain; carried to extremes, it can be fatal.

The basic solution to the question of planned growth does not lie in formulating before–and–after organization charts. In organizing for growth, the focus should be on the behavioral mechanisms which allow structure to evolve and not on the structure itself; by so doing, the constraints to organizational growth can be removed or, better still, prevented from occurring. The question is basically one of how human beings handle organizational change. Much of the theoretical or academic orientation thus far has been focused on the individual and his relationship to the organization. However, as John Gardner, former Secretary of Health, Education and Welfare, has stated: "What may be most in need of innovation is the corporation itself. Perhaps what every corporation (and every other organization) needs is a department of continuous renewal that could view the whole organization as a system in need of continuing innovation."[1]

The need for adaptability to rapid change in the industrial marketplace forces us to reexamine the traditional relationship between strategy and structure. Structure, in the formal sense, implies stability. If strategy in modern organizational life is to be adaptive, fluid, and dynamic, can structure be otherwise? A large chart on the chief operating officer's wall, depicting the formal organization, has become the security symbol of many an aggressive and dynamic executive. Both he and his staff usually recognize that the organization chart in no way shows the actual functioning of the company. When organizations are viewed as interpersonal social systems accomplishing an accepted goal or task it becomes evident that, like biological organisms, there must be mechanisms for balance and information flow. Without them, increasingly differentiated departments—each with its own goal, each maximizing to its utmost—will ultimately result in a form of organizational anarchy that makes coordination impossible.

These mechanisms are management teams that plan both strategy and the policies which prescribe steps for implementation. Strategy has been defined as the "pattern of objectives, purposes, or goals and major policies and plans for achieving these goals, stated in such a way as to define what business the company is in or is to be in and the kind of company it is or is to be."[2]

It should be apparent that the whole organization must supply the inputs to such a pattern. The input process serves two functions. First, it provides all necessary data required for strategy formulation. Second, it allows men to participate in decisions that ultimately affect their personal futures. If the processes are in existence, if there is strong executive presence, if the organization is a dynamic viable entity, then formal structure can fall where it will.

Organizational Development

Research in organizational development supports an argument based on the idea of responsive, participating people operating in a relatively unstructured, fluid environment. Likert focused on the problem of interdepartmental communications and group relationships; his thesis is that factors promoting internalization of objectives can be realized by involving all subgroups of the organization in group decision making of a task–oriented character.[3] Separate organizational groups with overlapping common members (linking pins) serve to provide vertical and horizontal communications as well as a task orientation toward common organizational goals. Specific responsibility for decision making is delegated to each organizational group.

Bennis approached management of change directly, anticipating that bureaucracy will decline because of its inability to manage tension between individual and management goals as well as its inability to adapt quickly to the increasing pace of change in the environment.[4] More decentralization of authority is considered the replacement for bureaucratic organizations as democratic organizations evolve.

Bennis points out that implementation is the least understood factor in bringing planned organizational change about. Speaking as a professional consultant, he views implementation of planned change as involving four factors. First, the change agent, through his prestige, consultation, and psychological support, reduces resistance to change. Second, the client system must develop understanding and help to control the fate of the change while trusting the change agent. Third, the change effort should be perceived by the client and workers as being as self–motivated and voluntary as possible. Legitimization and reinforcement by top management and key reference groups adjacent to the client system should aid in accomplishing self–motivation and voluntary perceptions. Fourth, the change program itself must obtain emotional as well as rational commitment from those affected.

Lawrence and Lorsch examined organizational structure, the economic and technological environment, manager decision-making behavior, and the overall performance of the firm within the context of the organization as a social system. They concentrated their efforts on application of a "differentiation-integration" model. Differentiation is defined as the "difference in cognitive and emotional orientation among managers in different functional departments." Integration is defined as "the quality of the state of collaboration that exists among departments that are required to achieve unity of effort by the demands of the environment."[5]

More simply stated, this study examined how managers of different departments view their jobs and how well different departments cooperate with each other in accomplishing overall organizational goals. Although this model was not directly applied to the issue of change, such application may provide new insights to change caused by an altering environment or company growth.

More recently, Lawrence and Lorsch offered some "how to" inputs.[6] Organizational development is decribed as an application of behavioral science through a process of diagnosis, action planning, implementation, and evaluation. Diagnosis includes defining the existing organization and prescribing what the organization should be in order to attain determined goals. Action planning requires identification and description of key people in the organization as well as selecting the type of action to be taken. Action may be educational (change people's expectations), structural (change the organizational relationships between individuals or groups), or strategic (change the basic strategy of the organization).

Implementation normally consists of a program for phased change. Drucker has also implied that in order to reduce resistance to change, sweeping total change should be made when a completely new concept of operation is implemented.[7] Finally, the evaluation of the preceding three diagnostic steps requires that original goals be compared with the results actually obtained. A new diagnosis is made and the cyclic process is repeated, effecting a continuing process of adaptation. This may be one cause for the frequently heard statement, "in our society today, the only thing that is constant is change itself."

Lawrence and Lorsch also discuss the relationships between different organizational features and environmental characteristics. Table 17–1 is derived from a combination of ideas presented in their discussion and expanded. The newer book is concentrated on the examination of three organizational interfaces: organization-environment, group-to-group, and individual-and-organization. Different task or environmental requirements at any of these three interfaces require different organizational characteristics.

Table 17-1
Management Relationships for High-performance Organizations

Environment Characteristics	Organizational Feature			
	Rules and Communication	Time Horizon of Management and Professionals for Future Planning	Goal Orientation of Management and Professionals	Interpersonal Style of Management
Stability	Formal (vertical organizational structure) Bureaucracy	Short-narrow (no need for new ideas or a reluctance to accept them)	Concentrated (specialization)	Task orientation
Change	Informal (flat organizational structure) Federal decentralization	Long-broad (new ideas may be implemented to maintain or improve organizational effectiveness)	Diffuse (job enlargement)	Personal orientation

Note: An organization in a stable environment would be most efficiently managed by using formal rules and channels of communication. If the environment evolved into one of rapid change, high organizational performance could be maintained by switching to informal rules and communications which could more easily adapt to the changing environment.

After a diagnosis of existing relationships at each interface, the desired direction of change is specified. The more promising variables which should be altered to allow the organization to move in the desired direction must then be identified. Action is planned and implemented. After results are evaluated, the gap between actual and desired results may be closed by tailoring the new change methods to the nature of the existing gap.

The authors point out that the cycle for the process of diagnosis, action planning, action implementation, and evaluation requires a rather long time at the top management level (possibly five or more years) and progressively shorter periods at the lower echelons. For example, the second echelon might have a one-year cycle, the fourth echelon a one-month cycle, and so on. In this way, the type of change implemented at each lower management level (where the time cycles become progressively shorter) must show faster results in order to provide meaningful feedback into the next higher echelon of management. This means that the type of change which may be initiated at lower management levels is quite different from that initiated at the top.

Recently, several ideas have been advanced which provide further insight into the management of change. Learning and training have proven to be cogent fields of interest, which is based on the premise that lack of opportunity to learn generates resistance to change. Dill, an IBM executive, feels along with others that better learners make better peiformers in a changing environment; Marquez, president of Northern Electric Company, Ltd., points out that, because of our increasing rate of social and technological change, the ability to learn has replaced experience as the prime manager asset.[8] However, this change of asset value does not mean that younger men are necessarily destined to replace older ones in the management hierarchy. In fact, acceptance of change by workers has been shown to increase with the length of time a superior has held his job. However, younger supervisors have more initiative regarding change and are more successful in this respect. Regardless of age, the amount of support and interest (reinforcement) shown by the supervisor's immediate superior improves the effectiveness of training and change implementation.

Departmental Myopia

The most accepted view related to organizational design is that strategy determines organizational structure. The key question related to strategy formulation is probably, what business are we in? The answer to this deceptively simple question will determine the organizational environment within which the business operates. For example, is the producer of bottle caps in the capping business or is he in the packaging business? His understanding of his own strategy will radically affect his approach to customers, product line, competition, and the resources he must employ. It will mean the difference between narrow restrictive planning and innovative positive growth.

Strategy ultimately determines, then, how the firm will compete in its environment and the relative importance of various departments. It is the independent variable which management controls to bring about desired changes in the environment. Departments which are critical to strategy success will obviously be run differently in terms of the level at which key decisions are made, the need for information, how managers are rewarded, and the need for coordination with the rest of the organization.

The traditional relationship between strategy and structure, however, is becoming more obscure in an age of rapid change and technological advance. The need for diversification and growth has required organizations to adopt multistrategies. The internal stability that has marked traditional organizations predicated upon division of labor, structure, scalar and functional processes, and span of control were a reasonable attempt for large-scale organization and distribution of responsibility throughout a bureaucratic form. However, as Lawrence and Lorsch point out, the internal environments of the complex organization can vary with each functional department. Division of labor and traditional reward systems promoted and, indeed, fostered interpersonal and interdepartmental competition. The prevailing ethos within which any individual operated was that success meant competition and the best man would win. The emphasis on segmentation between departments and between individuals is responsible for the basic phenomenon in organizational behavior which causes managers of functional departments to develop a kind of departmental myopia and to lose sight of organizational goals.

Thanks to Gestalt psychology, behavioral scientists, and, most of all, sad experience, we are learning that if subparts maximize, the total does not always maximize. We are beginning to realize that corporate form is analogous to biological form in that each entails homeostatic or balance systems, and each needs mechanisms of integration to keep the parts of the system in proper balance.

Increasing specialization forces each manager to interact with only one particular part of the total organizational environment. His preoccupation with that particular part is understandable, Lawrence and Lorsch point out, when we consider that each segment of the total environment differs in its degree of uncertainty and predictability according to clarity of information, certainty of cause/effect relationship, time orientation, and goal orientation.

When the differences among departments that interact are great, the firm is said to be highly differentiated. It has been found that specialized attitudes are more prevalent in high-pressure organizations where the nature of the environment is complex and unstable. Because of the vagaries of growth and technological change, more and more organizations that have been usually classed as stable are falling into the differentiated category.

In a highly differentiated organization, such as an electronics firm, it is not uncommon to find greater specialization among departments, greater potential for interdepartmental conflict, greater differences in operating styles among departments, and more explicit control procedures. Such organizations need decentralized decision making, supporting staff, and elaborate integrating/coordinating mechanisms.

A real problem in rapidly expanding organizations is that certain departments have different goal and time orientations during and after transition. For example, sales will usually have a very short time perspective and a greater need for quick feedback and clear information, while R&D may have a longer time perspective and a lesser need for fast return of information. The degree of differentiation determines the amount of difficulty likely to be experienced in maintaining a desired state of organizational cohesiveness.

In a stable environment, operating decisions can usually be made centrally at the top levels of management because of the low differentiation among functions. Roles become established over time, and in relatively simple production processes it is not at all uncommon for one or two individuals to have a good workable idea of what every department is doing and how the department is doing it. Little upward communication is required in order for executives to formulate strategy and to design policy. Little is required in the form of downward communication beyond the issuing of orders, because the orders usually reflect the stable repetitive nature of the environment.

In a more complex and changing environment, these well–established roles become a measurable barrier and impediment to adaptability, change, and growth. High differentiation caused by increasing specialization requires more upward communication to top management in order for optimal executive decisions to be made. It also forces implementation decisions downward into the departmental areas closest to the point of action. As roles become specialized, there is a corresponding need for top management to coordinate the activities of departments and to ensure that organizational perspective is shared by all decision makers at all levels. This increases the need for integrative mechanisms, such as management teams, to facilitate information flow and to ensure proper coordination of increasingly complex specialized activities.

A Question of Leadership

No serious student of leadership phenomena will prescribe a particular type of style to cover all organizations and situations. If one general rule can be defined, however, it is that the most effective leaders are those who best meet and fulfill the needs of their organization. The use of management committees and other necessary integrating mechanisms does not mitigate the need for a strong executive presence. A strong leader will produce a strong organization. Conceptually, the problem has been that power equalization techniques, such as participative management and management teams, have implied that those who use them must abdicate their leadership role.

Operationally, nothing can be further from reality. What is needed is a different form of strong leadership calling for presence rather than prominence. By presence, we mean that state of leadership which permits a manager to achieve a close relationship with his people. He does this by building a climate in which people are free to reach their potential and to grow along with the organization. Two-way communication, participation techniques, and the tools of an "environmental creator" require strong leadership presence, primarily because in a dynamic organization the emphasis is on lack of structure. Most of the research has been aimed at mitigating the negative effects, such as rigidity, inability to change, and so on, that formal organizational structure causes. An important point is that structure provides some very necessary behavioral benefits—namely, it is a psychological crutch.

None of us could endure very long in a world without structure. As individuals, we constantly test reality by seeking out interpersonal relationships. We can then "bounce" our self-image off the mirror of our associates, family, and friends.

When employees are free to participate in decisions that affect them on the job and to help mold the environment within which they will work, we are taking away an element of stability that must be replaced by a strong goal-oriented executive presence. Too many executives feel that participation is fine until trying times, but then someone has to take chances. A particular style of leadership at a particular moment tells us little until we can assess the entire leadership climate. Those who have been in the military might ask themselves which organization they would rather be a member of—a peacetime or a wartime military unit (assuming no one is shooting in either). Most will choose the wartime unit. Why? If wartime units are marked by strong autocrats yelling "charge!" at enlightened, intelligent modern men, why choose the wartime unit? Precisely because most combat units are also marked by participation, goal orientation of all members, quick response, little red tape, and little role differentiation, even between officers and enlisted men.

The most effective officers, military or corporate, are those who supply confidence and psychological structure to meet the needs of their people during anxiety-producing periods. Psychological support is quite different from order giving. Like the combat unit, it might be argued that organizations are at war. To grow, to survive in a rapidly changing marketplace requires adaptability and commitment to organizational goals. The responsibility for that state of organizational climate which permits growth, rather than forces it, is with the chief executive.

Strong leadership communicates the goals, ideas, and policies of top management. The goals, ideas, and policies of top management, however, should be based upon upward communication of information about risks, concepts, capabilities, and competition.

Some aspects of leadership cannot be delegated. In matters of strategy and corporate growth, the chief executive should be the final arbiter. This does not mean, however, that the formulation of strategy should lie wholly in the hands of one individual, regardless of his title. In operational matters, the participative approach presupposes that the chief executive cannot run the organization alone, and that those on whom he depends must have free access to information and decisions if they are to personally develop and the organization is to maximize its growth potential. Without integrating mechanisms, without sharing of corporate information and ideals and objectives, interpersonal fights for influence can adversely affect organizational growth.

More than one organization has somewhere on its grounds a multi-million-dollar white elephant, the production of one man who was successful in maximizing his particular department's goals without regard to organizational requirements. Such successes, without concern for overall organizational effectiveness, stand as monuments to the need for a planned approach to organizational development, an approach which recognizes that the key to natural organizational growth can be found not in charts but in people.

Notes

1. *Time* magazine, Nov. 7, 1969.

2. E.P. Learned, C.R. Christensen, K.R. Andrews, and W.D. Guth, *Business Policy* (Homewood, Ill.: Richard D. Irwin, 1965), p. 17.

3. R. Likert, *New Patterns of Management* (New York: McGraw–Hill, 1961).

4. W.G. Bennis, *Changing Organizations* (New York: McGraw–Hill, 1966), p. 209.

5. P. Lawrence and J. Lorsch, *Organization and Development* (Homewood, Ill.: Richard D. Irwin, 1967).

6. P. Lawrence and J. Lorsch, *Developing Organizations: Diagnosis and Action* (Reading, Mass.: Addison–Wesley, 1969).

7. P. Drucker, *The Practice of Management* (New York: Harper & Row, 1954), p. 392.

8. W.R. Dill, "Changing Concepts of Executive Development," *Executive Thinking,* Harvard Business School Association, Cambridge, Mass., 1969; V.C. Marquez, "The Managing of Change," *Executive Thinking* (April 1969).

18 Planning That Begins and Ends with People

James E. Tebay

Most professional managers today recognize the need for a high degree of employee commitment and participation, and the concomitant need for effective leadership, to effect significant change. Achieving the participation of those who will be affected by change involves them in planning their own destiny. Unfortunately, that is easier said than done, for the definition of just what that destiny should be is seldom agreed upon easily. In practice, this approach is often limited to having people participate in those aspects of planning for change that affect only themselves.

In this chapter, James E. Tebay, president of Tebay Management Resources, Inc., gives us some further insights into the challenges and rewards of participation. Contrary to some, he advocates leaving the establishment of controls to the last step in the process of managing change, and validly points out that planning techniques alone will not guarantee results. It should be noted, however, that the budgetary process that Mr. Tebay advocates putting last is often a useful management technique for determining whether the goals that are adopted by the organization are realistic to begin with. In actual practice, planning, resource allocation, and budgeting are an ongoing process that should not interfere with your efforts to obtain people's commitment to change.

One large industrial firm had been lagging behind the competition for some time. Past policies of stressing daily tasks rather than goals and keeping key employees in the dark about sales, profits, and other operating conditions had resulted in the company's managers being slow—even reluctant—to initiate or respond to change. Idea output and innovation dragged, although the president who had fostered this climate had since retired and been replaced by one who was open, oriented to profits and growth, and unafraid to make changes.

To improve the performance of his company, the new president decided to implement a program of management by objectives. Unfortunately, though, in applying his idea, the president placed his reliance on the technique alone, failing to recognize that effective planning depends as well on the attitudes, expectations, and willingness of the management team to take risks and to alter work styles. The president took almost a textbook approach to planning, forgetting that his company's managers had been conditioned for years to taking orders and performing tasks, not to setting and achieving objectives.

Danger of Textbook Planning

While the president believed that his management team had become committed to the plan because it had participated in the actual planning, the team in fact had agreed to the plan simply to please the new president. Little commitment to the plan had actually occurred, as the results after the first six months indicated. Profits were lower than planned, the company's new-product program was behind schedule, and all the operating departments were turning in mediocre performances.

Realizing his mistake, the president held another series of planning meetings with his management team. Before these meetings began, however, he cautioned his managers to be more realistic and honest in their planning. Moreover, he reminded them that they should feel the same sense of responsibility for achieving the objectives set that they felt in paying a mortgage on their home.

Although the president accepted the fact that a status quo company could not in a few months become innovative and objective oriented, he continued to invoke change as rapidly as possible. At the end of the first year, a small profit had been made, the morale of the company's employees was up, and managerial performance had improved.

In implementing a planning and control system, many managers commit the same error that the president first did and forget that the initial acceptance and effectiveness of planning is subject to the existing attitudes of employees. Greater success can be achieved with planning when a manager, corporate planner, or outside consultant takes into account the attitudes and experiences of those persons involved as he installs the planning system than if he concentrates only on the methodology. In fact, just as the indiscriminate use of a textbook system not tailored to the peculiar characteristics of a company can cause inefficiencies to be built into the system, planning, without taking into account the peculiar characteristics of the persons involved, can negate many of the advantages of the technique.

**The Role the Environment Plays
in Implementing Planning**

Consider, for example, what happens when a manager who has been in the past overly critical of the mistakes made by his staff decides to set up a planning program for his department. Although the department manager may be sincere about wanting to give his staff more opportunity to make decisions, harsh penalties imposed in the past for decisions that proved wrong will cause members of his staff to use any device at their disposal to preserve the status quo. It will take the manager some time and positive demonstrations of tolerance to persuade his staff that it will not be crucified if it makes the wrong decisions. In the meantime, however, idea output will drag. A delicate balance must be struck by management—a balance that is designed to produce sound judgment on the one hand and a willingness to gamble intelligently on the other. The manager must convince his staff, by actions as well as words, that innovation will be rewarded, not penalized. This will require the objective evaluation of mistakes as learning experiences and, where possible, a reward system that encourages members of the staff to take well-reasoned risks.

Of course, management teams that already participate in some form of planning activity more readily accept the entire planning process than those that have no previous planning experience. For the latter, an orientation seminar on the value and methodology of planning can be very valuable. Participation in such a course also would be worthwhile for those managers who doubt the value of the technique, for all managers must understand and support the planning process for it to be successful. Token support from managers in key positions within an organization is easily recognized by their subordinates and can result in halfhearted participation and nonattainment of goals.

Benefits of Total Participation in Planning

Although it is difficult, getting all managers—line and staff—to participate in the planning effort is worthwhile due to the fact that participation in the process generates within each participant a sincere desire to accomplish the objectives set. People forced to change, it is important to remember, often resist as a protest against their lack of control over what is happening to them; however, such resistance can be curtailed by giving those affected by the planning as much opportunity to participate as is practical—even if this only entails voicing their opinions on whether to accept and how to achieve goals already set by top management.

Most small companies—and many medium-size ones, too—rely heavily on their controllers for leadership in planning. This stems from their erroneous belief that planning is really only a form of budgeting. However, a president who fails to lead the planning effort—especially in determining corporate opportunities, objectives, and strategy—may find that the final plans reflect the controller's more narrow view of the company. This imbalance will undoubtedly cause problems in implementing the plans and measuring their results.

For example, it is possible that the controller will approach planning in the same way that he does budgeting—that is, first defining areas of responsibility, then developing budgets and plans for each. In doing this, however, the controller focuses attention on individual department operations, particularly where profit centers are defined, thus setting the stage for department-centered planning, which in turn can lead to managerial maneuvering and manipulation to get the most money for specific areas.

To minimize the bad effects of department-centered planning—for example, disregard for interdepartmental relations and neglect of organizational problems—a company should encourage participants in the planning process to adopt the overall goals of the organization as their own objectives. One way to do this is to begin the planning process by determining corporate goals, leaving budgeting as the last consideration.

Need for Objective Evaluations
of Goals Set

Besides the danger of department-centered planning, there is also the problem of unrealistic goals being set. People react in different ways to the prospect of taking part in planning their own performance. Some managers set overly optimistic goals without adequate programs to achieve these goals, while others tend to set very conservative goals. Both problems, in general, can be avoided by comparing objectives set by the manager to the opportunities available and corporate strategy.

One natural-resource corporation developed a planning guide to help its managers to evaluate objectively the opportunities available, thus ensuring that realistic objectives are set that are in keeping with corporate objectives. The guide contains a list of questions to be answered by the manager before he decides on the goals for his department. The questions force the manager to determine such factors as the foundation he has to plan from, the personnel available to achieve the job, and the potential costs involved in the prospective activity.

Many different points of view are voiced during planning. Remember, planning is a creative process in which such conflicting viewpoints are encouraged so that the best of several ideas can be selected. Some managers, though, do try to dominate the planning process by pressing their own ideas, while others may withdraw from active participation in the planning sessions due either to fear of executive disapproval of their ideas or to the belief that their views will be ignored.

To prevent either situation from happening, each participant involved in the planning process should be informed prior to the start of the program that all opinions will be respected and solicited and that final decisions will be based on the evidence and reasonableness of the suggestions.

Although a well-integrated planning and control system can do more than any other technique to increase a company's profits, not all companies that implement such systems achieve successful results. Unfortunately, too many companies install planning systems, expecting results from the technique alone. Stressing the motions to be gone through in planning and ignoring the spirit that must accompany them can result in halfhearted participation and nonattainment of goals. Consider, for example, what happened at one company where supervisors were invited to participate in the planning effort. When management told the supervisors that their frank opinions would be welcome, the supervisors just sat there and nodded their heads. Said one executive, "We knew they weren't saying what they felt. I guess they were afraid of management disapproval." And management knew that it did not really have their support.

19 How Polaroid Gave Women the Kind of Affirmative Action Program They Wanted

Susan C. Ells

A striking and important change that has taken place in our country in recent years is the significant change in the roles of and attitudes toward both women and minority-group members in our business organizations. Interestingly, much of this change can be attributed to the forced adoption of affirmative action programs by the business community. It should be useful to examine such programs, to view in microcosm how important social changes, involving fundamental changes in people's attitudes, can be effected within the business environment.

In this chapter, Susan C. Ells, coordinator of Polaroid Corporation's Equal Opportunity Administration, discusses some of the subtle changes in language and underlying management attitudes that must be addressed in making any change of such great social significance. You should have no trouble in making analogies to other changes of fundamental social significance, many more of which lie ahead.

As society's views toward women began to change during the late 1960s and early 1970s, top management of one large industrial firm began to issue white papers and memoranda stating corporate commitments to equalize opportunity for its women workers. In addition to putting its benefits, pay, and promotional plans into line with new laws and federal guidelines prohibiting specific discriminatory practices, it published an "affirmative action plan" for women and various booklets on the historical discrimination against women workers in America; its 1972 and 1973 annual reports were picture books of women in professional jobs.

Unfortunately, though, in dealing with sex discrimination, top management placed its reliance on the same techniques used to handle budget reviews and to meet sales goals. It failed to recognize that equal job opportunity for women within its company depended on corporate commitment and the willingness of the management team to accept and communicate change. As a result, women employees still remained in the lowest-level jobs, were forced to take unpaid childbearing leaves, and were enrolled in separate "female management training programs." Although the company had published an affirmative action plan for its women employees, the document and its proposed actions steps remained unknown or unavailable to the women workers.

When Methodology Is Emphasized

When the women employees tried to discuss their complaints with supervisors, managers, or the personnel department, they were ignored; therefore several took their sex discrimination cases to court. One divisional director, encouraged to upgrade women within his area, had promoted his secretary to an administrative post previously held by a man. "You're much better than your predecessor," he told her after she had completed two months in her new job. One year later, the ex-secretary realized that she was earning 40 percent less than her male predecessor and filed an equal-pay suit. "But she's earning good money for a woman," said the confused manager when told of the impending suit. So far, management of the company has signed one back-pay settlement for $350,000; additional cases against the business are expected.

In implementing an equal-opportunity program, many firms commit the same error that this company did. They forget that the initial acceptance and effectiveness of the program are subject the the existing attitudes of employees. Greater success can be achieved when management takes into account the attitudes and experiences of the women involved that when it concentrates only on the methodology. Participative management is a must when dealing with human needs, as the experience of Polaroid Corporation illustrates. It is smart, Polaroid has found, for management to work with its women employees if it wants to understand what is troubling them. This is the first step in developing a nonpatronizing, relevant affirmative action program.

Supportive Approach to EEO

Polaroid's current approach to equal job opportunity for women is based on a report, submitted by the women employees themselves, on their status within Polaroid. The women, who had been meeting for some time after work hours to discuss how they could encourage management to deal with ongoing sex discrimination, were asked by management to research their status at Polaroid and to report their findings to the company's Personnel Policy Committee. A divisional director, appointed by the company's management, served as liaison between the women employees and management and met at least once a month with the group.

Upon receiving the request from management, the women divided themselves into five task groups on the basis of their own personal interests and immediately went to work researching the areas they selected. The task forces were on the status of women employees, corporate policies, company practices, management awareness of the problem, and company compliance with equal-opportunity legislation.

The task force on the status of women found that women were overrepresented in the lowest-level exempt and lowest-level nonexempt jobs throughout the company. On the nonprofessional (nonexempt) levels, women tended to enter hand-assembly or secretarial positions, while men entered the more upward-mobile areas of machine operations and skilled trades. On the professional (exempt) level, women appeared to be virtually nonexistent in department and senior management slots, line production positions, and throughout the sales force.

The masculine pronouns "his," "he," and "him" were used consistently throughout all written policy statements, the task force on policies discovered. Typical of the statements was, "When a company employee has a complaint, he should talk with his supervisor." Such pronouns, the task force felt, left women psychologically "out in the cold."

Investigating more tangible issues, the policies task force learned that single women employees were not eligible for obstetrical coverage under the corporate Blue Cross/Blue Shield contract, while the wives of male employees were eligible for these benefits; therefore, the wives of male employees had better hospitalization coverage than single women employees. The temporary disability of childbearing, the task force also noted, was the only disability not covered under the corporate sickness benefits plan.

Informal and formal training programs within Polaroid were also studied by the women employees. Their task force on corporate practices found that almost all the participants in secretarial training programs were women, while supervisory and skilled-crafts training classes were made up predominantly of men. In this manner, the group reported, the company's training program helped to perpetuate sex discrimination.

Management Awareness

While the task forces on the status of women, policies and practices, and compliance with EEO legislation researched their particular areas and prepared recommendations for management, the task force on action/education organized management awareness sessions for interested departments.

The group designed role plays, discussion groups, and questionnaires in an effort to heighten male employees' knowledge of women's work status within the company. Questions such as, "Who earns more, a clerk or a custodian?" and "Of the 300 production supervisors in Polaroid, (a) 20, (b) 3, (c) 11, or (d) 52 are women" were used to generate discussions on the need for a women's action plan during these sessions, which are still being held on request of department managers throughout the company.

Upon completion of their research, the task forces together prepared a written report, along with recommendations, for review and approval by the Personnel Policy Committee, a group made up of representatives of top management as well as of the personnel function. Specific goals, timetables, and implementation procedures were included in the report, which was approved almost totally by the committee.

Polaroid now has a Women's Action Plan based on the recommendations of the women's task forces and the committee. The plan is increasing, slowly but surely, the representation of women in every job area. Convinced that management is serious about implementing the action plan, women are utilizing the corporate bidding system and entering jobs as production supervisors, sales representatives, forklift drivers, security guards, chemical processors, drafters, and maintenance mechanics. Certain inequities in policy have been changed; for example, the discriminatory policies concerning childbearing and obstetrical coverage were amended to assure equitable treatment.

Although, at this writing, the Women's Action Plan is not yet a year old, continued progress appears certain. By collaborating with the women's task forces and selecting an equal opportunity coordinator for women from among their ranks, top management has illustrated an apparent conviction that women have a right to be heard and that management has a need to hear.

Women's Commitment

Two major barriers, though, must still be broken before women workers will gain equity. The first barrier (now being attacked in the management awareness sessions) is male managers' stereotypes of what a female worker should or should not do; the second barrier is the woman herself. Lacking models in management or in skilled-trade jobs, women are not yet convinced that secretarial and teaching positions are not the only available or appropriate options.

One method Polaroid has just created to increase women employee's awareness of skilled and semiskilled trade fields is a traveling road show. Consisting of slides and tapes, the twenty-minute show pictures women mechanics, machine operators, drafters, and security guards on the job at Polaroid. The accompanying tape has the women describe the pros and cons of their positions, tell why they chose these new fields, and give advice to other women who might want to join their ranks. The show will be presented to women employees who are now concentrated in the lower-paying hand-assembly jobs throughout the company. The hope is that once these employees see "fellow women" performing nontraditional, higher-paying jobs, their interest in entering "men's ranks" will increase.

A second show is being developed for women in upper-level technical and clerical jobs. This one will focus on entry-level professional jobs, such as production supervisor, buyer, production planner, computer programmer, and sale representative. Again, the few women who have entered these fields will be shown on their jobs, discussing how and why they chose their careers.

The films are expected to be useful tools in the management awareness sessions as well as the road shows. If a picture says a thousand words, films may make it easier for managers to realize that women can and must enter these traditionally male job areas.

Any corporate problem as complex as equalizing opportunities for women requires that management follow a step-by-step organizational approach. Without truly involving a large number of women employees in the definition of and solutions to the problem, much time and money can be wasted.

20 Developing Creative People

Charles E. Watson

Organization, participation, and creativity are essential elements in the effective management of change. In this chapter Charles E. Watson, associate professor of management at Miami University of Ohio, identifies those traits that carry with them or encourage creativity in individuals. He also provides some useful insights into the development of creativity.

Dr. Watson's analysis of the characteristics of creative people and the environment that enhances creativity places heavy emphasis on the human attributes of change. Consider also, however, the organizational attributes of the change process as you read this chapter. It is particularly important in the management of change that an organizational structure be developed which permits people's creative attributes and talents to be used to their greatest extent. In larger organizations it is often the case that the opposite is true—a relatively safe generalization until you consider certain large organizations in which (either in spite of the organization or because of enlightened management) creative people are put in positions designed to elicit their best contributions. In practice you will find that creativity enhances organization, and it is through organization that creativity is made most effective.

The process of creative thinking is not restricted to a chosen few. All people are to some extent creative, although some are more so than others. Therefore all can develop their creative abilities and profit from the benefits it can bring.

In recent years as knowledge about creativity has grown, increasing amounts of attention have been given to ways of fostering creative thinking in individuals as well as in group settings. Over fifty universities are now offering courses in the techniques of creative thinking or in creative thinking applied to specialized subjects ranging from art to engineering. The *Journal of Creative Behavior* was established in 1966. In 1972 alone, about sixty new books were published on the subject of creativity and creative problem solving. In 1973 eighty more were published, and during 1972 and 1973 over thirty doctoral dissertations were written on some aspect of creativity or creative behavior.

This chapter is based on an article that originally appeared in *Research Management,* May 1975. Copyright © 1975 by the Industrial Research Institute; reprinted by permission. All rights reserved.

Although much is still to be learned, out of all this activity have come a number of practical techniques and procedures for improving creativity that are applicable to individuals in the R&D environment.

Creativity Traits

Psychological or personality tests aimed at identifying creative individuals have not yet been developed to the point where they are very reliable. The trait approach for identifying creative people suffers from the same basic problem that trait theory has had in the study of leadership. But pushing aside slightly the many valid criticisms of trait psychology, the following traits are most often cited as being associated with creative persons.

1. He keeps an open mind. He does not take a stand and then seldom change from it.

2. He is not a conformist. He establishes and lives by his own standards. This does not mean he is a weirdo; there is no support for the idea that the creative person is neurotic, frail, or socially inept. He does value his own self-respect more than the respect others may have for him. The less creative person tends to have a great need for affiliation and is highly dependent on social norms and the opinions of others.

3. He is aggressive, self-assertive, and quick with suggestions.

4. He works by his own timetable—that is, he works when he feels like it. He does not turn his thinking "on" at 8:00 A.M. and "off" at 5:00 P.M.

5. He works hard for long periods of time. He does not give up easily on solving complex problems. Instead of saying there is not a solution to my problem, he is more likely to say that he must be asking the wrong question or that he is going about solving the problem in the wrong way.

6. He is willing and able to consider and express irrational ideas and impulses. He is able to reduce external inhibitions upon his thinking process, and he will entertain in his mind the bizarre, absurd, and unusual. This does not mean that he acts this way, however.

7. He is not bothered by working on problems which may not have clear cut and unambiguous answers. He takes satisfaction in attacking complex problems and resolving conflict, confusion, and ambiguity.

8. He is not a rigid rule follower. As a matter of fact he may even enjoy working outside the prescribed routine.

9. He likes to toy with new ideas, even if they turn out later to be a total waste of time. He enjoys ideational activities which may or may not have any practical value.

10. He is more impressed with what he does not know than with what he does know. He enjoys discovering new ideas, concepts, words, and so on.

11. He does not make black-and-white distinctions. He can accept and tolerate ambiguity.

12. He thirsts for new and unusual experiences, and very often has a background of varied experiences.

13. He wants and likes freedom to explore new things and ideas on his own.

14. He does not take things too seriously, and likely has a sense of humor.

15. He is above average in intelligence. However, this does not guarantee creativity. In general, there is not a simple, positive correlation between IQ and creativity.

Barriers to Creativity

Most creative people are usually victims of one or more of the three common barriers to creativity. The first barrier is laziness. Thomas Edison, perhaps one of the most creative people who ever lived, would often say, "Everything comes to him that hustles while he waits." Unfortunately, most people do not follow this advice, and as a result most are not very creative. A person should not wait for the perfect idea. Instead, he should work on what he finds at hand.

The second barrier to creativity is the inability to perceive opportunities where one can be creative. Henry David Thoreau once said it this way: "Many an object is not seen though it falls within reach of our visual view— but because it does not come within range of out intellectual view." Dr. Russell H. Conwell, founder of Temple University, and a similar message in his talk, "Acres of Diamonds." Diamonds, according to Conwell, are opportunities which can be found everywhere—even in our own backyards. People do not need to travel far and wide searching for opportunities— there are many all around them already. They will become successful if they can see them and take advantage of them. Creativity is often severely limited because one's perception does not permit him to see the problems and opportunities which are immediately before him where he can apply his creative energies. Before one can become creative, he must usually increase his perceptive powers to see and identify opportunities where he can exercise his creative thinking.

The third barrier to creativity is the attitude or belief that one is incapable of becoming creative. Jonathan Livingston Seagull faced the same kind of problem in trying to get the other gulls to discover that they too could be free. "Why is it," Jonathan puzzles, "that the hardest thing in the world is to convince a bird that he is free, and that he can prove it for himself if he'd just spend a little time practicing? Why should it be so hard?"

With what people have to work with, their brains, they should not lack confidence. It has been said that if a computer were to be built to match the capabilities of the human brain it would be larger than the Empire State

Building and would take Niagara Falls to cool it. Yet too many people act as if they do not even know they have a brain.

There are two types of creativity: primary and secondary. Primary creativity is the unconscious process of insight and inspiration, seeing things in a fresh way. It is the "once-in-a-lifetime new idea." It is unplanned, unintentional, haphazard, and occurs by chance. Secondary creativity is deliberate, conscious, planned problem solving. It occurs as a result of logical and scientific processes of deduction or laborious trial and error.

Developing Creativity

While a few people ever come to enjoy primary creativity, most can develop ability in secondary creativity.

Attitudes and Concentration

A positive, optimistic attitude is essential if one is going to become more creative. This is the attitude of, "I am going to work hard, make my brain work toward its potential, and find new and better solutions to real problems. I am not going to sit back and wait for the perfect idea to come to me, because it probably never will. I will go out, on my own, and discover creative approaches and solutions to problems. Moreover, I can be creative if I will try, work hard, and stay with it until I triumph." The creative person remains optimistic about the possibility of finding the better idea or a creative solution to a problem. He does not worry about what he cannot do, but optimistically busies himself at working toward his objective.

Selecting or Defining a Problem

Creativity rarely occurs in a vacuum. Instead, it results when hardworking individuals rise to solve specific challenges or problems. Necessity is indeed the mother of invention. The history of American business is replete with examples of this. In 1880 George Westinghouse was asked by his wife to take her on a shopping trip to New York from Pittsburgh. Westinghouse had heard that Thomas Edison was planning a demonstration of his electric lamp in Menlo Park, New Jersey, near New York, and, eager to see it, this was all the motivation he needed to oblige his wife's request.

At the demonstration, one of Edison's engineers told Westinghouse that electricity could be made to light lamps no more than a mile from the generator—a severely limiting shortcoming of the marvelous invention.

Returning to Pittsburgh, Westinghouse wasted little time in working on this problem. Direct current limits you to low voltages, which in turn means distribution of electricity only within short distances from the generating source. How could electricity be transmitted over long distances? His inquiry led him to the investigation of alternating current and yet another problem: how to transform alternating electric current from low voltage to high voltage and back to low voltage. The solution to this second problem found itself in the form of the Westinghouse transformer.

Acting on the Problem

As indicated before, creativity results from hard work. It very rarely occurs by chance. Studies of the biographies of great, creative individuals reveal at least one trait they had in common. They wasted no time in searching for creative solutions to those problems which challenged them. A person becomes creative through acting on specific problems. He does not waste his life away thinking or worrying about these problems—or by avoiding them either. One humorist classified four different types of unproductive problem handlers: (1) the ulceroidal type who worries about the problem, (2) the thyroidal type who runs around the problem, (3) the adenoidal type who screams and yells about the problem, and (4) the hemorrhoidal type who sits on the problem and waits for it to clear up.

Exploration and Preparation

The raw material of creativity is knowledge. It has to be gathered, refined, digested, and organized. Contrary to notions held by a few, drugs and alcohol are useless to the creative process. A structure cannot be built out of air, and creative approaches to problems do not arise out of thin air either.

The gathering, refining, digesting, and organizing of data and information require great effort. Browsing, scanning, reading, attending lectures and seminars, and engaging in discussions are all useful sources of the raw material—knowledge. Investigation and study of diverse fields also enables one to expand his breadth of knowledge. Travel, meeting new people, and varied experiences also contribute to a person's wealth of knowledge. Systematic, planned study of a specific subject area in which a problem lies is a good first step in finding a creative solution to it. The more one learns about the particular subject area, the better are his chances of finding a creative solution to his problem.

Another incident from the life of the remarkable Thomas A. Edison is illustrative of the exploration and preparation step. Up until 1914, the

United States imported all of its carbolic acid, chiefly from England and Germany. Edison used this in large quantities in the manufacturing process of disc records. As the war broke out in Europe, England placed an embargo on the material. What could be done? His answer was to produce it synthetically. Other chemists were not optimistic. Edison remained undaunted. He spent the next three days and nights looking up and examining the different known processes of making synthetic carbolic acid. He narrowed these down to one or two and took them into his laboratory for experimentation. At the end of the third day, he had decided on one known as the sulfonic acid process.

Unlike Edison, most people need months and usually years to gather and prepare the knowledge necessary for creative ideas. Regular visits to the library to read books and journals in one's field of study and in related fields usually must persist over long periods of time. Moreover, one should have the capacity for absorbing knowledge, for retaining principles and concepts and even relating other new information gathered to it.

In its simplest terms, the mechanics of creativity may be represented by the following:

$$A + B \rightarrow C$$

A and B represent two concepts (or a problem "A" and a concept "B") that come together to produce a new concept, or insight, C. The purpose of exploration and preparation is, given a problem, A, to generate as many concepts and ideas, Bs, as possible, with the expectation that at least one will provide a useful solution, C. Here are some examples:

A: Glass jars with metal lids are often difficult to open.

+

B: Metal expands more than glass under a given change in temperature.

↓

C: Hold mouth of jar under hot water. Metal lid will expand more than glass and make opening of jar easier.

A: In the late 1870s Gustavus F. Swift became aware of a strong demand for meat in the populous areas in the eastern United States which had outgrown the regional supply.

+

B: Swift also became aware of a recent invention—the refrigerated railroad car.

↓

C: He arranged for a few cars to be built, and began shipping meats—thus the birth of Swift & Company.

A great amount of study and preparation and a background of wide and varied experiences will increase the likelihood of a person finding a suitable solution, C, to a defined problem, A. Sometimes the combination of problem with solution can arise from the association of two people—one with a problem, the other with a solution.

Generating Creative Ideas

Creative ideas evolve slowly if they are left to occur by chance. Therefore, conscious and deliberate means, such as brainstorming, wild thinking, or forced relationships, are often used to hasten the creative process. In essence, these techniques are designed to bring a wide variety of solutions and problems together with the expectation that there will be suitable matchups, thus yielding creative ideas.

Brainstorming is a free-association technique popularized by Alex Osborn. The intent of this technique is to bring out as many ideas as possible to bear on a problem. Usually six to twelve people are involved in this conference-style process, with one appointed as leader. The leader's chief responsibilities are to see that everyone has the opportunity to express his thoughts and ideas, that no one person dominates the discussion, and that the following ground rules are observed: (1) criticism is absolutely barred; (2) modifications of ideas or their combination with other ideas is encouraged; (3) quantity of ideas is sought; quality is not of concern because it implies judgment—a form of criticism; and (4) unusual, remote, or wild ideas are sought.

The Phillips 66 Technique allows for small groups, usually composed of six people, to discuss a problem for approximately six minutes. Hence the name "66." The small-group atmosphere is conducive to freer flow of communications because most people find it easier to speak to a small number in a closed circle than before a large group. The leader collects the best thinking from the group members and then presents it to the larger group, of which his small circle of six people is a part.

The Gordon Technique, developed by W.J. Gordon of Arthur D. Little, Inc., was aimed at overcoming the possible problem of a person in a brainstorming session coming up with an idea, feeling it is the best, and stopping there, not going on looking for more ideas. The Gordon Technique, designed to last about three hours, involves five to twelve people. However, only the group leader knows the exact problem. He states the problem in vague, general terms and encourages the members of the group to suggest their solutions. These are carefully recorded. The success of this technique rests heavily with the leader, who must keep the discussion flowing freely. As the session continues he may narrow down the definition of the problem so that the other members of the group can focus more specifically on it.

In addition to these free-association techniques, there are analytical techniques and forced-relationship techniques. Analytical techniques generally force people to seek ways to adapt, modify, or eliminate products or parts of products to meet old needs better or to satisfy new needs. One of the many analytical techniques is the Input-Output Technique. The Input-Output Technique is a structured process but relies on the freewheeling thinking of a small group. Outputs and inputs and key conditions and constraints are specified at the outset of the session. Then the group engages in wild thinking to arrive at a creative conversion process.

The checklist is another analytical technique. In its simplest form, the checklist contains nine questions:

1. Can this (article, part, product) be put to another use?
2. Can it be adapted to a new use?
3. Can it be modified?
4. Can it be magnified?
5. Can it be minimized?
6. Can it be substituted for something else, or something else be substituted for it?
7. Can it be rearranged?
8. Can it be reversed?
9. Can it be combined with something else?

Forced-relationship techniques are aimed at bringing together unnatural or unusual combinations of things or ideas. The catalog technique is the most commonly used forced-relationship technique. Generally, a merchandise catalog is used. It is opened at random and an object is selected. Next it is closed and then opened again, and another item is selected at random. The two are considered in combination, and an effort is made to arrive at new ideas or products through whatever combination of the two might be discovered.

Listening to gripes and complaints is another good way to generate new ideas—for example:

Ironing clothes is a big waste of time.
I hate to spend twenty minutes looking for a beer can opener. When I find one, it usually pricks my finger with its tip.
When I am away on a trip for a couple of days it is a real hassle to have to lug around eight-inch cans of shaving cream and deodorant.

Thus we see stay-pressed clothing, the pop-top beer can, and miniature aerosol cans of toilet articles.

Stealing ideas is also a useful new-product source—for example:

If my gasoline station attendant can be very friendly, why cannot the grocery store clerk?

If driving a big car can make people feel they are wealthy, can the wearing of a certain brand of shoe or suit do the same?

If gentlemen prefer blondes, might gentlemen also prefer a particular automobile, or cologne, or hair dressing?

Incubation, Illumination, Verification

Incubation

The old Egyptian wisdom had the saying, "The archer hitteth the target, partly by pulling back, partly by letting go." Although people, temporarily, consciously stop working on a tough problem to sleep or eat or engage in other activities, their subconscious mind continues at it. Sorting through the myriad of facts, data, and situations, the subconscious continues the quest. Sometimes it is something entirely unrelated to the problem that makes a match up, connecting a hidden or lost piece of data or idea to the problem and thus leading to a creative solution. Sherlock Holmes allowed his subconscious mind to work on tough problems while he played his violin and paced to and fro in his flat. Hobbies and sporting activities such as fishing are excellent pursuits to engage in while allowing the conscious mind to rest and the unconscious mind to continue working on the problem at hand.

Illumination

This is the most joyous of all moments. It is the flash of brilliance when the conscious mind signals that a solution or creative idea has arrived. In many cases illumination occurs at unsuspected times—while walking, or reading, or intensely working at some pursuit, or even sleeping.

Thomas Edison sat at his worktable studying his notes and experimental data. For thirteen months he had searched, without success, to find a suitable material to serve as a filament for his electric lamp. As he sat pondering this problem, yet remaining optimistic, his hand idly strayed to a little pile of lampblack-and-tar mixture which his assistant had been using in a telephone transmitter project. Picking up a little of the substance, he rolled it into a thin rod between his thumb and forefinger. After a half-hour or so, he looked at what his hand held. Could this substance work? It met all the requirements. Putting it to the test, he discovered that he was indeed on the right track.

It is important to capture the creative inspiration when it occurs, lest it be forgotten. This is why most creative people usually keep paper and pen at hand, so as to be ready to write down their inspirations immediately.

Verification and Application

This last step serves to test the soundness and appropriateness of the solution. Will the idea work? Does the suggested solution meet the conditions and needs of the problem? One should not take this last step so seriously that it causes one to become discouraged if a solution or idea is impractical. Perhaps it needs to be modified only a little bit to be workable.

**Part IV
Maintaining Change**

Perhaps the most important challenge facing modern management is to create an environment in which change is accepted as a constant, a way of life, rather than something to be dealt with from time to time.

Now that we have considered the identification of change, the characteristics of change in social organizations, and techniques for creating change in such organizations, it should be useful to consider those characteristics of the environment that can be managed to permit change to take place on its own. Hopefully, such change may occur at better than a merely evolutionary rate.

The chapters in this section are not held together by any essential homogeneity. This is because the task of maintaining change is, by definition, a disparate process itself. Many approaches can be used to maintain change in a business organization. They deal, among other things, with the relations between employee and employer; they relate to the human systems needs of the organization. Accelerating the analytical process within an organization helps to deal with most conventional day–to–day changes. Recognizing and adapting to the tremendous changes now taking place in personnel administration can help structure change as an ongoing phenomenon.

One approach to contemporary organizations asks what causes them *not* to change. Why are they not changing? What has to be done to make them more adaptable to their environment?

Finally, the housekeeping attributes of managing change can well be met, in some cases, by formal structures such as group participation systems. The following chapters examine each of these points of view.

21 The Psychological Contract: A Conceptual Structure for Management/Employee Relations

Michael H. Dunahee and Lawrence A. Wangler

What are the principal factors that affect the relationship between a business manager and those whose work he manages? How did these factors come into existence and what causes them to change? Much of the structure of human relations in a business organization is related to the definition of responsibilities and authority, which in turn is affected by feedback between the parties and their performance and impact on one another's output.

An interesting explanation of how these characteristics interrelate is presented in this chapter. Obviously, psychological contracts may exist in organizations of all types—within families, in the educational environment, in military organizations, and in business enterprises. Michael H. Dunahee, vice president for marketing of the Bank of A. Levy, Oxnard, California, and Lawrence A. Wangler, director of personnel for Six Flags, Inc., Los Angeles, California, present a well-organized discussion of the concept. An effective psychological contract provides the basis of security that you will need to create change, and that others will need to allow change to take place.

When human resources are poorly managed, a whole host of employee behavior problems are likely to occur, including excessive absenteeism, poor performance, tardiness, theft, and high turnover. Most managers have recognized that making optimum use of the human resources at their command is one of the most important aspects of their job, and have tried to improve their relationship with subordinates with the goal of creating an improved work environment and resultant increased productivity.

Many managers, however, and entire companies as well, have found that the field of management/employee relations is a complex one. When the manager begins to do some homework on how to go about understanding and improving the interpersonal work environment, he discovers that he is faced with an enormous amount of literature replete with research studies, case studies, and more theories on how employees want to be handled than any one person could count, let alone comprehend. And if he does any amount of digging into the wealth of information, he soon realizes that he faces many diametrically opposed explanations for employee behavior problems, a classic example being the importance of money to the average worker. At this point, all too many managers give up trying new management techniques and go back to what is familiar. As one supervisor put it, "My job is complex enough without trying to become a behavioral scientist."

The subject of employee behavior is as difficult to handle as any other facet of human psychology. In addition, the fact that the findings of the behavioral scientists have not been translated into day-to-day guidelines for front-line managers causes several problems. First, the individual manager wonders which management style to use. Should he follow theory X or theory Y? Should he try to create a system 1 or a system 4 work environment? Should he try to provide opportunities for each employee to be enriched and self-actualized? Should he appeal to the employee's social need or play on his ego? More importantly, can the manager himself behave differently than his own personality dictates?

Next, the manager wonders how he can keep his thinking current with all that is being written on the subject of management/employee relations, especially considering the new thinking and conflicting concepts. How can he integrate this knowledge into some usable pattern of possible responses?

Another problem for the manager who wants to do a better job in managing his human resources, but does not know how, is deciding how far to go. "I want to create the right environment, but I do not want to give the company away to the employees." How much is too much? When do employee relations programs reach the point of diminishing returns?

Finally, how can management feel confident that any efforts have some impact on the bottom line? We talk of productivity, but how often do we see any real payoff? Yet, because of the rather nebulous rationale for many employee relations programs, the direct relationship to profitability is dismissed as impossible to quantify.

What management really needs is not a disjointed array of behavioral schools of thought, but a systematic understanding of the application of the concepts and the implications of their dynamics. To help managers obtain such an understanding, some sort of structure or communications vehicle should be used which provides a common ground for making one's self heard and understood. Such a device is the psychological contract.

**Theoretical Framework of a
Psychological Contract**

The concept of a contract between the employer and his employees usually brings to mind a situation involving a union. While the union contract is a formal written document, it bears many similarities to the psychological contract. The formalization of a union contract, at least initially, is intended to legalize what the employees felt was fair in the first place. Usually, employees are dissatisfied with various aspects of the work relationship and are "ripe" when the organizer appears. Their initial demands are usually intended to bring the "pluses" and "minuses" back into balance, as they perceive the discrepancy. Then, over the years a union contract becomes very specific and detailed as more and more facets of work relationships are spelled out in the legally binding agreement.

Where there is no union, no such legal document exists. Yet organizations should realize that there is a contract of sorts that binds every employee and the employer together. Like the union contract, it becomes very specific and detailed over a period of time. However, unlike the union contract, it is not written. Rather, it is a psychological agreement between two parties, and it is a much broader concept than the traditional use of the word "contract" in industrial relations. It is a reality that has a great many implications for productivity and individual satisfaction. This contract is concerned with the organization's expectations of the individual employee and the employee's attempts to meet those expectations. It also includes expectations of the employee, and the employer's continuing willingness to satisfy his needs.

The dynamic quality of the psychological contract means that the individual and organization expectations and the individual and organization contributions mutually influence one another. In other words, the relationships between the manager and the managed is interactive, unfolding through mutual influence and mutual bargaining to establish and maintain a workable psychological contract. This contract is not written into any identifiable formal agreement between employee and organization, yet it operates as powerfully as its legal counterpart. Furthermore, it is not static; it is an evolving set of mutual expectations. Thus neither party to the transaction, since the transaction is such a continuing one, fully knows what he wants over the length of the psychological contract, although each acts as if there were a stable frame of reference which defines the relationship.

Development of the Contract

While this theoretical conceptualization has been discussed in the literature, although not in detail, the way that these concepts translate into examples of day–to–day interaction between management and employees has yet to be presented. Demonstrating the pragmatic consequences of the psychological contract helps to show its value as a conceptual framework for all managers.

Preemployment Negotiations

When an applicant sits down for a job interview with a prospective employer, he comes with certain expectations regarding this new position. Likewise, the employer has expectations regarding the prospective employee. During the job interview each party satisfies himself that the employment relationship will satisfy most of these expectations. For example, the employer expects that if an individual has had prior experience in a related job, training time should be less. In the same vein, an individual who has had no previous experience expects that adequate training will be provided by the employer.

The specificity of this first agreement depends on job availability and manpower availability, with one party or the other being not as demanding for definitions if the scarcity is not in his favor. While each has a whole host of expectations, the structure of most job interviews allows for only the most basic of these to be explored. For the employer these include proven special skills as shown by prior experience and education. For the employee, wages, days off, and benefits are perhaps discussed. Generally, however, these clauses comprise only a small fraction of the provisions of the total work relationship. The entire agreement not only covers how much work is to be performed for how much pay, but also involves the whole pattern of rights, privileges, and obligations between the individual and the organization. Indeed, as Maslow has pointed out, the individual has a whole hierarchy of needs that he expects the organization to meet in varying degrees. Furthermore, the employee fits these expectations into the framework of his own version of the psychological contract. Thus based on the employment interview the employer and the employee both develop a comprehensive psychological contract based on minimum interaction and discussion. In fact, much of the initial contract may be based on what is not said. The employee may draw inferences from the employer's body language or from certain perceived characteristics of the organization.

Further Refinement of the Psychological Contract

Hopefully, during the initial employment interview, if there is sufficient agreement on the major provisions and if a mutuality of expectations exists, employment begins and continues as further definitions and agreement evolve. This contract by its very nature will be expanded, modified, and interpreted daily by both parties. In the first few days of employment, the individual will be looking for clues, either verbal or nonverbal, which will help him further solidify provisions for the contract. The employee determines what the job really is, how much authority and independence he will have, which management person is really the boss, and how soon promotions and raises are likely to occur. The employer, too, is further expanding the contract. Does the employee observe accepted norms of behavior and can he really do the job with all the subsidiary duties not mentioned in the job interview?

As time goes on, more and more provisions are added and the contract becomes quite complex. Furthermore, it is often based on information which is not factual or, at best, incomplete. Thus numerous conflicts in the daily work environment are likely to occur. This is especially true where the psychological contract between employer and employee conflicts with other contracts developed between the individual and his peer group or the individual and his subordinates or the individual and some nonwork entity. The most important point to remember is that the contract between employer and employee may be only one of the many contracts in existence at any particular time. And in fact there may be more than one contract between employer and employee.

Unfortunately, situations may also arise that require contract adjustments which were originally not anticipated. The employer suddenly finds that he can no longer remain in business and breaks his contract of continued employment with the individual. Such unanticipated factors produce a certain degree of distrust on the part of each individual and ultimately complicate contracts with subsequent parties.

Plurality of Contracts

If the supervisor and the employee sit down shortly after employment, and at intervals thereafter, to discuss aspects of the employment relationship which are of interest to both of them, it is likely that each party's interpretation of the contract will be fairly close (unless it is not truly a mutual negotiation of contract clauses, but instead a one-sided presentation of demands). More often than not, however, a continuing negotiation is the exception rather than the rule. In this case, because neither party has adequately verbalized his understanding of the provisions of the contract, the separate contracts begin to evolve. As time goes on. these two contracts are likely to become quite dissimilar. Yet each party behaves as though there were a stable, well-defined framework within which continuing employment will occur.

Furthermore, both the individual and organization feel completely free to amend and expand the contract at will without overt notification of the other party when dissatisfaction with the current contract is prevalent on the part of one or both of the parties.

Maintaining Contract Equitability

When one party senses that the other has in some way altered the contract (whatever that contract is perceived to be), there is a tendency to modify other provisions in order to maintain equitability or even gain a tangible or psychological advantage. Thus the employer who senses that his employees are not returning a fair day's work for fair pay may institute a work measurement program, or increase the assembly-line speed, or institute stringent supervisory practices. What the employer is attempting to do is to bring equitability to the contract as perceived through his eyes. Whether the existing contract is in fact inequitable is immaterial. Also, such concepts as "equal pay for equal work" are matters which typically have not been quantified between the employee and employer—they are "perceived" concepts, with each party perceiving them differently.

Continually, throughout the life of any psychological contract, adjustments are being made. Each adjustment is based on an "acceptable" pattern of behavior as perceived by the parties concerned and an "equitable" employment relationship. Thus the individual who demands more money, not because of increased productivity but to be compensated with additional material rewards for having to endure a lack of psychological rewards, is attempting to equalize what he perceives as an unfair provision of the psychological contract. Again, it matters little whether in fact the contract provisions are equitable. What is of primary importance is the individual's perception of the contract. Also, very few people follow a reasoning process of saying, "my psychological rewards are lacking, so I am going to ask for more money." Rather, they sense that some inequity exists (very few individuals even recognize what exactly the inequity is, if in fact one exists) and then attempt to rectify the inequity through some counteraction. Thus management reschedules coffee breaks so that employees cannot take more than ten minutes to equalize for excessive talking at the work stations (even though the individual's psychological contract said that fifteen minutes was "acceptable" and that talking with co-workers at the work stations was common practice).

It is clear from the above that a "correcting" cycle can begin with each party to the contract making adjustments to the contract to maintain his sense of equitability. When adjustments to the contract cannot be made or when adjustments occur too rapidly, either party may reject the contract.

Rejection of the Contract

Because the psychological contract is usually ill-defined, and interpersonal communications lacking, a vicious cycle develops where contract violations on the part of one party result in offsetting actions by the other which in turn force the first party to adjust again. As this working relationship becomes less and less acceptable, more serious actions are taken by both parties. For example, the employee may initiate actions including:

Gripes. The individual begins to express his dissatisfactions; he is asking to renegotiate. He may complain about all kinds of problems, many of which are not closely related to the basic problem or contract violation.

Quitting on the Job. The employee refuses to give his all for the job. Increased absenteeism, frequent tardiness, sloppiness in work, and decreased productivity are just a few examples.

Retaliation. Grave employee dissatisfactions can take the form of overtly blocking management from reaching its goals, destruction of company property, and concerted efforts with other employees to thwart organizational success.

Outside Assistance. Since the employee by now feels that voluntary reconciliation with management is impossible, he may turn to power politics—union membership, Equal Employment Opportunities Commission, and so on.

Termination of Contract. If during the time of employee dissatisfaction the contract becomes completely unacceptable, or if the employee feels that another employer can offer a better contract, the contract is terminated by the employee.

All of the above actions are designed to "equalize" the contract as perceived by the employee. Again, whether the contract is in fact inequitable is immaterial. What is material is the employee's perception of contract equitability.

Just as the employee can take actions for perceived contract violations, the employer may also take recourse to:

Oral Counseling. The employer advises the employee that his actions or job performance are not within acceptable limits. This may result in a job threat.

Tightening Work Rules. The employer institutes work rules which prohibit certain nonacceptable employee actions. These may become highly formal (in writing) or informal (oral).

Written Warning. The employer may give a written warning to the employee advising him that certain perceived job behavior is unacceptable and may result in termination. Such threats may or may not be based on facts.

Disciplinary Layoff. The employer may send an employee home for a few days in hopes that such an action will bring about the required behavior.

Termination of the Contract. The employer may become so dissatisfied with the employee that he feels termination of employment is the only course of action.

The Psychological Contract in Practice

Thus far, the concepts involved in the development of the psychological contract on the job have been discussed in the abstract. Let us now take a look at a realistic example of how this actually works in a typical work relationship.

Mary Ann is a prospective employee applying for a job at the XYZ Bank as a teller. She has come into the bank for an interview with the manager. During the employment interview she has a number of things she wants to do. The first, of course, is to create an impression that is sufficient to get hired. Of secondary importance, but quite necessary, is the ensureance that there are going to be the right kind of conditions present to satisfy her needs from the job. The manager, likewise, has some things that he wants to do. He wants to create the proper impression too, so that the prospective employee looks forward to working there, as well as to determine if she will be a productive addition to his staff. To keep our example simple, we will deal only in a few key ramifications of a psychological contract. In practice, however, the negotiations would take on far more complex and complicated dimensions.

During the employment interview Mary Ann is trying to satisfy her major requirements—namely, that proper training will be provided so she can be a competent employee; that there is an opportunity for advancement, since she has a lot of ambition; and, finally, that there is a good working environment that provides pleasant surroundings in which to do her work. She feels that these are minimal requirements for a job with the bank. The manager has a couple of key requirements as well. He is looking for someone with experience who does not require a great deal of training. He also wants someone who will produce at a satisfactory level.

Mary Ann and the manager make favorable impressions on each other. The manager offers her a job as a teller at a salary that is acceptable to her. They agree that she is to report to work the following Monday, and the initial phases of the contract are finalized.

When Mary Ann reports to work on Monday, she finds that she will not be working for the manager at all but instead for the supervisor. Luckily for Mary Ann, the supervisor expects roughly the same things as the manager does—that is, experience and production—but he requires one additional thing that he regards very highly, and that is loyalty to him and to the bank. However, since he does not bother to tell Mary Ann about this, she has an incomplete idea of what is expected of her.

During the first three months, certain things occur which tend to distort the original contract and thus two contracts begin to develop. First, Mary Ann discovers that there is very little training available. She also finds that the procedures used at the XYZ Bank are far different from those at the bank where she gained her experience. Second, she learns that there seems to be no opportunity to move into other positions at the bank. Indeed, many of her co-workers have been tellers for upward of ten years and have never been given a chance to work into any kind of managerial position. Finally, she finds that the atmosphere in the branch is one of extreme pressure, with generally more work to do and more customers to handle than she or the other tellers can possibly handle.

Also during the first three months the supervisor finds that while Mary Ann claimed to have experience, her experience was not applicable to the job and that, indeed, she had to be trained almost as if she were a novice to banking. He grants that she is extremely productive and is very pleased at that, but her manner of dress is not acceptable. She wears clothing that is far too provocative, in his opinion, and not at all in keeping with the conservative atmosphere of the bank which he and the manager attempt to maintain.

Therefore, at the end of the first three months both parties to the psychological contract feel that there are several provisions that are unacceptable to them. Since no further negotiations have taken place, they take steps to bring the contract back into a state of equitability. First, Mary Ann adopts the attitude that the mistakes for which she is criticized are not her fault. After all, she was not given adequate training to do the job. Second, since she has not been allowed by the supervisor to wear the clothes which comprise the majority of her wardrobe, she is forced to go out and buy new clothes which she had not planned on purchasing. This gives her the feeling that she must make faster progress in here salary range as compensation for expenses that she had not anticipated. Finally, she begins to develop a bitter attitude toward the supervisor and an unwillingness to support him and meet his demands for production.

The supervisor is also adjusting the contract. Since the experience that Mary Ann was supposed to bring to the job is not up to the level he expected and he has had to do more training than he had anticipated, he feels he can expect in return an even greater production rate from her to compensate for his extra efforts. He interprets her poor attitude and increased demands as a lack of loyalty—one of his requirements for the job. He begins to show her less warmth, less personal attention, and less positive feedback.

During the next six months Mary Ann finds that the work environment created by the supervisor has resulted in new problems. She is required to produce even more on the teller line, but she sees no salary increase coming with this additional performance. Indeed, she has not yet received her first salary increase. She felt during the initial interview that salary increases came at a reasonable time, so she assumes the supervisor is not satisfied with anything that she does. And recently he had become quite angry when her coffee breaks exceeded the allotted ten minutes in the morning and afternoon. She feels this is unwarranted since she often forgoes breaks in order to complete her work.

The supervisor is also seeing some provisions of the contract change. He sees Mary Ann's attitude change, her loyalty lessen. Only recently she was not feeling well because of a slight headache, so she stayed home, even though it was one of the busiest days of the month for the bank. The supervisor considers such lack of loyalty inexcusable. Also, he finds that Mary Ann is making more frequent salary demands, faster and larger than the Personnel Department guidelines.

After a total of nine months on the job, Mary Ann's concepts of the psychological contract has become quite different from what she expected at the beginning of employment, and she feels that steps have to be taken to bring the contract back into some semblance of equitability. First, she lets down on production. She feels that if nine months of working as hard as she possibly can has not produced positive feedback, promotion, or adequate salary progress, then she is not going to continue to work herself to death. Second, because of the lack of warmth on the part of the supervisor, she is adopting a rather callous attitude toward him and the entire management crew.

The supervisor likewise feels that the psychological contract is becoming unacceptable. He goes as far as to give Mary Ann a warning that if her attitude does not improve, she may be subject to discipline or termination. The deteriorating condition of the psychological contract and the wide discrepancy between the two individuals' views of what that contract should be forces its conclusion and results in the following: Mary Ann decides that the contract is not salvageable and quits. She does not have another job to go to, but feels that this contract is so bad that any other contract would have to be better. Furthermore, it would be much easier to develop a new contract elsewhere from scratch than to attempt to salvage this one. She goes looking for a job with a more cautious view of the employment interview and a more skeptical attitude toward management.

The supervisor is glad to be rid of a problem employee. He tells himself that new employees are going to have to pass much closer scrutiny before being hired. The manager who was only in on the initial interview is puzzled. Mary Ann appeared to be a nice girl. She seemed competent and had a good work record. He is also puzzled by the high rate of turnover in his bank. Perhaps he should look a little more closely into the management of the operations of his bank.

Key Elements of the Contract

The significance of the psychological contract is simply that it is the responsibility of each individual manager to maintain a workable psychological contract with each employee under his control. This becomes a simple process when the manager realizes that the concept of a psychological contract is not a new or different managerial style but a base on which any managerial style can be built. Thus whether the manager is a practitioner of theory X, system 3, motivators and hygiene factors, or sensitivity training, he is working under a psychological contract with his employees. Any managerial style will work in practice as long as there is a workable and equitable (as perceived by each party) psychological contract in existence.

If this is so, then how is such a contract brought into existence? There are several key elements to a psychological contract:

1. A well–structured job with clear job responsibilities. This must be mutually understood at the beginning of employment and at successive stages during the employment relationship. The job responsibilities do not have to be written; what is vital is the understanding between the two parties to the contract.

2. Continuous feedback between the two parties to the contract. Again, whether this occurs in a written format (performance appraisal) is immaterial. What is vital is a continuous dialogue between employer and employee concerning the conditions of the contract. This must occur in an open and free environment, with either party to the contract feeling free to approach the other with contract clarifications or modifications. This can be achieved only through management awareness that each employee brings to the work situation certain expectations. It is these expectations that must be dealt with on a daily basis through effective two–way communications. The employee must be given the opportunity to communicate with his employer about his expectations and fears. There must be a constant interchange of thoughts and feelings to avoid misinterpretation of the contract, and ultimately dissatisfaction for one or both of the parties.

It is evident that the superior and subordinate must frequently negotiate and renegotiate the provisions of the psychological contract. This is basically the communication concept, but it is also something more, because it is possible for two people to communicate to a great extent but not communicate about the right things. It is possible for superior/subordinate communications to degenerate into a discussion of minor points that really have no significant bearing on the total work relationship. The psychological contract is more. It gets right down to the nitty gritty of man/job relationship. It is the superior saying, "This is what I am willing to give you in exchange for your giving the following to me and to the job." It is the employee saying, "I will give you what you ask if you will give me the following things." Thus the concept of the psychological contract limits the discussion to the key and most important factors.

3. Continuous emphasis on the man and the job. Current popular thinking about emphasizing the man (that is, Hertzberg) or the job (that is, Taylor) must be modified and combined to include the man and the job as a total system. What should result is an integrated theory of job design which meshes the beliefs and practices of the industrial engineering approach to job design with more recent behavioral science theories.

4. Relevancy of the psychological contract to the bottom line. That is, the compensation received for a job must have a relationship to the psychological contract that is in existence. If the negotiations of the psychological contract throughout the organization can be documented and tracked by the corporate personnel department, it is possible to find out what kinds of things employees are looking for as important provisions to their psychological contract, and thereby gear employee relations programs to those things most desired by employees. The individual supervisor can also provide valuable feedback to the organization if he finds that he is unable to negotiate satisfactory workable psychological contracts with a significant number of his employees because of an identifiable deficiency on the part of the organization. Employee relations programs aimed at solving those deficiencies can be related to profitability. For example, a simple case would be where a supervisor would say, "I cannot fill this job with competent people if we are going to pay such a low salary and ask people to work in this kind of environment. I cannot negotiate that contract." Therefore, in order to fill that job we would have to either increase salaries or spend money to improve the environment, and this then could be related to the bottom line.

Recommendations

How can the psychological contract be established in a typical work environment? First, employee orientation and the employee handbook can be stated in such a way as to become a contract of sorts for both employer and employee. It may well be that psychological contracts should be patterned after typical union contracts, spelling out hours of work, pay, working conditions, benefits, rights of grievance, transfer, promotion, and so on.

Second, it should be the responsibility of every manager to sit down with the employees under his control and renegotiate the contracts that were established earlier to determine if they are still being satisfactorily fulfilled or if new provisions of the contract need to be added. The employee should, of course, be allowed to express himself as to the overall desirability of the contract.

Everyone deals with psychological contracts in their everyday life. They exist between husband and wife, student and teacher, and employee and his peer group. While the manager has a psychological contract with his employee, he also has a contract with his superior. This must be recognized so that effective adjustment of this contract can be accomplished as the need arises.

22 A Human Systems Approach to Coping with Future Shock

Gary B. Carlson

As noted in the preceding chapter, it is important to recognize the stated and unstated arrangements and understandings that exist between individuals in an organization. This is true whether the individuals are boss and subordinate or fellow volunteers on a community service project. Just as important as the need to maintain a high level of motivation in an organization is the need for the organization to be structured and managed so as to permit changes to take place as needed in the psychological contract and in interpersonal relationships.

In this chapter Gary B. Carlson, senior vice president and director of human resources for the Central National Bank of Chicago, describes a number of systems that can be used to maintain a desirable rate of change and permit adaptation within an organization. The idea of providing positive reinforcement for human needs within a structure of planned organizational development is a good one. Although Mr. Carlson's ideas are expressed in terms of a bank's operations, similar systems and approaches should be valid for other organizations. Not too many companies realize that their personnel departments could, as Carlson suggests, provide the behavioral technology for change, with line supervisors acting as change agents. The idea deserves your consideration.

If you were to single out one word to characterize the banking business since the close of World War II, it would probably be "change." Perhaps no other industry has seen so many traditional concepts challenged and changed in so short a time.

In fact, change has been occurring at such an accelerating rate that it can realistically be called "future shock." And quite possibly the most exciting and positive change of all is just now emerging. It is not where you would expect to find it, in the operations or marketing areas, but in the relationship between the people within the organization itself.

And it is happening just in time. For the most part, the economic and material resources in banking have been beautifully orchestrated, but the third and most vital asset of all, the people who make a bank work, have received little more than pitch–pipe attention from management. And while everyone was preoccupied with innovative financial instruments and the capacities of new computers, these overlooked wallflowers have undergone impressive transformation.

Today's employee, who is here to stay, is completely different from his counterpart of a previous generation. Not only does he tend to be younger, with a median age now under thirty, but he is far better educated and more mobile, skeptical, and vocally aware; and he has higher expectations.

Managements are becoming aware that traditional methods and relationships just won't wash with this new breed, and that if the challenges of today and tomorrow are to be met, some changes are in order.

Humanistic Approach

Some of the more advanced institutions in the early 1960s cautiously began to explore the "human systems" concept—a humanistic approach that anticipates employees' needs and values and constructively caters to them so that corporate goals can be achieved.

The impetus for the human systems approach is "organization development," or "OD" for short. It refers to all programs used in a systematic way to improve organizational effectiveness, including an array of behavioral technologies that can be applied to enhance productivity through a fuller utilization of human talent. The concept, which has been developing into a bankwide system at Central National Bank in Chicago, seems startlingly simple and right. It is an idea most managements have given the nod to for many years. And that has been part of the challenge, too.

Managers have always been quick to agree that the people who run an organization, from the trainee on up, should be well cared for. But this has mostly added up to the usual paternalistic, maintenance–type benefits that cater to basic physiological needs, security, and a few social values.

Jobs with Meaning

Although their demand for material gratification has intensified, it is not the major concern of today's bank employees. They no longer are content to know that in fifteen years of quiet, nonboat-rocking diligence, they may move up from trainee to the next available rung of the hierarchy. They want their career paths timed and charted. But more importantly, perhaps, they want their present jobs, whatever they are, to have meaning. Employee benefits, which were valued by their parents, are taken for granted, just like adequate plumbing.

Adding to the confusion, the labor needs of banks have changed too. No longer is the ability to run a simple addressing machine at statement-rendering time considered an optimum back-room skill. The requirements have shifted from manual to mental dexterity, from envelope stuffing to computer programming. Clearly, those banks that have overlooked their human resources are in for a future shock. The eleventh hour has come and gone.

Management Support

When the writer joined the Central National in 1967, the bank had the typical personnel operation of the period, with nothing even remotely resembling the OD system approach. It was necessary to start from near-zero base, but there was one very distinct advantage in that top management not only was aware of the need but also was completely receptive to building toward and participating in the total human resources system as it exists today.

Management's positive attitude stemmed from several advantageous conditions. As a medium-size bank, the Central National has been flexible enough to move fast with programs that are statistically significant in terms of judging impact. Decisions can be made quickly and informally. And the bank's history has been one of successful anticipation of and adaptation to many changes and challenges.

Upgraded Personnel System

Before planning could begin for the human resources system, an integrated personnel program had to be developed. From 1967 to 1970, benefits were upgraded and policies and procedures for salary administration, employment practices, employee relations, manpower planning, training and development, and many other programs were examined, improved, and woven into a cohesive system.

In the employee relations area, communications were improved by regular monthly publications, memos, and bulletins. Employee surveys were conducted to reveal attitudes, needs, and, yes, feelings. Feelings may seem an odd commodity to consider in the cold hard logic of the business world, but cold hard logic, unfortunately, will not always tell us what we need to know about a person's growing need for greater self-esteem and self-actualization.

A series of reference guides and manuals were revised and introduced. A more productive method of soliciting questions and suggestions from the staff was implemented. Employees were provided with yearly computerized statements of benefits and related values. Counseling on a variety of credit and financial problems was made a formal part of the new human resources department's services, as was preretirement advice.

An array of training and development programs were also part of the program. Early in 1967 a leadership skill program for potential managers and first-line supervisors was put on-stream. Next, a program in management training in advanced motivation concepts was launched. Supervisory skills were shaped in interpersonal problem-solving discussion groups, and workshops and seminars were initiated in such areas as salary administration and the concepts of job enrichment.

Since the Chicago labor market has not always yielded an adequate supply of applicants qualified for all positions, the bank introduced a program to develop trainees in specialized skills through planned instructions and on-the-job training techniques. Then the bank developed its own version of the highly productive management by objectives concept, and in 1970 a bankwide MBO program was initiated for managers and supervisors.

Although simple in concept, MBO is often extremely difficult to apply in a practical way. The success of MBO at Central National is attributed to one key factor: top management support and participation. Without high-level involvement in the goal-setting process, MBO would not be possible. MBO is a process and not a training or personnel program. It is not only a way of achieving results but a way of managing. It is no coincidence that most effective and successful managers are highly goal oriented and influence their subordinates in the same way.

Motivational Programs Launched

With the personnel programs developed into a unified system and an MBO program under way, the next step was into the motivational areas to construct an OD model that would serve an employee's need for self-actualization and self-esteem. A conventional model consisted of three basic elements: values, process, and technology.

The first element—values—philosophically sees the bank in humanistic terms as an integrated part of corporate goals. If the organization is viewed as an integrated system, an action on the part of one individual or a major element will cause a reaction on the part of other individuals or elements. For example, the feelings and needs of one individual can affect others in a work group, and the actions of one group or department can affect the total organization. Thus the values of organization development develop staff members to their fullest potential as human beings, rather than as units of production. To accomplish this, it seeks to create a work environment that is exciting and challenging by providing opportunities for employees to influence the way they relate to their tasks, their fellow staffers, the organization, and their world outside the company.

For example, such problems as job absolescence or misapplied aptitudes are dealt with as opportunities to help the individual to redirect himself to a more enriching work experience. The bank is not doing the person or the organization any favor by allowing him to stagnate on a job or to underutilize talents. People are always capable of becoming more than they have been. If anything, there is a definite need to continue to grow and develop, and this need can be satisfied to the benefit of the total organization and its members through the organization development process.

The second element in the conventional model—process—translates philosophical values into reality. This phase starts with identifying problems, needs, and opportunities. Various surveys, group and individual discussions, and suggestions are some of the devices used to provide input for measuring, analyzing, and diagnosing the organization from a human resources standpoint and establishing appropriate courses of action.

The third element—technology—utilizes many behavioral techniques to anticipate and deal with problems and opportunities at their germination stage. One of the most basic techniques is team building, which improves the interrelation of groups and individuals so that corporate goals can be reached. Most OD "purists" would insist on encounter or sensitivity sessions, or some other laboratory technique to achieve confrontation, "unfreezing," and finally group or team cohesiveness. However, Central National Bank believes that an artificial environment is not necessary to obtain positive change. By relying on the realities of the actual work environment, when opportunities occur or are anticipated, it is possible to intervene with more practical and effective techniques. In this way, team building is achieved through some distinct yet thoroughly interrelated techniques such as supervisory training, application of motivational concepts, analysis of managerial styles, interpersonal problem–solving sessions, MBO, and job enrichment.

Transactional Analysis

The subject of some recent best–sellers, transactional analysis (TA) is a technique for understanding and dealing with the basic ways people interact with each other. TA says that each person has three ego states—parent, adult, and child—and that one of them is used in communicating. The TA program shows how to recognize these states and how to adjust a relationship to the problem-solving adult-to-adult level. The adult relationship is what most people are looking for, whether in business or in their personal lives. The beauty of TA is that a person does not need a background in psychology to learn to better understand and cope with the interpersonal communication process. TA has the potential of turning communication away from typical win–lose encounters toward more productive and satisfying win–win situations.

Positive Reinforcement

This new program is based on the idea that behavior is determined by its consequences. If a task, or even a portion of it, is rewarded—positively reinforced—every time it is done right, a person's performance level can be dramatically improved.

Theoretically, if productivity can be increased by 10 percent in a department of ten people, the net result is a staff increase of one highly trained person, and since some behavioral scientists estimate that the average person uses only between 30 and 50 percent of his abilities, 10 percent represents a modest increase. In a job market where qualified applicants are sometimes difficult to recruit, a positive reinforcement program is not only an economic gain, but also helps to create an atmosphere that holds good employees. Its value in building self–esteem and self–actualization is obvious. Most people want to do a good job, and most are capable of doing it. This program has the potential of eliminating barriers to performance and providing the feedback systems necessary to recognize and reward desirable performance.

By contrast, too many organizations manage through threat, fear, coercion, and criticism. This is unnecessary punishment, and the members respond by punishing each other. If punishing relationships prevail, members lose their ability and desire to jointly share and solve problems, and the negative drag on the organization can begin to show up in the profit column.

Central National Bank believes that an atmosphere of positive reinforcement is well worth the time and effort. When there are capable people, growing and developing in a positive environment, profits, productivity, and satisfaction are all bound to increase. The exciting thing about positive reinforcement is that it need not take a long time or cost a fortune to implement.

Agents of Change

To develop and grow, a company must be open to change, open to the needs of its people. Organization developments techniques and other programs provide a rational basis for planned change within the organization, as well as a means for anticipating the side effects of those changes. The human resources department provides the behavioral technology of change, while managers and supervisors act as the agents of change.

Banks have got to shake off the old ivy image and attitudes to attract and hold today's new type of employee. After all, they compete for qualified people in the same job market as the country's largest firms. Prestige and security just are not today's employees' major concerns. They want satisfaction —enriching jobs that clearly mean something to them.

The larger banks have the resources to build a human resources system like that at Central National, but like many monolithic structures they have become too rigid and bureaucratic to move swiftly into these new areas. Those banks and other organizations not prepared to cope with change, especially with changing human resources, will be in for a shock. Recognizing change in human attitudes and values is vital for continued growth and success. Take the area of business restraints alone: as they continue to increase in number and complexity, earnings will lag unless services can be expanded. You cannot move an inch without qualified people whose personnal goals are related to those of the corporation.

Correspondent banks have begun to seek advice and some have requested assistance in developing their own comprehensive human resources systems, complete with advanced motivational techniques—a service that may be a formal offering in the near future.

The cost of developing and implementing Central National's human resources system has been minimal, and the ratio of the human resource department's staff to total staff is 50 percent below national averages. This has been done by relying on key senior officers who are innovative, receptive, and willing to try new ideas and assume the sometimes precarious role of agents of change. The momentum and impact of social change has been anticipated and preparations made for the new era of banking that lies just ahead.

23

Now You Can Be Ready for Quicksand or Fire Storm

Mack Hanan and
Arnold Amstutz

Thus far we have examined the structural and human elements of change. We have also considered some of the technological and social factors leading to and arising from change. To maintain a desirable rate of continuing change, attention must also be paid to considerations of short–term and long–term strategy.

In this chapter Mack Hanan, managing director of Hannon & Son, New York City, and Arnold Amstutz, chairman of Decision Technology, Cambridge, Massachusetts, describe a short–term strategy planning model from which the would–be instigator of change can take some leads. Their discussion focuses on the short–term sales plan, but the concept is equally applicable to the management of organizational dynamics. If it is valid to review your sales plan quarterly, it should also be valid to review the progress of your managerial evolution on a short–term basis, with revisions to the plan considered and reviewed at periodic intervals. In reading this chapter, consider its applicability to strategy revisions for agents of change.

Don't look now, but your next year's sales plan is probably obsolete already. Come to think of it, you'd *better* take a look. Thanks to the combined pressures of the energy crisis, materials shortfalls, and unpredictable cost and price patterns, plans that seemed impeccable when they were drawn up a few months ago appear to have little relationship to the "real world" of today's marketplace.

It is bad enough to try to follow a sales plan after your supply base has shifted seriously. The current business climate is even more complicated, however, as sales managers are discovering every day. Their market demand base is shifting, too, as customers react to crises by altering their own sales mixes, production schedules, and inventory policies.

Under such conditions, the annual sales plan is all but useless. What is needed is short–term strategy planning, which requires the sales manager to chart a new course every quarter. The payoff: he can react confidently to rapidly changing conditions. Anyone who has listened to the agonizing in most sales offices these days must realize that the extra effort is worthwhile.

"The problem isn't just guaranteeing an energy supply and obtaining raw materials," says one sales vice president. "There are other factors. We have to order from open–ended purchase agreements whose cost to us will be whatever our suppliers say it is at delivery. Then we may find our customers can't use our product because they can't get other components that go with it; or they can't sell what they make out of it because there has been a shift in demand in their own markets."

A sales manager sums up the situation: "We spent the last ninety days of last year putting together a plan we thought would be good all this year. It took just two weeks in January to wipe the whole thing out. Without a plan we can trust, where do we go from here?" Answering that question may be the most critical problem for sales managers this year.

But two things are clear right now. First, the answer probably is not going to come from good old Uncle Henry, the veteran of past crises who seems to be on the staff of almost every company. Even if Henry has been through the shortages of World War II or long–lasting industrial work stoppages, he is not apt to be much help. The problems of today's crisis are different because they reach into many previously unaffected aspects of production, distribution, pricing, and sales. Second, because today's business community is an incredibly interdependent mechanism, it is often impossible to shift strategies or adopt replacement materials in one sector without setting off shock waves in another.

Nor are the futurists who dwell on the outlook for the year 2000 likely to provide relief. They, too, have been caught with their plans down—a good quarter of a century earlier than they expected. The future is now, and marketers must take that into account if they want their business to survive. Thus the answer to planning in a crisis economy will have to meet at least three criteria:

1. Any solution must be grounded on the assumption that short–term crisis will probably be the name of the game for the foreseeable future. Sales managers who are waiting for things to "settle out and go back to normal" are planning for the past. Because short–term crisis may well become the normal context for doing business from now on, short–term planning will have to become the norm for managers.

2. Planning will have to provide alternative sales strategies for managers to choose from so they can deal quickly with shifts in their supply base or their market base. This means the planning cycle must be condensed. No longer will an annual plan be considered short term. True short–term planning will be done quarterly, and semiannual planning will be about as long range as any manager will dare risk.

3. To enjoy any chance of success a plan will have to be based on a proven system. By that we mean a system that has demonstrated its ability

to be applied to the sales decision making of virtually any business, whether large or small, consumer or industrial, capital intensive or labor intensive. Therefore it must be highly cost effective and reliable.

How To Be a Ninety–day Wonder

For an increasing number of companies, short–term strategy planning (STSP) provides a viable approach to maintaining profits, preserving market share, and even improving brand positioning. Every quarter, sales strategies are planned for the next quarter. Thus the "term" of short–term strategy planning is ninety days. The sales executive continues to set an annual sales objective, of course, but that is regarded simply as a loose envelope for the four quarterly plans.

Thanks to the flexibility that comes with short–term strategy planning, the quarterly projections may differ widely from each other as materials or market conditions change throughout the year. Unlike traditional sales planning, no quarter can be planned much further ahead than the last month of the preceding quarter.

Short–term strategy planning is true strategic planning. It is not simply innovating an existing plan, making marginal changes, or plugging in contingency strategies. Nor is it tactical planning that merely dictates such minor moves as reallocating a cooperative advertising budget or adding a contest to the sales force's incentives.

As the five–step outline in figure 23-1 shows, STSP provides an acid test of just how market oriented a sales manager really is. If he knows his principal markets and those of his key customers, playing the short–term strategic planning game may become the ultimate application of his skills to a real–world market that is constantly changing.

Try Your Trusty Computer

Because a real–world market model is a self–contained information system, a sales manager could perform his quarterly manipulations just using his own brainpower. But short–term strategic planning demands such rapid response that a simple computerization of the model is highly desirable. Teamed with a computer, the manager can alter the model when required and, if necessary, use it to create new strategy options.

Does the computer threaten to make the line manager's job less important? On the contrary, it often permits him to exercise his authority fully for the first time. "Finally I'm free to manage," says a sales manager who plays his market model regularly. "Here's how I can tell: I used to think I was managing when I went around asking people questions that began with,

Step 1. Build your real-world market model.

A. In order of importance, rank the key needs of your principal customers in each of your major market segments. This gives you your "key need base."

B. Rank the key benefits of your main products and services that satisfy the needs you have listed for your key account customers. This gives you your "key benefit base."

C. Call a small sample of key customers and check out the validity of the "plannable factors" in your need/benefit base. Are the key needs really what you think they are? Are the key benefits really the most critical? How well do you really know the characteristics of your key customers that cause them to be in your market segment? How committed are they to your product and service benefits? If your knowledge checks out, plug in these added facts:

Your net profit from sales; the share of market that generates it; the dollar and unit sales volumes that give you your share; the price/cost relationship that gives you your volume.

These same facts for each of your chief competitors. The key "unplannable factors" in your industry that can seriously affect you: legislative acts, materials (or other) shortages, business cycle ups and downs, competitive actions, new technologies or processes coming on-stream, new market trends.

Step 2. Play the model.

Get comfortable with your market model. Learn to read it like the diagram below.

Step 3. Insert changes into the model.

As soon as a major change occurs in any of the main elements of your model, your profit and share-of-market figures may be subject to change, too. Every important shift presents these questions: Now that the real world in my market is different, how can I maintain my forecast profit? If I can't maintain it, how much of it can I safeguard? Is it even possible to improve it?

Step 4. Create new strategies to deal with changes.

Once your market changes, your planned strategies may no longer work. So create new ones and test them on the market model. The model will predict the profit outcome of each alternative short-term strategy you can think of.

Step 5. Choose your best new strategy.

Select the best strategy to safeguard or improve your profit. Put it to work in the field as quickly as possible. Then start work on your next small-sample key customer research and go through the STSP process again.

Putting the Real-World Market Model to Work

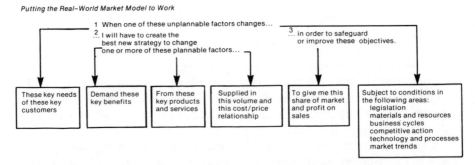

Figure 23-1. The Five Steps of Short-term Strategy Planning

When are you going to do this? Who's responsible for that? Now I ask a manager's question: What if we did this or that? That's what management is all about—creating new strategies to reach your objective.''

The economic crisis of recent months is unusual because it is double-barreled, affecting not just materials sources or market demands but both. It has changed the marketing ground rules so radically that many sales managers have been stumped. A few have panicked and forsaken profits, market franchises, and brand positions for sales at any price. Others have been paralyzed into inaction, waiting for "sanity" to return. But today's apparently irrational market behavior may well be the norm for the foreseeable future. The time to start getting used to it is now.

For the next six years it is likely that most industries will experience recurrent shortages of materials and even of certain services. Energy may remain in that category for even longer, so may transportation services. Virtually every industry will face supply or cost problems that will be impossible to solve "for love or money."

Another Quarter, Another Plan

Market demand changes must also be expected to occur over shorter cycles. Customers will continue to seek new ways to maintain and improve their profits in the face of continued cost inflation. They will also have to contend with frequent changes in requirements for capital investments, just to keep current with shifts in their own markets' demands.

The good old days of "another year, another plan" are all but over. From now on, "another quarter, another plan" will be the rule. In the second month of every planning cycle, sales executives will determine if the plan's objectives are going to be achieved within budget. So managers who now come under the gun only on an annual planning basis will have to learn to live with quarterly evaluations.

Actually, short–term strategic planning could turn out to be the sales manager's best friend. Here's what one man, who started out hating the idea, has to say about it: "When I became a manager, they told me, 'Now you have to learn to manage according to plan, not personality.' So three months of the year I planned, and the other nine months I managed by my personality. Now I'm managing according to plan most of the time because I live with my plans all the time. I have to. I'm so plugged into my markets that when my suppliers or customers itch I scratch. Sometimes I scratch even before they itch. By my definition, that's managing my business."

Come to think of it, that should be a definition of managing anybody's business in the decade ahead.

24 Preparing for Change

William F. Holmes

*In this brief chapter William F. Holmes, executive development director of
Lever Brothers Co. in New York, indicates that he intended to present some
basic ideas about planning for change. His comments, however, have more
to do with maintaining change than with planning and preparing for
change.*

*In considering the organizational principles affecting the management
of change, relate the change management principles set forth in this chapter
by Holmes to the creativity-enhancing principles expressed by Watson in
chapter 20. There are more similarities than differences. Both address the
organizational dimension, though Holmes goes one step further conceptually in suggesting that emotional appeals are necessary in addition to
organizational appeals.*

*Obviously, there is no one ultimate objective that is valid for every
organization. You will find it equally true that a change management
system must continually be reviewed and re-reviewed to assess its appropriateness and effectiveness.*

Change is upon us. Traditional management methods for leadership and
control are giving way to new forms. Structures and systems for planning
are increasing in importance. Whole organizations are becoming more
flexible in structure.

The question is: How can management deal with revolutionary forces
of change which are now impacting companies when only evolutionary
methods for development are available? The answer is: training and
planning.

What, then, are the bare-bone requirements for accomplishing change
in an organization?

1. Impetus for accomplishing change must come from the top. There is
a big difference between a company philosophy to simply react, and a
general management tone which bases change efforts on well-planned
premises about the shape of things to come. Top management's attitude sets
the tone for the company.

2. A strategy for accomplishing change must incorporate the behavioral, structural, and systems dimensions of change. These three dimen-

This chapter is based on an article that originally appeared in *Administrative Management,*
October 1970. Copyright © 1970 by Geyer McAllister Publications, Inc.; reprinted by permission. All rights reserved.

sions are interdependent and require parallel attention in any well–planned change effort.

3. Managers must be actively involved with the accomplishment of change at all levels, as change agents. This concerns the manager's own responsibility for continuous self–development and, continuous self–development and renewal of his organization.

4. The change effort must be continuous and have long–term emphasis so it gets built into the organization's bloodstream and becomes a management way of life.

Three flexible organization arrangements that can be used to solve today's problems and also fit the future include task forces, project teams, and problem solving. Where there is a knotty problem to be solved, a task force is put together from different parts of the organization to properly define the problem and recommend solutions. The advantage here is that people get turned on by this kind of assignment and learn through participation.

Project teams apply where the job to be done is so complex and involves so many divisions that practically every part of the organization needs to be pulled in.

Problem–solving groups are used to get hold of an immediate crisis, like a dangerous customer service problem. The group members are taken from different parts of the organization according to their skills to solve the immediate problem and recommend ways to prevent it from happening again. But what is even more important for the future is behavior change— new styles of managing, attitude change, and motivation of people which results from behavior and organizational climate.

This kind of value, attitude, and behavior change requires a special kind of learning which we cannot get from books or the standard pragmatic training programs. Behavior change requires reaching people at the emotional as well as the reasoning level. For this reason, laboratory learning, group process, team building, and other behavioral–science–based programs which are designed to accomplish emotional learning are effective. The aim of this training and development makes management and the organization responsive to the social revolution in the company's inside and outside environment, and is in concert with new structures and systems necessary for improving performance in the future.

25 Future Shock for Personnel Administration

James M. Mitchell and
Rolfe Schroeder

This chapter is excerpted from an article by James M. Mitchell, director of the Advance Study Program of the Brookings Institution, and Rolfe Schroeder, supervisor of employee development in the U.S. Office of Personnel Development. In reading the chapter, substitute the term "manager" for the term "PA" [personnel administrator]. As in other chapters in this volume, the authors have identified future shock in terms of physical and psychological stresses that arise from overloads of the human adaptive system and decision–making processes, primarily in governmental and other large institutions. In their view the "shock" part of future shock is the human response to overstimulation.

The change agent has a position similar to that of the personnel man in the excerpt. To maintain a satisfactory rate of change, you will need to [1] maintain a long view of what is occurring in your own organization, [2] review your own role in the situation, [3] evaluate your capabilities [and those of the people for whom you are responsible], and [4] periodically reassess your strategic situation.

Consider the personnel administrator (PA) as a change agent. He has the resources to forecast change as well as to do something about it. He is one of the few people with the "big picture" of what is occurring throughout the organization. Unlike the budget officer, the PA is almost solely concerned with people and is thus in a good position to signal some future shocks. As a change agent, he is out of the mainstream of final–policy decisions. He can make appropriate recommendations to the city manager, for example, and can thus play something of an outsider's role.

In order to develop the role of change agent, the PA must look closely at himself and his organization. His preparation for future shock should involve examination of the following four principal areas:

1. He must assess his own place within the organization. While we may debate where on the table of organization the personnel operation should be placed, there is a strong requirement that the personnel man have the confi-

---

dence of the top executive. From the standpoint of the budget and the accomplishment of goals, the employees of an organization must be a prime concern of the top executive.

2. The PA must look at his own staff and their capabilities for meeting challenges of the future. If they are not capable of meeting those challenges, they should prepare the capability. The personnel staff must be in a position to separate the important from the unimportant in a meaningful way and to respond quickly to change.

3. There must be a willingness on the part of the administrator to take risks, because he does not have a laboratory in which to experiment. Far too many ideas are lost becaue of an inability or unwillingness to be innovative or original in our thinking, and the constant change of the future requires new ideas and new alternative solutions to problems.

4. If the environment in which the administrator functions will not permit action as outlined above, he should consider finding a new environment. If he does not, he may find himself overwhelmed by future shock.

While being innovative themselves, PAs should seek to foster creativity among all employees in the organization. This has been attempted for years through suggestion systems and award programs. However, such devices have been termed "crutches" and "creativity contraceptives." All members of an organization should be stimulated to continuing creativity, possibly through an occasional think session for department heads that gets them away from the daily routine to objectively analyze their organization and develop new ideas in problem solving. Conferences and meetings do this now, to some extent, and the literature of learning has demonstrated that people removed from their normal environment for short periods of time are usually more creative. This is not to suggest that we become stagnant during our regular office hours but that some additional time should be set aside for creative activity. The future—and future shock—obviously hold much challenge and excitement for the PA.

26 The Anachronistic Factory

Wickham Skinner

As noted earlier, our institutions have a tendency to get out of touch with reality. Fortunately, something can usually be done about this. A similar problem is often encountered in maintaining an appropriate rate of change, with the result that disruptive and sometimes revolutionary changes are necessary to overcome the "buggywhip factor." It should be useful to examine the characteristics of organizations that become outdated in relation to their environment.

In this chapter Wickham Skinner, professor of business administration at the Harvard Business School, addresses the need for fundamental changes in our methods of planning and managing to accommodate new values and new expectations. Although his recommendations are expressed in terms of a manufacturing organization, they are equally applicable in other, less conventional systems. You should find an understanding of the myths, problems, and anachronistic elements detailed by Dr. Skinner helpful in dealing with barriers to change.

How might top managers of manufacturing go about making profound changes in the stubborn infrastructure of the conventional factory to make it less anachronistic, more productive, and more relevant to today's social and economic facts of life?

Analysts of the current scene approach such a difficult question with a humble confession of their own inadequacies and uncertainties. Who knows really, how to solve the complex problems of our time? Nevertheless, I move to the other side and offer my opinion that there is a great deal that managers responsible for manufacturing can do to make their factories more productive and less anachronistic.

My recommendations are simple yet vital, and fall into two groups:

1. Changes *in conventional concepts* of managing manufacturing.
2. Changes *in meeting human needs* in manufacturing careers.

This chapter is excerpted from an article that originally appeared in *Harvard Business Review,* January–February 1971, and was subsequently published in the author's book, *Manufacturing in the Corporate Strategy,* published by John Wiley & Sons, Inc., New York City. Copyright © 1978 by John Wiley & Sons, Inc.; reprinted by permission. All rights reserved.

Conventional Concepts

Manufacturing management was derived in a conceptual sense from engineering and technologically oriented variables. Because manufacturing requires specialized expertise and constant improvement of often complex equipment and processes, its foci as a sector of management have been on technology, efficiency, and equipment. As a result of this legacy, manufacturing executives have typically been more expert in those areas of their work than in other parts.

Indeed, the potential of manufacturing as a competitive weapon and the concept of using manufacturing as a strategic asset have been almost always overlooked in management's single-minded attention to efficiency, costs, and engineering.

Manufacturing can be managed quite differently from the way most companies manage it. What is required are three fundamental changes to bring about (1) the recognition and banishment of a number of fallacious myths and assumptions about manufacturing, (2) the management of manufacturing as a corporate strategic weapon, and (3) the widespread acceptance of a concept of manufacturing as an institution, with an extensive and influential infrastructure of internally consistent technological and sociological elements.

Myths and Assumptions

By having led us into planning and managing plants in ways that result in disappointments and unnecessary hard work and away from more fruitful approaches, myths and assumptions have seriously hurt our progress.

The main criterion for evaluating factory performance is efficiency and cost.

This statement is wrong. Manufacturing can also be a competitive weapon when it is less "efficient" but more flexible in terms of product change, in managing inevitable ups and downs in volume, in getting new products into production quickly, in providing for and consistently meeting short-delivery promises, and in producing with a minimum investment in inventory and fixed assets. Criteria for judging a factory should not be limited to efficiency and cost, for these criteria ignore the fact that in the context of a particular company's competitive strategy, other criteria may be vastly more important.

A good factory can simultaneously accomplish low costs, high quality, minimum investment, short-cycle times, high flexibility, and rapid introduction of new products.

Wrong again. A factory system—like an airplane or a building—can be designed to do only certain things well. The failure to clearly identify design objectives or to compromise among many criteria results in manufacturing systems which do not perform well by any criteria.

The management of factories is essentially a task for engineers.

This assumption is a grievous mistake—blindly employed since the turn of the century and now made even more seductive by advancing technology— that has generally entrusted the direction of manufacturing to people conditioned with a technical point of view. The technical dimension is important, but time is proving that social and strategic dimensions are at least equally important. Moreover, the technical obsession often delegates the production function to those who are inadequately trained and oriented toward human and social factors, financial problems, and the strategy and markets of the entire firm.

Increasing mechanization is a job for industrial engineers and operations researchers.

Another wrong assumption. Tackling complex multidimensional problems with the limited array of disciplines offered by even those broadly intentioned professionals is simplistic.

The systems approach and a high level of conceptualization are a substitute for experience and substantive knowledge.

This fallacy is implicit in excessively theoretical and conceptual planning exercises which have caused a multitude of errors in judgment and swarms of "bugs" in automated factories.

The ultimate objective of automation is to reduce the numbers of people required; problems with and costs of people can be avoided and overcome with automation and mechanization; people problems can be bypassed with good equipment.

These three interrelated misconceptions should have been demolished by the experiences of the past ten years.

Economics always favors machines.

This is a myth because the fantastic abilities of people to plan, remember, and use judgment, wisdom, and intelligence extend far beyond the capabilities of computers and mechanization. To try to make such facilities substitute for people has repeatedly proved expensive, especially when reliable backups are built in to achieve a hands–off operation. When a skilled person is to be replaced by a machine, the cost of the equipment replacing the person may run into hundreds of thousands of dollars. Therefore, economics often favors the use of people.

In total, these myths and assumptions about plants and people have led us into an excessively technically oriented point of view of the factory. They have allowed us to overlook key dimensions in industrial change and to attempt to introduce machines and equipment without changing organizations, responsibilities, job content, information systems, promotion and pay systems, and control and motivational approaches—in short, the stubborn total infrastructure of the factory as an institution.

The simplistic view of the factory as measured largely by efficiency not only drives away good men and women but fails to use the factory as a competitive weapon to meet specific manufacturing tasks demanded by corporate strategy. Delegation of their own responsibility by top managers allows too many plants to be managed by technologists who do not have a general management point of view.

Wise managers recognize the multidimensional complexity of the problems with which they deal. To bring about change in the infrastructure of manufacturing involves a great deal more than new technology and technological innovation. Production managers are asking for heartache, frustration, and frequent defeat when they attempt to go it alone.

We walk innocently into an ambush when we attempt to develop new production systems without looking at their strategic and social implications as well as their technological aspects. Present know-how and skills will be multiplied enormously, and failures and delays will be prevented when we recognize that factory problems are just as complex and demanding as all the other problems involved in renewing major social institutions. They require a multidimensional team approach.

Strategic Weapon

Suffice it to say at this point that the concept of manufacturing as a strategic weapon is powerful in my experience because, once understood and assimilated, the concept has a dynamic effect on managers. Its use automatically lifts them out of any narrow, parochial corner into a broad, total view of the production system and its relation to the corporation and its strategy. The concept gives them a means and a framework for thinking about the design of manufacturing and requires them to think of the production process in policy—rather than solely operational—terms.

Concept of Manufacturing

Seen as a major institution, manufacturing at once takes on new dimensions which have existed often unrecognized all along. Certain conclusions then follow:

1. Elements of the infrastructure must be mutually and internally consistent.
2. Everything counts, since one overlooked element may ruin the total.
3. Manufacturing decisions must span the infrastructure; changes can no longer be made piecemeal if they are to be successful.
4. The span of changes must be broader and take in more elements.

The interaction between the various elements of the infrastructure is complex and often not easily understood; but their resulting effects warrant attention and improved expertise.

Meeting Human Needs

A different kind of recommendation from those representing conceptual changes involves the organization and operation of production systems in terms of societal and personal values. If an institution is to be productive in the short run and viable over the long run, it must (1) meet or change the felt needs and expectations of employees so as to be generally satisfying and (2) develop an image that attracts sufficient numbers and varieties of people to allow for the selection of an able total cadre of employees and managers.

As stated earlier, we have much evidence that the factory as a social institution may be rapidly growing outdated. Who, after all, wants to work in a factory these days? And what does the common answer, "Not very many," mean? To me it suggests that the values and demands that today's factory institution imposes on its members are beginning to conflict with the values and expectations of an increasing fraction of modern Americans.

Specifically, table 26–1 suggests a number of these conflicts and growing incongruencies and anachronisms. What can be done with this vital "people segment" of the factory infrastructure? While it is probably the most difficult element with which to cope, I suggest, albeit cautiously, that the people area is not so impossible to deal with as is often assumed. It can be resolved more satisfactorily, but it will take some daring and innovative management nerve, for changes in people policies can be explosive; and this means that top management must take responsibility and be involved.

But the picture is not all negative, for the factory can offer a great deal that employees want and need. Employees, particularly in metropolitan, big-city environments, are often lonely in the crowd; do feel needs for group memberships and cooperative, nonaggressive, nondefensive, fulfilling experiences; wish to identify with a successful organization and quality products; and seek outlets for their ideas and opinions.

Seen in this sense, the factory can be attractive if it meets some of these needs. Some factories are already doing a superb job in certain facets. In

Table 26–1
Conflicts Between Current Factory and Societal Viewpoints

Factory Expectations and Values	*Social Expectations and Values*
Employees are to perform jobs designed by management.	Employees know better than their boss how to do their own work.
Advancement is to be by seniority and long–proven performance.	Employees want continued and steady advancement.
Experience is important.	Experience is overemphasized.
Time is important.	Time is pressure.
Work, activity, achievement on one's job are to come first.	Family, leisure, and balanced life are most important.
Decisions are to be made quickly and efficiently.	Employees don't want anyone to decide anything that concerns them as individuals without first getting their opinions.
Employees are to adjust to the demands of expensive machinery.	Employees don't want to be treated like machines.
Following orders is essential.	Freedom is essential.
The individual is to be paid what he or she is worth.	Employees are entitled to a decent standard of living.
Productivity is essential to economic well–being.	Friends, conversation, and social interaction are essential to human well–being.
Employees are to perform well (even under adverse physical conditions).	Employees don't want to work under adverse physical conditions.
Seniority entitles employees to job protection and privileges.	Each person has one vote.
Loyalty to the company is owed by employees.	Loyalty to one's belief is more important than loyalty to the corporation.
The corporation cares for its people.	The corporation cares little about its employees.
Employees are to perform work per schedules, quotas, and budgets.	Schedules, quotas, and budgets are mechanisms to exert control over people.

fact, it appears to me that the factory is in an ideal position to meet many of today's unfulfilled social needs and expectations.

But to do so, what must be changed? Consider these anachronistic elements of many conventional factories:

1. Pay systems based on hours worked.
2. Physical arrangements that treat employees with disrespect and supervisory assumptions that fail to treat them as individuals.
3. Decision–making processes that leave out the opinions and ideas of involved employees.

4. Promotion and job security policies that emphasize only experience and seniority.
5. Communications practices that withhold information or present only one point of view.
6. Job designs and work content that focus solely on motor-mechanism/physiological aspects of an employee's capacities and leave out the emotional and spiritual dimensions.
7. Union contracts and governance systems that restrict change and stifle initiative.

Innovative Examples

Lest the foregoing discussion strike the reader as recommendations from an ivory tower, let me cite several real-life examples of changes going on now in manufacturing management. These are typical of what some few innovative companies are doing in the light of the kinds of problems I have been discussing here.

Company A is a $50 million annual sales manufacturer of capital equipment whose manufacturing vice president and president became concerned enough about late deliveries, high costs, shortages of skilled technicians, and rising labor problems to decide that total organization—rather than piecemeal—changes were in order. Their factory is now being overhauled from top to bottom.

The changeover process started with a determination of the specific manufacturing task required by the company's competitive strategy, which the executives identified as offering short lead times on an ever-increasing number and variety of products with a trend toward shorter runs of more customer specials. Subsequently, they tackled each element of the factory infrastructure, such as analyzing scheduling and information systems, supervisory and wage policies, equipment, and layout.

In short, all of this factory's operations were reexamined and rethought (1) to be mutually consistent, (2) to provide short lead times on new product development and delivery, and (3) to cope with today's social and economic environments.

Company B is one of our industrial giants. At one decentralized division where labor productivity has been marginal at best, a totally new approach to supervision and work-force management has been installed on a pilot basis. The approach features a "self-determining work group," consisting of about thirty workers in a general-purpose, job-shop machine area who are permitted to govern themselves. The group members set their own rules and regulations within the framework of only the general and functional company objective of making parts as needed, per blueprint and on schedule. Quality controls, scheduling of machines, discipline and work rules, and productivity are all under the control and direction of the group itself with the help of a "trainer" who functions as a nondirective, consultative coordinator.

Companies C and D are pursuing a less drastic approach to a new kind of supervision and work-force management. Entirely independent of each other—they are located 1,200 miles apart and are in different industries—both have restructured traditional foremen jobs.

Concluding that the typical foreman's job is "impossible," Company C took four sections of thirty men each under four foremen and set up an enlarged section of 120 men with a team of the four former foremen in charge. One member of the team was asked to focus on quality, the second on training, the third on technical problems, and the fourth on scheduling, planning, and reporting.

In Company D the same kind of change took place, but with a three-man team in which the role of the quality specialist was omitted.

In each of these four companies positive responses to its innovative approaches and changes are taking place. Perhaps a kind of "Hawthorne effect" (in which experiment and change always seem to produce beneficiary results, regardless of the nature of the change) is at work. Then, again, perhaps the experiments are sound in themselves and will become models for other companies.

In any event, the climate for innovation and experimentation in manufacturing management has never been better. Real progress is taking place among a relatively small number of companies whose managers are recognizing the seriousness of problems in industry and courageously taking the risks of bringing about substantial change.

Conclusion

The factory system is anachronistic on two counts:

1. Its management concepts are outdated, focusing on cost and efficiency instead of strategy, and on making piecemeal changes instead of changes that span and link the entire system.

2. Its infrastructure contains such conflict and paradox that the expectations and desires of its people are too often incongruent with the imperatives of its technology, the demands of its markets, and the strategies of its managers.

This internal inconsistency marks a failure to adapt to environmental change in a key functional area of business—the production function.

How ironic that in production, where scientific management techniques began, these conventional approaches now seem out of date and out of tune with the social and economic facts of the times. Production management is perhaps bringing to an end a long cycle that began with innovation and new concepts for accomplishing productivity, developed in maturity of ideas, subsequently grew into a "conventional wisdom," and finally arrived at the point where we now see obsolescence.

Looking ahead, the changes in economics, technology, and society that now affect the factory may, if we dare, lead us to new kinds of production infrastructures that could absorb and harness new technology and new social values. With creative and substantial change, led by the more intrepid, the factory institution could begin to achieve the productivity breakthrough our economy so sorely needs.

27 Problem Resolution and Imposition of Change through a Participative Group Effort

Rossall J. Johnson

Often a good summary of conceptual reasoning on a particular subject can be found in a case study which embodies many of the principles to be applied.

In this chapter Rossall J. Johnson describes a typical problem situation in a large bureaucratic organization and how it was resolved through a participative group effort at change management. It is interesting to note that the situation described in this chapter involves imposing a series of specific changes in an organizational context of greater overall changes. Some of the details of this case may seem irrelevant at first, but such details suggest the full context in which a change in operating procedure was achieved in a particular department of a large company undergoing a strike. Here we have an example of evolutionary, managed change in an environment of revolutionary change.

You may find it helpful to read into this example experiences of your own in which seemingly small changes must be undertaken in the context of a larger and more turbulent environment.

In any dynamic organization changes are implicit, yet when the proposed changes are perceived as threatening, resistance can be expected. A number of research projects[1] have indicated that to bring about change it is more expedient to have the initiative for change come from within the group where the change is desired. All too often when an organization's procedures and processes have become inappropriate or obsolete, those working within the system are the last to acknowledge or even recognize the inadequacies. Often the group will make the system work through the use of increased manpower, expediting procedures, and other emergency actions, but when, in spite of these measures, the system falters, one can expect that a search for reasons or faults outside the system will be made before the internal procedures and processes are given a rigorous examination.

Because of this tendency to assign blame to the external environment for causes of internal problems, long delays may occur before the suborgan-

This chapter is based on an article that originally appeared in *The Journal of Management Studies,* May 1974. Copyright © by Basil Blackwell Publishers, London, England; reprinted by permission. All rights reserved.

ization will recognize the need for change. Suggestions for changes all too often must come from those who are not closely associated with the system. Such external inputs are frequently threatening to the system personnel and result in negative attitudes toward the outsider such as:

1. Viewing those who suggest the change as not knowledgeable enough about the problem to present realistic solutions
2. Questioning the motives of those suggesting change
3. Remaining unconvinced that a new approach would work

Resistance may also occur because issues concerning personal security remain unanswered and the idea of change implies:

4. An incompetence or criticism of present performance
5. An elimination of jobs
6. A shifting of personnel to positions of lower prestige
7. The learning of a new skill or the discontinuance of a present one

In reviewing these various reasons for resisting change, it can be inferred that if suggestions were generated from within the system, their chances of acceptance would be much greater. To obtain the internal inputs, it is necessary for those involved to examine the various possibilities for resolving the problem or adjusting to a change. This introspection process can be implemented through participative group effort. Such procedure was part of the approach in the field study described below.

This paper is divided into four parts. First is a description of the problem situation which is given in enough detail so that one can have a feeling of the pressure for change. This is followed by a description of the participating group efforts, with the recommendations for change. The results in terms of reduction in delays is then given. The last part contains general comments on the change procedure used.

A Field Study

While laboratory conditions attempt to simulate field conditions, a question still arises concerning the effectiveness of the participation procedure for bringing about changes in an actual organization. This paper is concerned with such an effort. The setting for this study is a telephone company that had experienced a five-month strike which began in June and was finally settled in October. During the strike, supervisory personnel functioned as maintenance personnel and, where time permitted, made some new installations. This was possible because, historically, the company had made it a practice of promoting from the rank and file to fill vacancies in management. Because these supervisory people had been away from the old jobs for some time, they were "rusty," and, in addition, there was not enough to fill all of the essential positions. This condition led to errors in installation and in record keeping and also resulted in the increase of a backlog of installation orders. However, over the period of the strike, phone service for the community was maintained at a respectable level.

When the strike was over, the backlog of orders for new installations and for changes in existing equipment had become so large that the regular workforce had been unable to keep pace with it, let alone reduce it. A program for the rapid expansion of personnel was instituted to cope with the backlog, with a resulting chain reaction in the promotion system which allowed relatively inexperienced employees to rise several notches in the organization structure. However, even with this expansion, orders were still being processed late.

The author was engaged in June, some eight months after the end of the strike, to give an "outsider's" views and recommendations on how to get the orders processed on time. One division of the telephone company, the Special Services Division (SSD), had been analyzed in some detail in an attempt to reduce the number of late orders. This division was concerned with such things as WATS line service, answering services, computer connections, and other specialized uses of the telephone circuits. While the number of customers receiving special services was relatively small, the billings represented a significant portion of the company's revenue.

The Special Services Division was mainly a paper-moving function in that orders were received from the marketing department, processed, and sent to the plant or installation department to be implemented. Special Services Division made up the order, indicating the appropriate design of the telephone circuit, designated the routing of the circuit, equipment to be used, and the terminals to be connected. When all was ready, the order was sent to the plant department for installation.

Quality of Service

The special-service customers were more aware of the quality of service than most home customers because of their greater dependence on the telephone equipment as a means of carrying on their business. Essentially the customer evaluated quality in terms of:

> Time: Did I get the equipment when I wanted it?
> Direction: Does it do what it is supposed to do?
> Price: Is it worth it?

The study is concerned with the time factor: did the customer get the equipment on the date promised?

Time and Quality

The time element is an insidious quality element since, as the delay time increases, there seems to be a tendency for other aspects of quality to diminish. To the customer, time is the first perceived indicator of the quality of telephone service. If the due date is met, the customer will perceive the company in a positive way, and the minor technical difficulties and the greater than expected service charge will be viewed in a less unfavorable way. However, if the customer is inconvenienced by a late order, the smallest flaw in the functioning of the equipment then becomes a major concern, and the monthly billing is examined in detail for possible overcharges. In short, time sets the stage for the customer's evaluation of the quality of the telephone service.

Seven months after the strike, customers ordering equipment through the Special Services Division were still not getting the equipment on the promised date. A sample of orders that missed the customer due date shows that 74 percent of all orders were not completed on the request date of the customers. An additional breakdown of the time results indicates that between 21 and 26 percent of the orders received by Special Services Division were late. However, SSD added its own delay to the orders, so that between 47 and 68 percent were sent late to the installation department. The installation department in turn contributed to the delay and, as a result, between 58 and 81 percent of all orders did not meet the customer due date.

Time and Cost

While the billing is not emphasized in this study, it is, of course, necessary to recognize that costs of processing orders are included in the total rate structure. But more important is the area of revenue lost to the telephone company when service is supplied after the customer due date. This impact is especially true when new service is being installed. Thus the company is faced with two negative factors when the due date is missed: (1) reputation for poor service and (2) lost revenue.

The telephone company's lost revenue due to late special orders (those processed by SSD) was conservatively estimated at $152,000 per year. In addition to lost revenue, there were more costs incurred when special procedures were established by SSD to expedite orders. Some of the most obvious costs to carry out special procedures in the SSD were extra salaries and paperwork procedures: (1) salary of six employees and a supervisor to answer questions from plant about late orders; (2) salary of teletype operators to resend messages that were sent incorrectly or were lost; and (3) cost of the various order forms (20 cents for each follow-up form), expediting costs for late orders.

It has been estimated from these cost figures that the company was losing at least $250,000 per year because of lost revenue from the late special orders, errors in orders, omission of information, and losses in the processing system.

Time and Errors

Emphasis on meeting the customer due date had, in the past, led to errors in the technical area. Technical here means the recording of the appropriate information that would allow plant (installation and maintenance) to install the correct equipment. Inappropriate or omitted information could occur at four major steps: (1) order received from marketing, (2) assignment of equipment and lines, (3) engineering design of circuits, and (4) teletype sending of order to installation.

A sample was taken from three of these work centers in March to determine the quality of output. Omitting information was a chief source of error. There were 420 items omitted from 105 orders that were sampled. In addition, there were 46 instances when the information was incorrect. While some of the information that was omitted or incorrect may not have been vital to the functioning of the equipment, it was a factor in delaying the order.

Two examples of customer complaints indicate the types of error which led to late installation and poor service:

Example 1

March 20: a manufacturing company

Complaint: poor transmission

Investigation results: A new design for transmission was made because new lines had been assigned to the company. During preparation of the new design it was discovered that another engineer had, due to error, received the original, but obsolete, order and had issued a design for the old lines.

Example 2

May 9: a wholesale company

Complaint: unable to secure WATS line

Investigation results: Line was requested on March 13, and customer was to receive service on April 14. The order was held by engineering because no circuits were available for the line. A recheck indicated that there were circuits assigned to other facilities that were not being used and should have been released that could be assigned to the WATS line.

Evidently the omission of information had not only led to errors which caused delays but also resulted in equipment lying idle when it was assumed to be in use. This condition would come about when circuits were requested for customer lines and then were not used. If the engineer requesting the circuit did not cancel the request, then the circuit would be presumed to be in use. Such a circuit might lie idle for some time before the error was discovered. The management of SSD thought that there might be a problem with employee motivation—motivation to meet the customers' requested date for service. After a review of the complaints and an investigation of the errors, the "why" of the condition seemed to be a result not only of the order backlog caused by the strike but of the rapid expansion of the division and the high turnover at the lower levels. The division had brought in additional trainers and, as indicated above, had promoted personnel to supervisory positions. These were long–term moves which would not alleviate the immediate crisis of excessive late orders. The immediate conditions in June are described in the following excerpt from the interim report.

Excerpts from Interim Report

There is a general recognition that a problem of quality exists in the processing of SSD orders. The top echelon recognizes the importance of the problem; their attitudes can be indicated by summarizing the quotations of several individuals: "There is a felt urgency to resolve it."

Steps have been taken to come to grips with quality. A team investigating the problem has outlined the dimensions of the situation through a series of inquiries and reports. The training activity has been expanded, and the upper levels of supervision have called the problem to the attention of the supervisors via reports, meetings, and on an individual basis. In short, action has been taken.

This action has had its impact on the supervisors, and they are reacting to the pressure from above. There are indications that the "I'm clean syndrome" is present. The I'm clean syndrome can best be described as a reaction of: "Our section is doing all it can to resolve the problem but circumstances beyond our control are at work. Look somewhere else for deficiencies—we are doing the best job possible."

It is true that no one work group has complete control over the problems; it is this interdependency that can cause a frustration within each work unit. The result is an urgency but a different type of urgency than is felt in the higher echelons. Each group busily engages in activities of correcting its own errors or of demonstrating that errors are due to the action (or inaction) of others. This type of behavior may give some relief to the group's frustrations but probably aggravates the problem by adding time to order processing. More important is that once a supervisor relieves his anxiety by the self–demonstration of "I'm clean," he gives less attention to working on solutions.

The condition described above should not be looked upon as a minus, since apathy toward the problem does not seem to be present. There is every indication that supervisors would expend considerable effort in solving the problem but they need some direction and coordination. This in turn should not be construed to indicate that previous action taken is inappropriate. To the contrary—the urgency is expressed and data backing up the demands for results are basic to resolving the problem. The supervisors, though, need a means of escape from the pressure, and therefore additional steps should be taken.

The above excerpts from the interim report should indicate that interdependency of the work groups within the division made it essential that cooperation exist in solving the problem which was defying immediate resolution. There seemed to be no one thing to be done to cut the number of delayed orders, and it was still not clear why errors, omissions, and delays continued in spite of increased pressure to eliminate them. It was also evident from the "I'm clean syndrome" that suggestions for change must originate from within these groups if acceptance was to be expedited.

Participative Group Effort

At this stage it was decided that representatives from each of the work groups organize to form a coordinating force to discuss the problem and that the force should limit itself to the examination of one area only (engineering, general design) and attempt to make some recommendations. Seven representatives, six at the lowest supervisory level and one engineer, met as a group on a full-time basis, with the author participating as an observer and as a guide to inaugural procedures. After the group understood its role, the author was mainly an observer. The selected representatives were intimately acquainted with details of the flow of orders through their own section, and several had worked in other sections. The formation of this group was in effect eliminating "suggested changes from outsiders who did not understand the problems" and creating suggestions for change from within the group. The group members were temporarily separated from their sections in order to allow them to give all of their attention to the problem. This was done by having them report directly to the division head and by relieving them of their duties in the section. The division head, along with the section heads, met with the newly formed coordinating force and explained their task. The division head emphasized two things: first, that the group was not brought together to establish blame; and second, that the recommendations of the group would be carried out if possible, and if not, he would meet with them and discuss the reasons why the recommendations could not be accepted.

It was anticipated that three or four full days of discussion would be sufficient time but, as it turned out, the first two days were spent determining if the division head meant what he said and in parrying back and forth on causes and blame, and reverting occasionally to the "I'm clean syndrome." While this process was time consuming, it did clear the way for a direct approach to the problem. After this initial fencing and testing, little effort was spent on establishing blame and, when such an input did arise, it was quickly stopped by the group. This then was another step in overcoming objections to change—the threat of negative evaluations of job performance was eliminated.

Resource People

The coordinating force was given the authority to request any information that it thought might be useful and also to call in resource people—that is, persons who might give pertinent information. This authority was used throughout the investigation period and proved to be helpful not only in obtaining information but also in involving others. Toward the end of the meetings, the group brought in a number of resource people to discuss the feasibility of the tentative recommendations. Not only was there the advantage that accrued when the recommendations were altered because of new suggestions, but again those who were brought in as resource people were participating in establishing more changes than was thought possible at the start. In all, thirty–four resource people participated.

Some of the old–timers were able to poke some legitimate holes in the original proposal and then recommend alternatives which were incorporated in the final draft. Even a seemingly minor item such as having a Xerox machine in the department to enable one to get immediate and clear copies was verbalized by several resource people. This suggestion was included in the recommendation and accepted by the division head, and the Xerox machine was installed in the department shortly after the group recommendations were made public. Such prompt acceptance and action led many in the division to feel that their own recommendations were being considered and that action was being taken on these suggestions to reduce the number of delayed orders.

The Recommended Changes

The coordinating force made the following recommendations: (1) increase the number of trainers, (2) enlarge the methods and procedures staff, (3) design a faster system for having circuits assigned for customer service, (4) obtain high–quality and faster service in obtaining Xerox copies, and (5) reorganize and update the order–tracking system for processing customer orders.

The last recommendation was to be the chief occupation of the coordinating force, since they felt that a new tracking system was essential to reduce the order processing time. They also felt that within the coordinating force was the necessary knowledge to work out the system details. The coordinating force, with the aid of a number of resource people, did set up a new system which was installed in December (14 months after the end of the strike).

Results

Immediately preceding the implementation of the coordinating force in June, the percentage of delays attributed to the Special Services Division was around 25 percent. As indicated above, prior to the strike the division was satisfied with a 5 percent delay result. In July the division was successful in heading toward this target and on five occasions had even been able to reduce the accumulated delays. The tracking system was implemented in December and, although the division contributed as high as 16 percent to delays after this period, the mean was probably around 7 percent. The average of the last six months was about 2 percent—that is, 2 percent of the delays were attributable to the SSD. The division's contribution to delays in the last three reporting periods was at the 1 percent level or lower.

The total period covered by the figure is a year and a half, and this leaves some room for speculation as to the impact of group participation over this extended period of time. First, it should be noted that there was a significant drop in delays in the immediate period following the report of the coordinating force. For the next six months the coordinating force continued to meet from time to time to check on the progress of the new tracking system. After the introduction of the system, it was necessary to follow up on its implementation. This was a continuous participative activity that had the impact of reminding many resource people that they had contributed to the changes.

There were also external inputs into the environment which cannot be ignored. Executives high in the organization showed their concern about delays. The president of the company answered his own phone to receive customer complaints and then followed up to see that the complaints were investigated and resolved. Other top executives bypassed the organization lines of communication and sat down with individual engineers and clerical personnel in an attempt to get a firsthand view of the problem. These overtures, of course, must have been an important factor in reducing delays. However, the coordinating force was of the opinion that the old system of processing orders had been outgrown and that, until changes in this procedurs occurred, an orderly processing could not be expected. It was the changes that the coordinating force and the resource people suggested and an acceptance of the new system that seemed to have brought about the desired results.

There was also a market decline in the number of orders (from marketing) entering the division late, and not shown; and there was a decrease in late orders in the installation department (plant). Part of the reason for this reduction can be attributed to the changes in the tracking system, which allowed the division to immediately pinpoint delays from marketing and in installation.

The cost area and company reputation must not be ignored when evaluating the results. Certainly the time–quality factor has been improved, with an end product of customer satisfaction. The time–cost factor is also better. It can be guessed that at least half of the $250,000 late–order cost was saved and, if a cost survey had been made, the saving might have been found to be considerably higher.

Discussion

The original objective was to determine ways in which the division personnel could be motivated to reduce delays and errors. The problem was looked upon as being behavioral in nature. Preliminary investigation revealed a great desire on the part of the employees to get back to the prestrike target of 5 percent—if for no other reason than to get relieft from the real or imagined pressure from supervision.

There was an awareness on the part of higher management of the need to make changes in training facilities and in methods. Some changes had been made; however, it was not until the investigation by the coordinating force that the extent of the needed changes and the fact that the problem was more technical in nature than behavioral were known.

The changes which should have been made, and which were not, were those connected directly to the job, and such suggested changes would tend to be threatening to the individuals. When the division manager instructed the coordinating force to look for solutions and not for blame, his instructions were instrumental in de-emphasizing the threatening behavioral aspect, thus allowing an examination of causes. The participative group effort was successful in resolving the problem and in implementing the change. This success in overcoming resistance to change can be attributed to the fact that the technique of participation was able to eliminate many of the threats enumerated in the introduction. While it is true that in this situation no jobs or skills were threatened, it should be noted that information about jobs and skills was generated internally and therefore accepted, whereas reassurance about jobs from an external source (that is, higher management) might have been received with apprehension.

While the intent was to obtain participation to a limited extent by having representation from each group, the extensive use of resource people broadened the participation considerably. Coch and French[2] used three types of groups in their experiments with change: (1) no representation, (2) representatives from each area, and (3) participation by all. In this project similar levels of participation can be seen, but the same group was involved rather than the use of separate experimental groups. A time sequence was also evident. At the beginning no substantial formal participation was sought—that is, no representation; this condition was of about seven months' duration. Following this was the formation of the coordinating force, which was essentially participation through representation from each area, but almost immediately this progressed into representation and partial participation when the resource people were contacted.

The project is not presumed to be a neat, controlled research study, but it does seem to support the reports of Coch and French[3] and also Marrow et al.[4] It should be noted that for the first seven months after the strike, little progress was made in reaching the minimum acceptable quality target and progress only seemed to accelerate when participation was sought and obtained. Because of a variety of uncontrolled factors, a causal relationship between participation and results can only be suggested.

While there was general agreement that the order–tracking system was obsolete, it was doubtful that a new tracking system imposed from the outside (by a consulting firm or an industrial engineering department) would have been readily accepted. In this instance it was the group's own system, and they probably would have made it work if necessary. The group did, in fact, make changes from their original plan without encountering resisting elements within the group. Those who used the tracking system were together on the goal of designing an efficient system. Thus what may be a most important result of this project is the positive employee attitudes developed by creating the opportunity for the lower levels to participate in resolving a most difficult problem.

Summary

A situation arose in the organization where a change was needed. In the classical and controlled experiments in change, group participation was deemed to be the best method for acceptance of change. This study was an applied test of the research findings. Because the study was situated in an ongoing company, it was not possible to rigidly control the variables.

For more than seven months prior to group participation attempts to bring about change from external sources were unsuccessful. One of the reasons for this lack of success was the incorrect identification of the problem—that is, the assumption that employee attitudes needed to be changed. When participation was encouraged, the problems of procedures and systems were determined as the areas where changes were needed. By having the group participate, the problems were correctly identified and changes suggested. This was followed by having the group implement their own suggestions. The result was that the percentage of delays was reduced to a level which was below their target. Thus this field study seemed to successfully follow the classical studies concerning group participation in change.

Notes

1. L. Coch and J. French, "Overcoming Resistance to Change," *Human Relations,* vol. 1, no. 4 (August 1948),pp. 512–523; A.F. Marrow, D.G. Bowers, and S.E. Seashore, *Management by Participation* (New York: Harper & Row, 1967), pp. 64–75, 95–109.
2. Coch and French, "Overcoming Resistance to Change."
3. Ibid.
4. Marrow et al., *Management by Participation.*

**Part V
Social Change**

We have considered many different views of the management of change. These views have been presented through a structure intended to convey certain ideas about the management of change in business organizations— ideas which have evolved over a number of years in the course of the authors' experiences in managing change in a variety of organization environments. Although there is a common thread running throughout the chapters of this volume, nowhere has this thread been explained as completely by one author as can be derived from the views of the many authors included here.

We have talked about the change agent as if he were an individual or small group of individuals seeking to amend the behavior of a larger group. This is a valid and useful exercise, for most often the responsibility for effecting changes in an organizational context falls to a relatively few leaders, consultants, or catalysts.

We live in an increasingly disaffected society, as evidenced by the shrill comments of those who would have us abandon all our old value systems and the moans and groans of those who would have us do nothing in the face of the many profound changes that are going on all around us. As such influences as the family and the church lose their impact on our society, our value systems will continue to change and will continue to be influenced by other elements of our culture. Value system changes are not made in a vacuum, however. Studies of political power indicate that a system of countervailing power exists between the larger societies in our world. Similarly, it is possible to conceive of countervailing power influences within our own culture and our own value systems. Perhaps the disaffection of our society with government, business, and the larger social institutions today is evidence of an imperfect mix of influence. Perhaps, too, our current concerns are evidences merely of the power that our major social institutions do have to effect changes in our value systems consistent with their own ends.

Our concluding chapters explore the impact of changing social values on business organizations and management philosophy.

28 Is Business the Source of New Social Values?

Otto A. Bremer

In this chapter Reverend Otto A. Bremer, pastor of the Lutheran Campus Ministry at the University of California at Santa Barbara, argues that business may be the most significant force in American society in shaping our social value system. This thesis is valid primarily if you accept the philosophy expressed by savant pitcher Satchel Paige: "Don't look back; something may be gaining on you." Probably business has been the most effective determinant of social values for some time now. That is not to say that this condition will continue, however, without some significant changes in the attitudes toward business that now prevail in our society. If businesses and other large organizations in our society are to change such attitudes, they must take a more active part in changing our society itself. To do this, they must adapt themselves better to the changes that are taking place within and outside their own organizations.

Reverend Bremer's presentation nearly says it all—a fitting way to put social balance into your efforts to manage change.

Business is today the most significant force shaping American life and the strongest influence determining the everyday values of the average citizen. The operative values in the management of a corporate enterprise tend to become the operative values in the daily life of society.

I have been making this suggestion to groups of businessmen in recent months, and I have not been getting much agreement. Most executives react by claiming that the opposite is true; business is fighting for survival of its way of life, and at times it seems as if all the rest of society is against it. They ask how I can support my statement when:

1. A steady stream of newspaper and magazine articles blame business for nearly every social ill, from pollution and racial tension to unemployment and the war in Vietnam.

2. A growing percentage of college graduates are eschewing business for other occupations.

3. A statement from Ralph Nader receives more positive public response than one from a thoughtful corporate manager.

All this surface evidence, however, may be misleading. We must be careful how we interpret it. If it is true that businessmen are being blamed

This chapter is based on an article that originally appeared in *Harvard Business Review*, November–December 1971. Copyright © 1971 by the President and Fellows of Harvard College; reprinted by permission. All rights reserved.

for so much of what seems wrong in our society, the foregoing points could actually be supportive evidence that the influence of business is indeed greater than ever before and that some people are reacting against what they perceive to be the negative aspects. An influence can be significant in the reaction it stimulates.

Consider what is happening on the campuses. "Surely," say those who disagree with my thesis, "values are being expressed there which were not shaped by business." Perhaps, but let us look deeper. The present student generation has grown up with less value input from traditional sources than any previous one. It is also the first to have had a lifelong exposure to non-traditional values through television. My experience with these students has convinced me that more than any older generation, they are keenly aware of the dominant influence of business on society.

Of course, they react in a variety of ways. Some are not aware of how much they have been influenced and accept rather uncritically the priority of economic values. This group is becoming smaller and smaller. More commonly, and with varying degrees of intensity, students sense the effect of business on nearly every aspect of life and are fearful of further domination in the future. The more vocal ones label the influence "oppressive"; the more active ones attempt to escape it by establishing some form of "counterculture."

The purpose of this article is to show why I am firmly convinced that the future of our society is going to be determined more by the day-to-day decisions of corporate managers—and the values that dictate these decisions—then by any other single influence. This conclusion is reached after twenty five years as a student of business, a pastor to businessmen, and a campus pastor in turbulent Isla Vista watching the Bank of America burn. I am convinced that if the business community will recognize the challenge that goes with the crucial influence it wields, we will not only ensure a better future for the American people but also provide a renewed sense of meaning, purpose, and fulfillment for business executives.

Supportive Evidence

I first became aware of the impact of business on a person's nonbusiness attitudes and values in pastoral counseling associations with businessmen. I had always assumed that the basic values of a person—in business and in private life—were shaped from mother's knee, church, community, and so on. But I discovered the following:

1. Those executives who were most confident about life, open to other

persons, and able to cope with present-day ambiguities and changes often described their corporate life in ways that showed they were influenced by very positive (from my point of view) values within the organization.

2. When businessmen discussed questions of religious belief, marital relations, and all kinds of interpersonal problems, their views were loaded with attitudes and opinions reflecting values operative in corporate life.

Moreover, I also discovered that corporate values were embedded in the lives of both business and nonbusiness people alike. It is difficult to find specific illustrations that adequately support my sweeping thesis. One problem is that the influence of business decisions on social values has two aspects: (1) the cumulative effect on people's values of the business decisions themselves, and (2) the way values which dictate these decisions tend to become the values determining nonbusiness behavior.

Most readers will be familiar with examples of the first aspect, such as products and promotion practices that reputedly affect people's behavior and values. Each of us could supply further illustrations by reflecting on recent nonbusiness behavior that was influenced by business decisions.

Less attention, however, has been given to the way in which economic and business values supporting these decisions have been transferred from business institutions to society in general. Here are some illustrations from my own experience.

Of all our institutions, the family is most vulnerable to the influence of business values spilling over society in general. In my marriage and family counseling I often encounter people who look upon the family as primarily a financial institution—usually without being aware this is happening. Success is judged by the amount of capital accumulation and the expansion of assets. Difficulties, such as divorce and rejection of younger members, frequently have their roots in the charge that someone is "unproductive" or "does not contribute to family success." Unconditional love, in the traditional, religious sense, has given way in these families to the standards of accountability appropriate to business.

Increasingly, other institutions are adopting business methods and the values that support them, such as efficiency, profitability, productivity, and quantitative criteria. There is no campaign by businessmen to bring this about, but demands to put public schools, universities, social service agencies, and churches on a "sound business basis" are receiving more and more support these days. In most cases I find myself approving, but should we not think long and hard about the future effects? For example, one group of churches is adopting planning, programming, budgeting systems (PPBS) as its basic administrative tool, and the church "executives" are attending explanatory seminars at the University of Michigan School of Industrial Relations. The present leadership is confident it can modify the assumptions of quantitatively measurable results to include the intangible aims and purposes of religion. Somehow, though, the two seem diametrically opposed.

Think about the way an average citizen invests in a pension fund. The value message he gets from the fund manager is most likely focused at maximizing his return on the investment in financial terms; he watches the fund closely and identifies his future with it. But are there not other returns on this investment, based on other values that are being overridden by the solely economic one? The investor thinks in economic terms about his future because he has been influenced in that direction. But what about his future in terms of a clean environment, racial equality, and individual dignity? There are corporations which further these virtues and make a profit, and corporations which do not further them and make a profit. Why not invest in the former to ensure a more "valuable" future? Most people do not think of this because economic values are dominating the others.

The Traditional Mix

I hasten to add that none of the foregoing illustrations proves that the values determining business decisions actually become the values which people in society accept as normal. Very few research instruments are available to assess the influence of business on society in the area of values. Even if the instruments were available now, only time would reveal what the actual consequences will be.

Obviously, we must do our own thinking on this elusive issue. We should probably start with a look at how the values of the average American have been formed in the past and what the roles of business and other institutions have been up to recently.

The United States has traditionally depended on the interplay of various "value input sources—farm life, communities, churches, business, education, and so on—to shape the values of each individual and, in sum, the values of society. The outcome, on the whole, has been very good. Each institution (or what I am calling value input source) made its contribution, but society—individually and collectively—made the final decision as to which values would prevail.

A parallel can be drawn between this process of value formation and classical economic theory. We have had a kind of laissez-faire approach to the development of our common values. The value input sources can be compared to the factors of production, each trying to maximize its own return or advantage. The community of individuals acts like the marketplace, with an "unseen hand" determining the ultimate influence that each value input source is to have. In the long run, competition has perhaps not been perfect, but the resultant mix of generally accepted values has been rather good.

Classical economic theory, of course, depends on each element seeking to maximize its own return in the marketplace. U.S. institutions have tended to perform similarly. A kind of advocacy tradition has developed in which each institution (as a value input source for society as a whole) is expected to support the maximum expression of its value position.

Economic theory also holds that the participants in the marketplace need not be concerned about the consequences of vigorously pursuing their own advantage—the process of individual maximization will always produce the result that is best for the total society. Likewise, a societal institution has not been expected to concern itself with the consequences of maximizing its own value position. There has always been the unspoken assumption that no one source will dictate the values of the whole society, that somehow the final mix of generally accepted values will be a balanced combination of the best from all value input sources. For example:

1. The church preaches absolute charity, forgiveness, mercy, sharing, and other values that, if actually adopted by society as a whole, would result in economic chaos. When the church becomes "practical" and starts modifying its maximized position (instead of just preaching "peace," it suggests a date for withdrawal of troops from Vietnam), there is often a great outcry from parishioners that the church has betrayed its advocacy role of standing firm for its absolute value position.

2. The university finds itself held to a similar self–maximizing role. If it responds to calls for relevance—from either a practical public or a socially conscious student body—the university is accused of betraying the objective, purely intellectual role of an academic institution. The assumption is that if it does not advocate its own unique position, the final mix of our common values will suffer.

3. Business—as a value input source for society as a whole—is the main focus of this article and will be dealt with in detail. Most readers, however, will be aware that many voices cry "betrayal" when business seems to compromise in any way the maximization of economic values.

A Competitive Advantage

Today the foregoing scenario is no longer applicable. In the language of our parallel in economic theory, the competition between the various value input sources has become quite imperfect. The influence of education, family, community, church, and so on, in forming the values that individuals live by, is greatly diminished, and the influence of business is consequently stronger than ever before. Think for a moment about what has happened to the traditional value input sources that influenced the everyday life of Mr. John Q. Citizen a generation or two ago.

Agricultural Society

Even when people were leaving the farm in large numbers, they did not do so without having internalized some down-to-earth values that lasted a lifetime. Farming itself is now a big business, highly mechanized with daily life influenced more by the values of nearby urban centers than by the agricultural routines of the past.

Family

The extended family of the past helped to secure the passing on of values from generation to generation. Today, few children have daily contact with grandparents who, as Margaret Mead says, "cannot conceive of any future for the children than their [the grandparents'] own past lives."

Town or Community

People are now more apt to experience short, rootless residential stops in innumerable indistinguishable suburbs than to live in the town where they were born and intend to die; thus assimilation of community mores is considerably weakened.

Religion

One does not really need the results of the many studies showing that people today look less and less to the churches and synagogues as a source of values. It is obvious that religion is not nearly the integrative and normative force that it once was.

Education

I suspect that most readers of this article can recall an elementary school experience characterized by uncritical transmittal of the values of the American way of life. To be sure, these values were usually seen from the perspective of a white, Anglo-Saxon, Protestant middle class imbued with patriotism and the puritan ethic, but the influence was strong. Today we are more sensitive to the pluralistic nature of society and less willing to impose the values of the majority.

Direct evidence of the demise of traditional value sources is seen in the attempt of many young people to reestablish meaningful contact with contemporary substitutes for them; mystical cults take the place of organized religion; earth food, ecology action, and closeness to nature substitute for the farm; and communal living replaces the extended family.

While the sources of traditional values decline in influence, in some cases as a direct result of industrial growth, people still make choices and decisions based on some kind of substantive input—although most do not think about where this input comes from. How are these choices and decisions made and what influences them? It is hard to actually prove that the values dictating business decisions are gradually filling the vacuum. My earlier illustrations, however, suggest that the influence of business has not declined and that now, by default, business finds itself with far more influence on society than ever intended—or desired.

The Emerging Monopolist

We are all familiar with cases where single institutions have dominated the values of other societies. In fact, many immigrants to the United States from Prussia and elsewhere sought to escape what they called a "military society." Other immigrants remembered with some nostalgia an "agricultural society" in which the farm, as a living ecosystem, was the pervasive model. For some, this nostalgia almost blotted out the fact that they had left their homelands because the domination by agricultural values stifled new ideas and possibilities for industrial development.

Experience taught both the early settlers and later immigrants that one way to safeguard freedom was to be certain that checks and balances were built into the formal and informal structures of American culture. Few concepts are more deeply embedded in our understanding of what the American way of life is all about.

During the past half-century, however, the description of the United States as a "business society" has been used more and more. The designation expresses a positive and appreciative recognition of the success of the business community in contributing to the highest standard of living in the world. But could business society also describe a modern counterpart to the church-dominated society of the middle ages or the military societies, both past and present?

In asking this question, I do not mean to imply that business has decided it wants a broad influence on society. Most corporate executives have been influenced by the traditional American understanding of the relation of business to the rest of society. "Most values," they would say, "are formed by the church, the home, the school, but not by business. Business may respond to these values, but it does not supplant or create them." To suggest to executives that business is somehow heavily influencing the values of society is, in effect, like changing the rules in the middle of the game.

Nobody I talk to wants such a description to be true—but what if a realistic look at the accumulated changes in society says that it is true? What if all the mobility, urbanization, affluence, and applied technology resulting from business decisions, as well as the values dictating such decisions, have so changed the way our lives are shaped that we have not only new rules but also a new ball game? In the old ball game, even so great an influence as the commercial control of mass media (particularly television) was not critical because the people listening and watching had had their values formed by significant input from a variety of traditional sources. The situation is drastically changed when these influences are absent.

Redressing the Balance

I realize that my argument is full of questions. And I am sure that the thoughtful reader has many more questions. Moreover, some readers will object that there has been a rather casual and undefined use of the terms "value," "values of business," and "values of society." My defense is twofold: First, the answers to the questions raised must come from the business community itself, out of its own sense of urgency and concern; second, it would seem unwise to get bogged down in the technical language (jargon) of sociology or philosophy, let alone of religion.

I can, however, offer a tentative answer to one question that is almost always raised when I discuss this issue. If this analysis is true, what does it mean to the businessman? Obviously, to be overly specific would deny the statement that meaningful response must come from business leaders themselves. But let me give some minimal suggestions:

1. Face the possibility that the analysis may be true. When it is admitted that the subject of societal values and the relation of business decisions to them is new and unfamiliar territory for most corporate managers, it must also be admitted that there is an ever-present temptation to avoid dealing with things so vague. This implies a commitment to finding the truth, one that challenges the most competent and creative leadership.

2. Think of social responsibility as an internal rather than external concern. If the influence of business on the values of society is as great as suggested, the first social responsibility of business is to ask whether the values

perceived as influencing the daily operation of the business are values that are desired for society as a whole. Attention to extra business involvements—such as contributions to charities and education or executives volunteering for community projects—becomes secondary to a concern for the values operating behind corporate decisions.

3. Increase your ability to discern the social consequences of management decisions. The kind of attention being given to environmental consequences should be broadened to include the effects on society and the values of its citizens. Experimentation might be made with someone—a kind of ombudsman for corporations and trade associations—who will alert management to the effect of corporate actions on societal values.

4. Develop a competence in setting social goals. The management function must be enlarged to include more than the ability to achieve predetermined goals. Managers need to develop a sensitivity to the effect of their pursuit of these goals on the configuration of society in general.

Concluding Note

At this point, the reader is likely to be very concerned about the issues raised, even though not necessarily in full agreement with the thesis I am presenting. Many readers are probably among those who feel most keenly the pressures which society is putting on business leaders.

My hope is that what I am suggesting will not be seen as another such pressure; rather, it is meant as a way of making sense out of the changes which are taking place and providing a framework for establishing present-day corporate priorities.

Moreover, I do not mean to deny the positive influences of business values on society, such as the quality of judging people on the basis of individual competence rather than on wealth, family, or connections. There are many other similar examples, but these should not lull us into complacency about the value crisis confronting us.

As I stated at the outset of this article, the operative values in the management of a corporate enterprise tend to become the operative values of the average citizen. If this is true, it seems clear that the future will be largely shaped by the business community. The central issue then becomes whether or not businessmen are going to make the kinds of decisions and establish the necessary priorities that will channel their growing influence toward furthering a better world.

29 Profiles of the Future: Changing Managerial Philosophies

George A. Steiner

Although there has been a profound change in recent years in our society's expectations of business and the private sector, there is still considerable debate as to whether the private sector is or should be the prime mover in the process of social change. One argument has it that business will inevitably do what's best for society in the long run, since whatever that may be will also be most beneficial to business. Another view is that business is simply a mirror of society as a whole and cannot be expected to do better than the system of which it is a part. And still another voice tells us that business cannot be counted on to do anything more than maximize short-run profits, which is (by definition, to those who hold this view) contrary to the best interest of society as a whole.

This chapter examines the evolution of management philosophy as we now see it. In tracing how we have come to think as we now do about the responsibilities of business management, George A. Steiner, professor of management and director of the Division of Research in the Graduate School of Business, University of California, may give you a better idea of what can be done to effect change in this important aspect of management in the future.

For the better part of our history, we have accepted the idea that a business has one and only one objective and that is to maximize profits. The notion is still solidly implanted in many elementary economics textbooks. This means, in the technical sense, that a businessman has no obligation but to push his production to the point where the greatest possible profit is achieved and to avoid producing less or more if it reduces total profits. This view holds that business managers exist solely to serve the best interests of common stockholders. The only social responsibility of a manager is to use the resources at his disposal as efficiently as possible in producing goods and services that consumers want and at prices they are willing to pay.

The first great change in this traditional view, at least as far as the larger corporation is concerned, came in the 1920s. The idea was advanced and widely accepted by top-level business managers, particularly in the

This chapter is based on an article that originally appeared in *Business Horizons,* June 1971. Copyright © 1971 by The Foundation for the School of Business of Indiana University; reprinted by permission. All rights reserved.

larger companies, that managers were trustees for the many interests focused on the company. The concept said that managers made decisions to maintain an equitable balance among the often competing claims of stockholders, customers, employees, suppliers, and the general public.

While decisions might be made which resulted in short-range profits at less than a maximum, many who held this view argued that if the balancing was correct, the long-range profit interests of the company would be maximized. Some felt that, within such a view of managerial responsibilities, actions might be taken which were not directly related to profits, but the acceptable impact on profits was negligible as compared with total corporate income.

A second major break from the older concept is now taking place. The thesis is that business must become deeply involved in the nation's major social problems and help society to achieve the many objectives it sets for itself. In this view, the involvement is partly justified because it may be done profitably, but a growing body of opinion, in and out of business, feels that significant business actions can and should be taken even though there is no direct relationship to profits. Indeed, actions may be taken legitimately which actually result in less profit than might otherwise be obtained. Incurring costs to install antipollution equipment, maintaining a marginal plant in a community where operations are important to community life, and training and employing hard-core unemployed are examples.

Some who hold this philosophy feel that what is done should be in the long-range profit interests of the company even though short-range profits may be cut. Others, however, think that much can and should be done irrespective of its direct profit impact—short or long range.

A major issue for today and through the 1970s, therefore, is how far a company should go in accepting a drain on short-range profits to assume social responsibilities which management thinks society may expect of it, or which management thinks it ought to assume either as a "good citizen" or to enhance long-range profits. There is no consensus about these current ideas, but it does seem clear that the underlying thought is distinctly different from the past views of balancing interests and of profit maximization. I see nothing in the future to change this third view. Indeed, all major trends point in the direction of an expansion of its scope and acceptance in both the private and public sectors.

I do not mean to assert that the social responsibility view has replaced the profit-maximizing or trustee views. Among managers, the public, government officials, and students of business, each view can be found today as a basis for action and thought. What I mean to say is that as the trustee view spread in the 1920s as an acceptable alternative to the profit maximization concept, so the social responsibility view will, in my judgment, become much more widely accepted in the 1970s as a replacement for older views.

This trend has and will continue to have a significant impact on managerial practice and business structures. Before discussing these, however, it is important to talk about limitations on the social responsibilities of business.

Limitations on Responsibilities

Some observers of the social scene assert that business is the last great hope in solving our social problems. Some businessmen also talk as though there is no limit to what they ought to do in finding solutions. There are not many who feel this way, but there are some.

We are in great need of generally accepted limitations on the assumption of social responsibilities by business. If business tries to do too much and fails, the social reaction will not be to the advantage of the business system. On the other hand, if too little is done, government will step in to do more, and this will not be attractive to businessmen.

Space does not permit a long discussion of limitations on business as it assumes social responsibilities, but it should be useful to block out a few criteria. I am not so much concerned about business going overboard in assuming social responsibilities as I am fearful that expectations of what business can and should do may get out of hand. I am not rejecting the view that business has social responsibilities; on the contrary, I accept this philosophy and think it is important. But it must be pursued with restraint.

There is no action formula that will apply to all businesses; each firm must choose its own. Four guidelines, however, may be acceptable as businesses plan to assume social responsibilities.

1. Each business should think carefully, before acting, about what its social responsibilities really are. A company must not underestimate the magnitude of major social problems. A proper estimate of the assumed task is important, for studies show that in the recent past companies have tended to move with more energy than discretion in dealing with social problems. Most companies surveyed confessed that they underestimated the tasks they accepted and that more money, time, and thought were required than they had originally estimated.

2. Business must be considered predominantly an economic institution with a strong profit motive. Business should not be used to meet noneconomic objectives of society in a major way without financial incentives. Will and Ariel Durant, after completing ten monumental volumes on *The Story of Civilization*, looked over the broad sweep of history and came to a few conclusions, one of them useful here. They concluded that "the experience of the past leaves little doubt that every economic system must sooner or later rely upon some form of the profit motive to stir individuals and groups to productivity." Substitutes like ideological enthusiasm are too unproduc-

tive, too expensive, or too transient, they added. Whatever we do, and whatever we expect business to do, it is of paramount importance that no action be taken to erode the profit motive. We must continue to judge business performance primarily on the basis of economic and not political or social criteria.

3. An effort should be made to determine which agencies in society are best able to undertake certain tasks in dealing with social problems, and proper responsibilities should be assigned to them. In some areas the government is clearly the best agent—for example, general education. In other areas business is best—for example, in producing goods or training the hard–core unemployed.

4. In a rough sort of way businesses have social responsibilities commensurate with their powers and impact. This criterion means that larger companies tend to have greater social responsibilities than smaller ones.

This list is certainly not exhaustive, but I think I have illustrated the need for much more thought on this subject. Developing an acceptable structure of limitations on business's assumption of social responsibilities is an urgent task for the 1970s.

Changing Practices and Structures

The question now should be examined: How are social expectations and changing environment altering managerial practices and structures?

1. The attention of top managers is shifting from the internal affairs of their companies to the external environment. This is occurring because the external environment is increasingly opening up new opportunities for profit and, at the same time, is a growing source of major threats. For instance, it is expected that between now and 1980 the federal budget will increase by at least $100 billion, a large part of which will go to such economic activities as controlling pollution, finding new means of transportation, and rebuilding cities. This expansion will contain, of course, great new opportunities for profit.

On the other side of the coin, the threats in the environment are mounting rapidly. For example, courts of law are taking a much more liberal point of view, from the standpoint of consumers, cconcerning manufacturer liability for product defects. Permitting class action suits intensifies this threat. We are on the verge of a new wave of suits from conservationists. A suit filed last year in federal court in New York, on behalf of "all the people of the United States" including "generations yet unborn," demanded $30 billion in damages from eight producers of DDT for punishment and restitution of damage allegedly done to the environment by the pesticide. This is a spectacular case, but exceptional only in terms of the dollar claim. Until recently a plantiff had to prove demonstrable economic damage, such as "because of this product my horse died." Now environmental litigants seek to prove noneconomic damages. Although the courts are not yet going overboard, there is growing disposition to protect intangible rights.

What I am trying to highlight is that the greatest opportunities for and threats to business today arise from external and not internal sources. In this light, the importance of long-range strategic planning is mounting in more and more companies. The effort is becoming more formalized in these companies, and a greater interrelationship exists between line managers and staff in developing company strategies. Top managers are spending more time on long-range planning. In a recent study conducted by the Conference Board, over 65 percent of 280 top executives said that long-range planning ranked first in order of importance of all their activities and that they spend about 44 percent of their time on this task.

2. Closely related to the above, social expectations and changing environment have produced a shift in types of forecasting of most concern to top management. Traditionally, economic forecasting of such environmental factors as gross national product, interest rates, prices, and wage rates has dominated company top-level forecasting efforts. Forecasting of non-economic factors in the environment is becoming more important as a basis for managerial decision making. I would not be surprised to see in ten years that forecasts of various social values and social indicators will stand beside such traditional economic forecasts as GNP as major projections important to management in decision making. In mind, of course, are projections of how people feel about such social values as work and leisure, materialism, esthetics, and so on. The social indicators will concern elements of life quality, such as medical care, health, clean air, clean water, and so on.

A management that can accurately identify and analyze change in these areas will find itself much better able to predict the course of those fundamental currents in society that will affect company health and survival. More companies are engaging in technological forecasting today because it is becoming clear that threats are arising from technological development in places other than the industry to which they are related.

A few businesses today have given to one staff man the single responsibility of looking into the distant future—the world toward the end of the century—as a basis for managerial thinking and action. This practice will become common. In scores of companies, in the meantime, various staffs are trying to penetrate the future to see what things will be like in twenty to thirty years in their companies, their industry, and their world.

3. Companies increasingly are establishing permanent departments at headquarters to coordinate and supervise their social affairs. One recent study of 247 firms in the *Fortune* 500 list showed that 201 have some sort of urban affairs program and only four of these were started before 1965. In

all but forty-six of these, someone has been assigned full-time or part-time responsibilities for urban affairs. Most assigned the urban affairs function to old established departments such as personnel, public and government affairs, or public relations, but fifty-six of them established a new organization at top management levels for the function.

William Stolk, chairman of the board of the Committee of Economic Development and former chairman of the board of the American Can Company, suggests that the chief executive officer of each company (I think he is talking principally about the largest companies) should appoint a qualified senior executive to manage the corporation's public business. He should be an executive vice president and a director because, he says, this area deeply involves the board. Indeed, two or three directors could constitute a committee to help the chief executive officer and the executive vice president.

Stolk's view is that this group could give advice and counsel to the chief executive across the range of social problems and opportunities. I do not know whether such ideas will catch on, but I anticipate that this sort of function will increasingly be taken out of the traditional departments of personnel, public relations, and government affairs and put in a separate new department or office reporting directly to the chief executive.

If a company has a formal long-range planning department, this function might be located there. By the end of the decade, the coordinator of corporate planning will probably move closer to the chief executive and tend to become his peer. In that event, this person may be the principal staff officer who will be concerned with the public business of the company as well as with its private business.

4. Over the past three decades government planning and business planning have interrelated at many points—for instance, government's aid to the petroleum industry in its planning of output, investment tax credits, export subsidies, accelerated depreciation, federal full employment policy, and so on. I look for a much closer relationship as the decade of the 1970s moves along.

It is clear that before we shall really come to grips in a major way with the outstanding social problems of today it will be necessary for business and government to pool resources and talents in new ways. We are witnessing, for instance, in coming to grips with hard-core unemployment, a new pooling of effort between business and government. Government puts up some cash and sets a few ground rules, and business is doing the training. This type of joint effort is going on in other areas and will be made more often.

In many other areas, business and government planning will coalesce. In the case of various pollutions, for instance, it is abundantly clear that if one company decides to take costly action it may find itself at a competitive disadvantage with the company that does not do likewise. As a result, businessmen who thought they never would ask government for controls now seek performance standards that each company is obliged to meet. The competitive structure of an industry is thereby preserved. I look for much more of this type of interrelationship between business and government.

If we are to manage our major evolving problems, we must anticipate them and preplan to make events conform to predetermined patterns. More of this will tend to bring business and government planning closer.

Although five-year plans for national economics, made by government and business, have become common throughout the world, such as the French five-year plan, I do not see a trend toward this sort of cooperative effort in the United States. I do not see, and I hope I am correct, any trend for a detailed overall economic long-range plan for the entire United States made either by the government or by the government working with private groups. I do see increased planning by business and government, separately and in partnership, in more areas.

Finally, organizations will be administered with greater reference to the individuals who participate in their operations. There is general recognition that individuals in organizations have rising expectations about finding self-satisfaction in their work, of being able to use their talents in their jobs, and of having a "piece of the action." Organizations do not now, and will not in the foreseeable future, satisfy all the personal interests of individuals working in them, but managements of businesses are recognizing these desires and will try to meet them. The reason is not necessarily to try to "do good" but to better use the talents available to improve profits.

I look for new ways to stimulate individual creativity and self-fulfillment, such as greater use of project management, more group participation in decision making, job enrichment, decentralization, and management by objectives. Such managerial methods will expand and outpace those forces in business that tend to foster conformity.

This does not, of course, exhaust the list of changes that are foreseeable in top management practice and structures. They are major developments which I see growing out of changing managerial social philosophies and changing environment.

Trends now obvious are likely to continue and change, in important ways, the views of managers about their responsibilities, and the practices and structures of top management in business. The view of business responsibilities has moved from that which centered solely on the monetary interests of stockholders to balancing the interests of those affected by corporate actions, to the assumption of social responsibilities at the cost of near-term profits. There are obviously important social advantages in this trend, but there are also great dangers; I have therefore suggested a few limitations to this view.

   Social expectations and a changing environment are altering and will
continue to alter top management practices and structures. Increased
emphasis on strategic planning and identification of opportunities and
threats in the environment will put a company in a better position to exploit
the opportunities and avoid the threats. Second, there is more emphasis on
forecasting noneconomic phenomena such as social values, social indicators, and technology. Third, companies tend to set up public affairs functions at higher levels in the corporate structure. Fourth, there is a growing
convergence between business and government planning. Finally, management will be more concerned with the interests of employees.

Epilogue:
You *Can* Do It Yourself

As we have noted before, businessmen often regard change as a transition between periods or conditions of stability. It is this viewpoint that lies behind such impossible quests as the "return to normalcy" or such nostalgic nonsense as the "good old days" (which, as one astute observer, Dr. Otto Bettmann, reminds us, were really terrible).

Given, then, that change is here to stay, and is to some degree a condition of every aspect of our existence, there are only a limited number of ways in which you, as an individual, can respond. Respond, in fact, is all that some will do: wait until change occurs and then simply react. Others will do even worse: stand by and do nothing.

If you respond in either of these ways, the chances are that you will be trampled in the rush or overwhelmed by forces beyond your control—either of which is almost certainly as bad as what can happen to you if you seriously attempt to resist. The principal advantage of resistance is the delay that can be achieved, during which time adaptive techniques can be devised. As Dr. Parkinson has observed, "delay is the ultimate form of denial"— and, as others have pointed out, it sometimes works!

In real life, most change occurs in an entirely uncontrolled manner. It is usually random and often it is not constructive at all. Thus those who control some change are likely to have a higher degree of adaptive ability than those who do not.

Business people and institutional creatures in general have a tendency to view problems from a limited perspective. That is why the multidimensional analysis advocated in these pages has advantages for those who would manage some change. My own experience as a business consultant suggests that the first thing to do in analyzing any problem situation is to consider the whole problem. What is the whole problem: its background and origins, its people attributes, its organizational dimensions?

Business people also tend to master technical changes and, with some notable exceptions, fail to master human and social changes. I am sure you can recall situations in which people deeply involved in a change management situation focused all their attention upon the apparent symptoms of need and failed to notice that the whole organization was in jeopardy of survival.

A Few Practical Suggestions

Although most change management situations respond to known and predictable stimuli, many do not. It is safe to say that nothing should be accepted as a given without testing it. Similarly, reliance upon a single strategy will run the risk of invalidity just as will the "truths" that are not true enough of their time to be relied upon.

Here are some other practical suggestions distilled from these pages:

1. Analyze the situation in all its aspects and dimensions; take the whole view.
2. Test every assumption, no matter how obvious it may seem.
3. Employ different strategies and different adaptive techniques; no one approach is always effective.
4. Organize your approach and use the act of organizing to involve others who will be affected by the change.
5. Require creativity.
6. Ensure that there are appropriate work disciplines for each and every job, and especially for every management job.
7. Use goals, goals, goals.

There are, however, certain dimensions of change management that cannot be simply distilled into such practical suggestions. These are the conditions in which one aspect of change relates to another, the interaction between the human dimension, the organizational dimension, and the environmental dimension.

Three Dimensions of Change

As our chapters gradually bring into focus, there are many ways to look at change, and each analyst or practitioner will look at some aspects more than at others. Behaviorists will tend to focus on the human dimension, sociologists on the environmental dimension, and so on. In practice, however, the most successful change management efforts tend to be those that have the greatest depth of inquiry and the broadest field of vision. Effectiveness requires more than studying the whole problem. It requires an understanding of the three primary dimensions: human, organizational, and environmental.

Each of these dimensions will have an effect on all the others. If you move something in the environmental dimension, it will affect each of the other dimensions. A practical example from my own experience as a public accountant has to do with the considerable pressure that our society, through Congress and the SEC, has been putting recently on the environment in which firms like ours now practice. One organizational result is the new requirement for rotating the partner responsible for our services to each client after a certain number of years. This in turn has led to great uncertainty and concern among our partners about their "worth" and their security. The net result has been to make it extraordinarily difficult for our partners to accept other types of change.

In another example, there is a company that specializes in polishing steel to a high luster for automobile applications. Some years ago, auto manufacturers started to explore alternative materials, such as plastics and aluminum. Then the major supplier of the steel used by this company introduced a high-strength alloy with very beneficial cost and performance attributes. For several years, when a downturn had appeared imminent for the company, its absentee owner and resident manager were getting along very well in a harmonious business relationship; they needed each other, or so they believed. But when production (and profits) spurted as a result of auto manufacturers' acceptance of the new alloy, the owner decided to try to sell the company and the manager started to look around for businesses to buy. The owner has tried to implement certain production and financial management changes in the business, only to be greeted with stubborn refusal by his employees.

In each of these instances, a change in the environment affected organizational relationships which in turn affected human and other dimensions, thwarting desirable change. If a broader view had been maintained by the change agents in these cases, perhaps more receptivity to change could have been achieved through the other dimensions involved.

Some Conclusions

Where does all of this lead us? It leads us to the several sensible conclusions that appear throughout this volume. It also leads us to considerable optimism that more change is possible than most people and most organizations would readily concede. It has been proved that people can be led to achieve more than they honestly believe is possible. They may not like it at the time, but significant change can be effected despite great opposition. Simply knowing in advance what change is likely to be required can accelerate the change process considerably, because planned and constructive change is always more effective than reactive change.

One final, highly personal conclusion. You *can* do it yourself, applying some measure of management to the otherwise random effects of change, controlling your environment to a greater extent than others will. Since most change is random, whatever you can control represents a significant advantage in managing your own destiny and in managing the efforts of those who look to you for leadership.

About the Editor

Peter H. Burgher is a partner in the international public accounting firm of Arthur Young & Company. He has been a management consultant and an auditor with Arthur Young in New York and Boston, and served as managing partner of the firm's offices in Rhode Island and, more recently, Michigan. A graduate of Williams College and Columbia University's Graduate School of Business Administration, he is a certified public accountant in various states.

Long active in both national and local business, professional, and political groups, the author has served on various committees of the Chamber of Commerce of the United States and as Chairman of the Greater Providence Chamber. He has also been active, at both the state and national levels, in the American National Red Cross, and has been chairman and a member of the board of directors of the Southeastern Michigan Chapter. He has also served in both Michigan and Rhode Island on various governmental commissions and statewide political organizations and is a frequent speaker and writer on business subjects. An accomplished pilot, he has served as chairman and a member of the executive committee of the Michigan Aeronautics Commission.